# THE ELIZABETHANS' AMERICA

*A Collection of Early Reports by Englishmen on the New World*

edited by
## LOUIS B. WRIGHT

HARVARD UNIVERSITY PRESS

Cambridge, Massachusetts

1965

Printed in Great Britain by
Butler & Tanner Ltd, Frome and London

# General Preface

WE HOPE to form this Library for the student, teacher and general reader who is interested in Elizabethan and Jacobean life and literature. It will not provide further editions of Shakespeare's *Works*, or *The Faerie Queene*, or Jonson's *Works*, nor will it duplicate readily available editions of any poet or dramatist. We hope to reprint what is generally unavailable outside the great libraries and microfilm and photostat collections, or available only in expensive and rare complete editions; we want the *Stratford Library* to publish important parts of the staple literature of the period.

The first volume was a selected Nashe, providing more than half his total writings and including four whole works. This present, second volume will be followed by a collection of Dekker's non-dramatic writings, including a full version of *Lantern and Candlelight* and other works not generally available; and a collection of narrative poems. We plan subsequent volumes of Sonnet Sequences, Lodge, Greene, Sermons, News Pamphlets, European Travel and Books of Rhetoric.

The texts are presented in modernized form. Editors have been asked to reparagraph, repunctuate, substitute italic type for roman, or *vice versa*, wherever they consider that such changes will avoid unnecessary confusions or obscurities. Modernization of spelling is sometimes difficult because of our slender knowledge of the spelling habits of authors and compositors, and our total ignorance of the many accidental decisions made during writing and printing: generally editors have retained archaic forms only where rhyme or metre requires, or where a modernized form does not give the required primary sense. Exceptions will sometimes be made where an author clearly distinguishes between two forms, for works surviving in autograph manuscript, or for verse carefully printed from authorial manuscripts. A textual note will define the editorial procedure for each volume. We believe that this presentation, in banishing the clumsiness of original editions and hyperconservative reprints, will often reveal liveliness and sometimes an added elegance.

Editors have provided brief annotations, a glossary or a glossarial

v

index, whichever seems appropriate, and also textual notes, collating substantive changes to the copy-text and briefly discussing its special authority. Each volume has an introduction dealing with any topics that will enhance the reading of the texts. We have not aimed at minute consistency between each volume, or even between each item in a single volume; editors have been encouraged to present these texts in the clearest practicable manner and with due consideration of the fact that many of the works reprinted have hitherto been 'known about' rather than known, more honoured or dishonoured in scholarly works than read and enjoyed as substantial achievements and records of Shakespeare's age.

JOHN RUSSELL BROWN
BERNARD HARRIS

# Preface

ENGLISH explorers, adventurers, and would-be colonists were fascinated with the New World and wrote narratives and descriptive reports that were equally fascinating to their contemporaries. Many of these accounts are not only historically significant for developments that they anticipated but they are also entertaining for a modern reader.

The editor has made an effort to select items that have both significance and interest. To make the documents more easily comprehensible for the reader who is not a specialist in sixteenth- and seventeenth-century literature, the spelling, punctuation, and capitalization have been modernized according to conventional usage today, but all obsolete words and grammar have been retained. Notes have been kept to the minimum required to make a passage clear or to provide needed information.

The editor is under a heavy debt to Miss Virginia LaMar and Mrs William L. Leonard of the editorial staff of the Folger Library, and to other members of the Folger staff, for help in preparing the text and notes.

L. B. W.

*The Folger Library*
*April 1, 1964*

# Contents

# Introduction

## The Wonders and Mysteries of Trans-Atlantic Lands

FOR the Elizabethans, the vast lands across the Atlantic were regions of mystery and wonder, where anything might be possible. There one might find hoards of gold, silver, pearls, carbuncles, and rubies; in those regions grew spice trees and herbs of such potency that they could heal all the ills of mankind; in those lands lived strange people, some as noble as Adam before the fall and others as evil as the Devil himself; some even had their heads beneath their shoulders and eyes in their breasts, as Sir John Mandeville had related. Even so eminent an explorer as Raleigh testified that he believed such people dwelt in the back country of Guiana. Some portions of this New World were as fruitful as Paradise before the serpent tempted Eve; indeed, it was believed that the Terrestrial Paradise—or something very like it— might be found across the sea, somewhere, Raleigh thought, along the thirty-fifth degree of north latitude. Nothing was too strange, wonderful, outlandish, or tempting to be believed about the New World, and the Elizabethans avidly read such accounts as they could procure and listened to tales, tall and otherwise, told by returning travellers.

Since England was a nation more concerned with trade than with military adventures and conquests, English merchants heard with envy of the rich cargoes that Spanish and Portuguese ship captains were bringing back from the East, the coast of Africa, and the New World. English merchants resident in Spain and Portugal could see with their own eyes the diversity of foreign products, and some of these commodities they bought and shipped to England. Englishmen could see no reason why they too might not find sources of the products that were enriching their foreign competitors.

The most effective propagandists for trade and settlement in the New World in the last quarter of the sixteenth century were the two Richard Hakluyts. Richard Hakluyt the elder, a lawyer of the Middle Temple, was the counsellor and advisor of London merchants interested in expanding English trade. In letters and papers that he prepared, he emphasized the economic benefits to be derived from exploiting the New World. His younger cousin, Richard Hakluyt the preacher and compiler of voyages, was equally insistent upon the economic as well as the political advantages of colonization. In a long treatise generally known by the shortened title of *A Discourse of Western Planting* he gave a detailed argument for settling some portion of North America. Its heading indicates that it was written as propaganda for Raleigh's colonial projects: 'A particular discourse concerning the great necessity and manifold commodities that are likely to grow to this realm of England by the western discoveries lately attempted. Written in the year 1584 by Richard Hakluyt of Oxford at the request and direction of the right worshipful Walter Raleigh, now knight, before the coming home of his two barks. . . .' Among many other benefits, Hakluyt declares that 'this western voyage will yield unto us all the commodities of Europe, Africa, and Asia, as far as we were wont to travel, and supply the wants of all our decayed trades'.[1]

John Hawkins, a member of an extraordinary family of Devonshire merchants and seamen, early realized the profits to be made in trade, illicit or otherwise, with the New World. His father, William Hawkins of Plymouth, had made three voyages between the coasts of Guinea and Brazil and had discovered that 'elephants' teeth', sugar, and Negro slaves were valuable commodities. Since African slaves were in great demand in New Spain, John Hawkins sought to reap a profit from this trade. In 1562 he made a voyage to the coast of Guinea, where, 'partly by the sword and partly by other means', he obtained 300 Negro slaves whom he took to the West Indies and sold. He brought back in exchange, 'hides, ginger, sugars, and some quantity of pearls'. So certain was Hawkins that he had ingratiated himself with the Spaniards that he loaded two vessels with hides obtained in Haiti and sent them to Spain, but, to his dismay, these vessels were confiscated and orders were sent to the West Indies forbidding further trade with Englishmen.

Hawkins, however, was not discouraged and received powerful backing for a second expedition. From the Queen herself he obtained a ship of 700 tons, the *Jesus of Lübeck*, and he added three smaller vessels. That Hawkins was not alone in these slaving ventures is indicated by the fact that he encountered before he was ten leagues at sea another expedition that included the Queen's ship, the *Minion*, and the *John the Baptist*. No one thought it ironical that the *Jesus* and the *John the Baptist* were going in search of slaves on the coast of Guinea.

Though trade with the Spaniards in the West Indies was forbidden,

Hawkins managed to get rid of his slaves, load hides and other products of the country, and explore the coast of Florida on his way home. The narrative of the voyage was written by a gentleman-adventurer, John Sparke, one of several who accompanied Hawkins, and provides one of the earliest recognitions of the potential value of Florida.[2]

On the third expedition that John Hawkins made to Africa and the West Indies, he again sailed in the *Jesus of Lübeck* and was accompanied by Francis Drake in the *Judith*, a little ship of fifty tons. They had also the *Minion* and two other small vessels. They cleared Plymouth on 2 October 1567, picked up between four and five hundred Negroes on the coast of Guinea, and sailed for the West Indies, where they secretly disposed of their slaves. The Spanish settlers were friendly and eager for Negroes but had to be watchful of their own officials because of an order from the King forbidding trade with strangers.

After encountering a hurricane between Cuba and the coast of Florida, the English ships had to seek shelter and repairs at the port of San Juan de Ulúa on the coast of Mexico. There, on 16 September 1568, they were surprised by the arrival of thirteen ships of Spain bringing the new Viceroy of Mexico. The Spaniards, after assuring Hawkins of the safety of his ships, treacherously attacked the little English fleet. Only the *Judith* and the *Minion* escaped, and Hawkins comments bitterly that the *Judith*, commanded by Drake, whom he does not mention, 'forsook us in our misery'. Since the *Minion*, with two hundred men packed aboard, had neither supplies nor space for so many on the long voyage home, approximately one hundred volunteered to go ashore. Twenty-three headed north, and three men eventually made their way to Nova Scotia, or some spot on the North Atlantic coast, where they were picked up by a French fishing vessel and returned to Europe. The other twenty were never heard of again.[3]

The remainder of the men went in search of the Spanish settlements. Some were killed by the Indians, but the survivors ultimately reached Mexico City where they suffered varying fates. They were all examined by the Inquisition and much of their testimony is still extant. Some were punished by death; others were condemned to the galleys; and the youngest were sent to monasteries for labour and instruction. A few obtained profitable employment and achieved some degree of comfort.

Drake in the *Judith* reached Plymouth on 20 January 1569. Hawkins on the same day sailed from Vigo on the coast of Spain, where he had been forced to put in for supplies. With many of his crew dying or so spent that they could scarcely work the ship, he reached Mounts Bay in the Channel on 25 January. The narrative of this desperate expedition was written by John Hawkins himself.[4]

Although some expeditions met with disaster, many Elizabethan adventurers and buccaneers brought back tangible evidence of the good things of the New World. Bristol fishermen had for years been making voyages beyond Iceland to the Grand Banks off Newfoundland and had come back to report that Newfoundland was a goodly land, worthy of settlement. They had made their voyages in summer, when the climate was less rigorous than at other seasons. Some had visited the mainland of North America and had tales to tell of its fertility, its vast forests, and the teeming fish in its waters.

The pillage of Spanish and Portuguese ships that English rovers encountered on the high seas showed the enormous riches that the enemies of England were accumulating from their possessions in the New World. Each galleon laden with gold, silver, pearls, and exotic products of America that fell into the hands of English mariners whetted the appetites of the English for more of this wealth. As Englishmen and other outsiders contemplated the economic power that Spain was gaining from her American possessions, the notion intensified that some means must be found to checkmate Spain and to gain some portion of the resources themselves. It was not enough merely to capture by chance a few stray galleons. Some part of the land itself ought to belong to England.

England had some technical claim to lands in the New World, at least in the north parts of it, as the result of a voyage of discovery made in 1497 by John Cabot, a naturalized Venetian, who had been born in Genoa and was at the time of his voyage in the employ of King Henry VII of England. Cabot sailed from Bristol in the spring of 1497 and returned in August after touching the mainland of America on the coast of Nova Scotia or Labrador. He had claimed the land for his royal employer, who showed his gratitude by giving him a reward of £10.

So long as England maintained close and friendly relations with Spain, as during the reign of Mary Tudor, for example, when Philip II of Spain was her consort, the English did not push their claim to American territory. The Spaniards, it is true, had not yet taken possession of the northern regions, but Spain still invoked the papal bulls of Alexander VI and the Treaty of Tordesillas, which had given her all of the territory west of a line drawn 370 leagues west of the Cape Verde Islands. Portugal had been awarded territory east of the line, a division that left her the hump of Brazil. But other nations were displeased at being shut out of the New World by the decision of a Spanish Pope, and Francis I of France scornfully demanded to see the will of Father Adam so that he could know how Adam had disposed of the patrimony of his descendants. After the Reformation, of course, the Protestant countries felt no compulsion to remember Alexander VI's division of the world.

As tension increased between Spain and England during the later years of the reign of Elizabeth, English buccaneers grew bolder in their depredations upon Spanish shipping, and the Queen herself was not above giving surreptitious aid to these sea-rovers—and taking a lion's share of the spoil. The demand also increased for England's active participation in the exploration and development of some part of the New World. One of the earliest and most active of the Elizabethans in fostering colonial enterprise was Humphrey Gilbert, a Devonshire man and half-brother of Walter Raleigh and closely connected with other West Country men who were concerning themselves with voyages designed to plunder the Spaniards and perhaps gain a foothold overseas.

In the late 1570's Gilbert was making various proposals to cripple Spain, enrich England, and gain bases for further attacks on Spanish possessions. On 2 November 1577 he prepared a state paper entitled 'A Discourse How Her Majesty May Annoy the King of Spain'. He proposed to annoy His Majesty of Spain by leading an expedition to capture the fishing fleets of Spain, Portugal, and France at Newfoundland when they were laden and ready to sail for home. Gilbert suggested that the government could disavow this action as the deeds of pirates. The best of the foreign vessels could be kept and the rest burned; fish could be unloaded in Holland until they could be sold.[5] A second project, to follow the first, would be the establishment of a base in the North where English sea-rovers could rendezvous while preparing for a mass attack on the Spanish West Indies. The English would then establish another base in the Caribbean area on Bermuda from which they would later move on to Santo Domingo and Cuba. Once seized and fortified, these islands could be used as staging areas for continued attacks on Spanish possessions on the mainland. Gilbert proposed that he be given a patent for a colonizing expedition to some distant place, and under that pretence he would carry out his forays. A ruthless and unscrupulous man, as he had demonstrated in the wars in Ireland, Gilbert was prepared to go to any lengths to checkmate Spain and enrich himself.

B

On 11 June 1578 Gilbert received letters patent from the Queen giving him permission during the next six years 'to discover, search, find, and view such remote, heathen, and barbarous lands, countries, and territories not actually possessed of any Christian prince or people as to him . . . shall seem good, and the same to have, hold, occupy, and enjoy to him, his heirs and assigns, for ever'. He was expressly forbidden to commit any act of violence against the subjects of any prince at peace with England.[6] Given Gilbert's character and the Machiavellian schemes that he had outlined earlier, it is not unlikely that he intended to use his colonizing expedition for piracy and plunder as well.

Gilbert's first expedition of 1578 is hidden in mystery. His fleet was back in Dartmouth harbour by the spring of 1579. Where his ships had been, or what they had accomplished, remains vague and uncertain. That a few of the captains were pirates is established, and when Gilbert was planning another expedition, the Privy Council ordered him to put up sureties guaranteeing good behaviour.[7] Professor Quinn thinks that perhaps Richard Hakluyt the elder drew up for Gilbert's guidance the pamphlet entitled 'Notes Framed by a Gentleman Heretofore to Be Given to One That Prepared for a Discovery and Went Not' (1578).[8]

That Gilbert was now determined to establish a colony in the New World under his patent is certain. From 1579 to 1583, when he set forth on the expedition to Newfoundland, he was busy with preparations and reconnaissance. Richard Hakluyt was engaged in collecting data about previous voyages and explorations for Gilbert's use,[9] and it seems likely that his first compilation, the *Divers Voyages touching the Discovery of America* (1582), was the outgrowth of his activities in Gilbert's behalf. At last on 11 June 1583 Gilbert sailed for the north parts of America with a fleet of five vessels. One vessel turned back, but four made their way to Newfoundland. On 5 August, Gilbert landed in St John's Harbour and formally took possession of the land in the name of the Queen.

One vessel was left in Newfoundland, and Gilbert started on his return journey with the *Delight*, the *Golden Hind*, commanded by Captain Edward Hayes who wrote the story of the expedition, and the *Squirrel*, a small frigate, in which Gilbert himself chose to sail. The homeward voyage proved disastrous. The captain of the *Delight* from sheer carelessness wrecked his vessel, which sank with the loss of over eighty men and all of Gilbert's maps and notes. Fearing that Gilbert's own vessel, the *Squirrel*, would also founder, Hayes some time later tried to persuade Gilbert to come aboard his own more seaworthy craft, but Gilbert made his famous reply, 'We are as near to Heaven by sea as by land'. On that very night, 9 September, the *Squirrel* capsized and sank with all hands. Gilbert had dreamed of an empire in the West and had paved the way for future colonization, but Fate left him only the empty honour of claiming Newfoundland for his queen.[10]

In the meantime, Francis Drake had made his famous circumnavigation of the globe in 1577–80. His ship, re-named at sea the *Golden Hind*, was so heavily laden with silver and gold captured from the defenceless Spaniards on the Pacific coast of South America that she nearly foundered on the long voyage home. Not only had Drake shown that an Englishman could emulate Magellan, but he had explored the Pacific North-west, visited the coast of California and named the land New Albion, and given fresh incentives for English interest in the New World.[11] That Queen Elizabeth was willing to knight him on the deck of the *Golden Hind* and thus give her royal approval of his deeds is indicative of the approaching open conflict with Spain.

The efforts of Gilbert to settle a colony in Newfoundland and the propaganda of the Hakluyts were not in vain. The year after Gilbert had proclaimed the Queen's rule in St John's Harbour, Newfoundland, Raleigh sent two of his captains, Philip Amadas and Arthur Barlow, to look for possible sites for settlement on the coast of North America. This expedition of 1584 explored the coast-line of what is now North Carolina and returned with glowing accounts of the goodness of the land, so fertile and fruitful that Barlow thought that he had had a vision of the Golden Age.[12] In compliment to the Queen, Raleigh named the whole region Virginia. The next year, 1585, he sent out his first colony in a fleet of seven vessels commanded by his cousin, Richard Grenville. Accompanying the hundred men who were to make the first settlement were John White, an artist, who made the first accurate paintings in water-colours of the North American Indians, and Thomas Harriot, a scientific observer, who wrote the first extended eye-witness account of Virginia and its products.[13]

Grenville planted the colony on Roanoke Island, at the upper end of Pamlico Sound, and left Ralph Lane as Governor. Lane was at first as enthusiastic as Barlow had been, but before the end of a year the colonists grew discouraged and were glad to go home in Drake's fleet, which called at Roanoke Island on its homeward voyage in 1586. Two weeks later Grenville returned, found the site deserted and left fifteen men as a token force to hold the region in the Queen's name. In the spring of 1587, Raleigh sent out another group of settlers. John White, the artist, was named Governor. They again settled on Roanoke Island, but, ominously, they discovered that all of Grenville's men had perished or disappeared. After a month's reconnaissance, White was persuaded to return to England to seek more settlers and a greater stock of supplies. He left behind his daughter, Eleanor Dare, wife of Ananias Dare, and their daughter, Virginia Dare, the first white child born in an English colony in North America.[14]

The fate of the Roanoke colony is enveloped in mystery. Because of the war with Spain, White was unable to return immediately. Ships intended for the succour of the colony went off on privateering expeditions or were commandeered for defence against the Spanish Armada. When White finally reached Roanoke in 1591, he found the letters 'CRO' cut in the bark of a tree and the word 'Croatoan' carved on a post. Perhaps the colonists were carried away by the Croatan Indians. Some North Carolinians believe that Croatan Indians still living in Robeson County show evidences of white blood that may derive from the 'Lost Colonists'. Other conjectures are that the colonists were annihilated by Spaniards from St Augustine, Florida, or that they grew desperate and attempted to return to England in a small vessel that had been left with them. Nobody knows what happened to Raleigh's unfortunate settlers. He, like Gilbert, was fated not to be the founder of a permanent English settlement in the New World.

The dream of colonization, of the establishment of profitable and strategic English bases in America, did not die with the failure of Raleigh's enterprises. Englishmen continued to explore the coast of North America and to bring back favourable reports of the richness of the country. In 1602 Captain Bartholomew Gosnold made a trading and reconnoitring voyage to the coast of what is now Massachusetts and, impressed with the abundance of cod-fish in the waters off shore, named a headland Cape Cod.[15] The next year another sea-captain, Martin Pring, sailed along the same coast, discovered Plymouth harbour, and returned with another favourable account of the fertility of the soil and the abundance of fish in the waters.

In 1605, an expedition financed largely by the Earl of Southampton and Sir Ferdinando Gorges and led by Captain George Waymouth again ventured to New England. Waymouth traded with the Indians and loaded his ship with furs and roots of sassafras, a small tree believed to have great medicinal value. He also kidnapped five Indians.[16] Gorges took charge of three of the Indians, saw that they learned English, and let them tell about the goodness of their native land overseas. He became an active promoter of colonization and for the rest of his life hoped to found a colony that would ensure prosperity for himself and his heirs. On the last day of May 1607, Gorges and Sir John Popham, the Lord Chief Justice of England, dispatched a colony consisting of 120 to the coast of Maine, where they landed in August. After a miserable winter spent at the mouth of the Kennebec River, the survivors, under the leadership of Raleigh Gilbert, son of Sir Humphrey Gilbert, decided to return to England. Although this colonizing venture failed, it is significant of future developments that Gilbert and his men were able to build a ship, which they named the *Virginia*, and load it with a profitable cargo of furs.

In the meantime, another group of colonists in May 1607 had landed at a site on the James River in what is now Virginia and had named their settlement Jamestown. The Jamestown colonists were sent out by the Virginia Company of London, which had received a charter from the King in the previous year. Although the little colony suffered many hardships in its early years, Englishmen had come to North America to stay. At last they had made a permanent settlement, and from this beginning a prosperous empire would develop.

The Virginia colony excited an enormous amount of interest throughout England. Since it was a joint-stock company, its shares were for sale and were readily bought by an astonishing cross-section of the population: tradesmen, mechanics, country gentlemen, clergymen, and nobles all subscribed to the stock of an enterprise that they believed would make them rich. The two Hakluyts and many promoters after them, as well as returning ship captains, had convinced the public that great wealth merely awaited exploitation by enterprising settlers.

The precise nature of this wealth was not always clear, but the promoters were certain that an abundance of all the good things of nature would be found in the new land. This confidence that emigrants could easily live off the land and find commodities that would bring them a ready profit helps to account for some of the disasters that befell the early settlers who came without experience and with inadequate supplies.

The belief in the infinite good things of the New World was one of the most persistent notions of the age.[17] The early colonial enterprises attracted numbers of gallants and gentlemen who came for adventure and, hopefully, for easy wealth that they would pick up along the way.

Everyone had heard of the vast quantities of gold and silver that the Spaniards had found and brought home. English adventurers saw no reason why they also might not have the luck of the Spanish *conquistadores*. The hope of discovering gold lingered in the consciousness of the early English emigrants and was a will-o'-the-wisp that led many to their ruin.

Writers about the goodness of the country across the seas succeeded too well in convincing the public. Such propagandists often begin by convincing themselves. Thus it was with Raleigh and with many others among the expansionists. Raleigh was certain that the Terrestrial Paradise or its equivalent would be found in America, and he succeeded in persuading others. This notion persisted for long generations after Raleigh and became a commonplace in the promotion literature, and indeed in the thinking of many colonials themselves. If they found their present conditions hard, they dreamed of better land, an easier life, and certain prosperity in some new valley beyond the settlements, or somewhere across the mountains. Optimism, often irrational optimism, became a dominant quality of restless Americans early in their history. Dickens was later to satirize the new Edens of the frontier in *Martin Chuzzlewit*, but already at the beginning of the colonial period, faith in the discovery of Terrestrial Paradises in North America was bringing emigrants from England. These hopeful settlers believed that in some fashion they would achieve prosperity in their new environment.

The merchants of London and other commercial towns, and economic planners like Richard Hakluyt the lawyer, also believed that colonies in America would bring prosperity, not merely to individuals, but to the realm as a whole. Although England had a population of less than five million, the number of unemployed who wandered from town to town convinced many people that the country was overpopulated and needed colonies to drain off this surplus. In the thinking of the economic planners one can discern clearly a doctrine that later came to be known as mercantilism: the notion that the colonies would supply raw materials to the mother country and provide a market for goods manufactured in England. A creeping inflation began to be noticeable in the early sixteenth century with the increased flow of precious metals into Europe. By the end of the century rising prices that affected everyone in England were of grave concern to thoughtful men in the government and to the embryonic economists of the day. They were disturbed about what we today would call the problem of

the balance of payments. Too much bullion flowed out of the country
in exchange for luxuries; too much money was spent on mere baubles,
so the argument ran. England should find a source within its own
jurisdiction for exotic luxuries that were draining away its treasure.
Worse than this, the money spent on exotics for the most part went to
countries hostile, or potentially hostile, to England—'doubtful friends',
the lawyer Hakluyt calls them. Two commodities that caused the
greatest drain of money were silk and wine, but other luxuries were
also costly. From her enemies England had to buy dyestuffs, olive oil
(used in the processing of cloth rather than in the diet of Englishmen),
raisins, dates, sugar, spices, drugs, and ships' stores. Hakluyt and
other advisers on colonial projects were constantly exhorting emigrants to try to find or produce these commodities.

The silk and wine delusion lasted until the end of the colonial period,
but England never found a satisfactory source for these two products.
Early in the history of Virginia, however, the planners in London had
high hopes of that colony. A treatise prepared by John Bonoeil on the
nurture of silkworms, the preparation of raw silk, and the care of vines
was equipped with a letter from King James himself and another from
the Earl of Southampton enjoining the colonists to set to work on these
two projects. Each head of a household was to have one of these useful
books of instruction, and King James confidently believed that this
treatise would be sufficient to ensure a supply of silk and wine from
Virginia. Such is the faith of theorists and economic planners.[18]
Unhappily for the success of these ventures, the Virginia colonists
were so busy trying to defend their settlements and to raise enough
foodstuffs to sustain life that they could not be bothered with silkworms
and vineyards. Never was there enough skilled labour in the colonies
to produce silk, even if other conditions had been favourable.

Another persistent delusion was the belief that cures for all of the
ills of mankind might be found in vegetable, animal, or mineral
products of the New World. John Frampton, an English merchant in
Spain, translated a treatise on the drugs of the New World, written by
Dr Nicolás Monardes of Seville, and gave it the alluring title of *Joyful
News out of the New Found World: Wherein Is Declared the Rare and
Singular Virtues of Diverse and Sundry Herbs, Trees, Oils, Plants, and
Stones, with Their Applications, as Well for Physic as Chirurgery; the
Said, Being Well Applied, Bringeth Such Present Remedy for All
Diseases as May Seem Altogether Incredible* ... (1577). This treatise,
which had three editions by 1596, popularized the idea that miracle

drugs would be forthcoming from America. Ralph Lane, writing back from Roanoke Island, reflects this belief in his report on gums and other vegetable sources of drugs.[19] Tobacco, which Harriot and his colleagues learned from the Indians to smoke in pipes, was described at length in Monardes' work as possessing wondrous curative powers. The roots and bark of the sassafras tree also were highly praised as a remedy of many of the ills of humankind, and for a time sassafras brought a high price on the European market. Captain Newport's crews after landing the first settlers at Jamestown, fell avidly to digging sassafras roots to take back on the return journey.

Since the belief was general that useful products in vast abundance would be easily available in the fruitful lands along the North Atlantic seaboard, many of the early settlers came with the notion that they could live without work, or, at least, with very little exertion. Captain John Smith, when he became 'President' of the little colony at Jamestown, had to exert strenuous efforts to force the indolent gallants to chop wood, clear land, and plant corn. When George Percy, a gallant himself and brother of the ninth Earl of Northumberland, took over the rule of the colony from Smith, the 'gentlemen' again resumed their idle ways, and one observer commented that they spent most of their time bowling in the streets of Jamestown.

The hardships of colonial life and the ever-present threat from hostile Indians eventually taught emigrants that the price of survival was hard work, watchfulness, and courage. Nature, they learned, would not rain down her bounties like manna. Although promoters of colonization continued to emphasize the fruitfulness of the country, a new note crept into some of the writing. Authors began to stress the profits to be made from humble products and say less about the exotics. No longer did writers promise that the north parts of America would produce raisins, dates, and figs. Men like Captain John Smith and others familiar with the realities of the New World described the abundance of fish, the vast sources of ships' stores (timber, masts, spars, turpentine, and tar), and the money to be made from trading with the Indians for furs.[20]

Interest in the Indians and Indian life mounted in England, and writers sought to satisfy this curiosity with reports of the native people. William Strachey wrote a fairly detailed account of the Indians for his *History of Travel into Virginia Britannia* (c. 1612).[21] The marriage of John Rolfe to Pocahontas created considerable excitement and a few odd reactions. For example, when she was described as an Indian princess, King James showed concern because Rolfe, a commoner, had not sought royal permission to marry her.

The Virginia Company of London was extremely sensitive to unfavourable criticism and was careful to see that reports praising Virginia and its products got into print. During the dark days of 1609, when the little colony seemed destined to failure, the Virginia Company enlisted several influential clergymen to preach about the duty of Englishmen to wrest a part of the New World from the Spaniards and to carry the gospel to the heathen overseas.[22] These sermons, however, emphasize earthly benefits more vividly than they do the spiritual values in converting the Indians.

One of the most enthusiastic and diligent of the preachers advocating colonial enterprise was William Crashaw, father of Richard Crashaw the poet. He was actively engaged in encouraging other ministers to preach about the desirability of colonizing Virginia, and he served as a sort of director of publicity for Virginia. He himself preached a famous sermon of farewell to the expedition headed by Lord De La Warr on its departure in 1610. Although Crashaw declares that the conversion of the Indians is a 'necessary duty', he shows more concern about the economic and political implications of colonization than about the Indians' salvation.

One of the preachers who actually went out to Virginia was Alexander Whitaker. He sent back a glowing account that Crashaw edited and the Virginia Company published as *Good News from Virginia* (1613).[23] Crashaw's long introduction asserts that the recent hardships and difficulties in Virginia are merely an indication that God tests those whom He designs for some great work. He notes that the miraculous preservation of Sir Thomas Gates and his company after the wreck of the *Sea Venture* in the Bermudas in 1609 is proof of God's favour, not only to Virginia, but to other colonial enterprises. For example, He took this occasion to reveal the Bermudas as a garden spot, a place like unto Paradise, especially reserved for the English. So concerned is the Almighty over English colonization, Crashaw points out, 'that assuredly God Himself is the founder and favourer of this plantation [Virginia]'. When at last the reader is permitted to get to Whitaker's own treatise, he discovers another laudatory tract emphasizing God's great desire for the English to find success in the New World. Though profits have not yet been realized from the enterprise, Whitaker declares, they are inevitable.

Preachers were so useful in advertising colonial enterprises that the promoters were careful to enlist others in their service. No less a person than Dr John Donne, the Dean of St Paul's, for example, was employed by Sir Edwin Sandys, the Treasurer of the Virginia Company, to preach a sermon before the Company on 13 November 1622 to help counteract the effect of news of the massacre of Virginia settlers by the Indians on 22 March. Within a few weeks Donne's *Sermon upon the 8th Verse of the 1st Chapter of the Acts of the Apostles* was printed by order of the Company. Although this sermon is not one of Donne's greatest examples of prose, he makes a number of telling statements about the virtues of settling Englishmen overseas. 'You shall have made this island, which is but as the suburbs of the old world, a bridge, a gallery to the new, to join all to that world that shall never grow old, the Kingdom of Heaven', he asserts in one memorable passage. Further evidence of Donne's concern for the Virginia colony is found in a poem written in commendation of Captain John Smith's *General History of Virginia* (1624). Perhaps it is worth remembering that Donne was a stockholder in the Virginia Company and, gossips reported, wanted to become its secretary.

Although Elizabethan England did not have the benefit of newspapers, sensational news travelled fast and was magnified in the telling. For this reason, the promoters of colonization were eager to have printed optimistic accounts of the country overseas and of their efforts to settle it—and to suppress or refute unfavourable reports. Raleigh was so convinced of the glowing promise of Virginia that he was willing for Harriot to make a scientific appraisal of the land and its products in *A Brief and True Report of the New-Found Land of Virginia* (1588), one of the earliest and best of the accounts. Later reports are frequently shorter and less detailed, with emphasis upon the promising aspects of colonization and with few warnings of the hardships involved. Those narratives that did give unfavourable news were sometimes suppressed. For example, William Strachey's 'letter to a noble lady', describing the shipwreck of the *Sea Venture* in 1609 and the difficulties that ensued—a vivid report that Shakespeare may have read in manuscript—was not published until Purchas included it in his *Pilgrims* (1625) under the title of 'A True Reportory of the Wrack and Redemption of Sir Thomas Gates'.[24] Sensational descriptions of Indian attacks on the colonists that did get into print were followed quickly with official 'Declarations' and other pamphlets giving an optimistic account of colonial prospects. The idea that colonies were pious undertakings that God would favour because of the adventurers' efforts to Christianize the heathen, that these efforts would be inevitably profitable, and that both the emigrants to the New World and the English commonwealth would grow prosperous through these endeavours receives constant iteration in the literature concerned with expansion. Even many of those who went overseas themselves and endured the hardships of the early years believed implicitly in the future success of their ventures, as their private letters indicate. A few wrote back sourly and realistically of their difficulties, but they were in the minority.

The doctrine grew that God had destined the English to be a power in the New World. For instance, Lewis Hughes, a minister writing back from the Bermudas in 1615 in *A Letter Sent into England from the Summer Islands* stresses the idea that God had especially reserved this portion of the world 'till now that it hath pleased His Holy Majesty to discover and bestow them [the Bermudas] upon his people of England'.[25] That the English were a chosen people, predestined to settle North America, was an accepted belief by others besides the Reverend Lewis Hughes, and it eventually developed into the notion of 'manifest destiny' invoked by English-speaking Americans in seizing the whole of the Great West in the middle of the nineteenth century.

Interest in North America continued to increase during the early years of the seventeenth century until almost any account, true or exaggerated, found eager readers. Captain John Smith's *General History of Virginia* (1624), telling of his own adventures and including reports of others, was favourably received and probably was influential in encouraging further efforts at colonization. Poets sang the praises of colonial enterprise, as evidenced by Drayton's famous ode 'To the Virginian Voyage',[26] John Fletcher's verses from *The Island Princess*,[27] and many other poetical effusions. Exaggerated stories about the New World became a theme for satire, as exemplified in *Eastward Ho!*, but, in general, readers accepted accounts of the wonders of the New World at face value. Throughout the late sixteenth and early seventeenth centuries, despite occasional reports of disasters, the public continued to believe that new Edens of infinite goodness would be discovered across the Atlantic. That belief grew with the years and provided a motivating influence upon thousands of emigrants who dared to risk the hazards of the sea and the even more fearful risks of death at the hands of savages to create commonwealths in the wilderness of America.

# Purposes and Policies to Be Observed in Colonization (1578)

Richard Hakluyt the elder, cousin of Richard Hakluyt the preacher and compiler of voyages, was a lawyer and a member of the Middle Temple. He was closely associated with an enterprising group of London merchants interested in trade and expansion overseas. Hakluyt himself anticipated many of the mercantilist ideas that became a part of British colonial dogma in the eighteenth century. His emphasis on the economic advantages of colonies overseas appears in various papers that he prepared for the encouragement of overseas expansion. The 'Notes' printed here were probably written out for Sir Humphrey Gilbert, who was planning an expedition in 1578. They were first printed by Richard Hakluyt in *Divers Voyages to America* (1582). More recently they have been reprinted by E. G. R. Taylor, *The Original Writings and Correspondence of the Two Richard Hakluyts*, The Hakluyt Society, 2nd Ser., Nos. 76, 77 (London, 1935), II, 116–22.

*Notes framed by a gentleman heretofore to be given to one that prepared for a discovery and went not, and not unfit to be committed to print, considering the same may stir up considerations of these and such other things not unmeet in such new voyages as may be attempted hereafter.*

That the first seat be chosen on the sea-side, so as (if it may be) you may have your own navy within the bay, river, or lake within your seat safe from the enemy; and so as the enemy shall be forced to lie in open road abroad without, to be dispersed with all winds and tempests that shall arise. Thus seated, you shall be least subject to annoy of the enemy; so may you by your navy within pass out to all parts of the world; and so may the ships of England have access to you to supply all wants; so may your commodities be carried away also.

This seat is to be chosen in temperate climate in sweet air, where you may possess always sweet water, wood, sea-coals or turf, with fish, flesh, grain, fruits, herbs, and roots, or so many of those as may suffice very[1] necessity for the life of such as shall plant there. And for the possessing of mines of gold, of silver, copper, quicksilver, or of any such precious thing, the wants of those needful things may be supplied from some other place by sea, etc. Stone to make lime of; slate stone to tile withal, of such clay as makes tile; stone to wall withal, if brick may not be made; timber for building easily to be conveyed to the place; reed to cover houses or such-like, if tile or slate be not; are to be looked for as things without which no city may be made nor people in civil sort be kept together.

The people there to plant and to continue are either to live without traffic, or by traffic and by trade of merchandise. If they shall live without sea traffic at the first, they become naked by want of linen and woollen and very miserable by infinite wants that will otherwise ensue; and so will they be forced of themselves to depart, or else easily they will be consumed by the Spaniards, by the French, or by the natural inhabitants of the country, and so the enterprise becomes reproachful to our nation and a let[2] to many other good purposes that may be taken in hand.

And by trade of merchandise they cannot live, except the sea or the land there may yield commodity for commodity. And therefore you ought to have most special regard to that point and so to plant that the natural commodities of the place and seat may draw to you access of navigation for the same, or that by your own navigation you may carry the same out and fetch home the supply of the wants of the seat.

Such navigation so to be employed shall, besides the supply of wants, be able to encounter with foreign force.

And for that in the ample vent of such things as are brought to you out of England by sea stands a matter of great consequence, it behoves that all humanity and courtesy and much forbearing of revenge to the inland people be used. So shall you have firm amity with your neighbours, so shall you have their inland commodities to maintain traffic, and so shall you wax rich and strong in force. Divers and several commodities of the inland are not in great plenty to be brought to your hands without the aid of some portable or navigable river or ample lake, and therefore to have the help of such a one is most requisite. And so is it of effect for the dispersing of your own commodities in exchange into the inlands.

Nothing is more to be endeavoured with the inland people than familiarity. For so may you best discover all the natural commodities of their country, and also all their wants, all their strengths, all their weakness, and with whom they are in war and with whom confederate in peace and amity, etc., which known, you may work many great effects of greatest consequence.

And in your planting, the consideration of the climate and of the soil be matters that are to be respected. For if it be so that you may let in the salt sea water, not mixed with the fresh, into flats where the sun is of the heat that it is at Rochelle,[3] in the Bay of Portugal,[4] or in Spain, then may you procure a man of skill, and so you have won one noble commodity for the fishing and for trade of merchandise by making of salt.

Or if the soil and climate be such as may yield you the grape as good as that at Bordeaux, as that in Portugal, or as that about Seville in Spain, or that in the islands of the Canaries, then there rests but a workman to put in execution to make wines and to dress raisins of the sun and other[s], etc.

Or if you find a soil of the temperature of the south part of Spain or Barbary, in the which you find the olive tree to grow, then you may be assured of a noble merchandise for this realm, considering that our great trade of clothing does require oil, and weighing how dear of late it is become by the vent they have of that commodity in the West Indies. If you find the wild olive there, it may be grafted.

Or if you can find the berry of cochineal with which we colour stammels,[5] or any root, berry, fruit, wood, or earth fit for dyeing, you win a notable thing fit for our state of clothing. This cochineal is natural in the West Indies on that firm.

Or if you have hides of beasts fit for sole leather, etc., it will be a merchandise right good, and the savages there yet cannot tan leather after our kind, yet excellently after their own manner.

Or if the soil shall yield figs, almonds, sugar-canes, quinces, oranges, lemons, potatoes, etc., there may arise some trade and traffic by figs, almonds, sugar, marmalade, suckets,[6] etc.

Or if great woods be found, if they be of cypress, chests may be made; if they be of some kind of trees, pitch and tar may be made; if they be of some other, then they may yield rosin, turpentine, etc., and all for trade and traffic. Casks for wine and oil may be made, likewise ships and houses, etc.

And because traffic is a thing so material, I wish that great observation be taken what every soil yields naturally, in what commodity soever, and what it may be made to yield by endeavour, and to send us notice home, that thereupon we may devise what means may be thought of to raise trades.

Now admit that we might not be suffered by the savages to enjoy any whole country or any more than the scope of a city, yet if we might enjoy traffic and be assured of the same, we might be much enriched, our navy might be increased, and a place of safety might there be found, if change of religion or civil wars should happen in this realm, which are things of great benefit. But if we may enjoy large territory of apt soil, we might so use the matter as we should not depend upon Spain for oils, sacks, resins, oranges, lemons, Spanish skins, etc., nor upon France for wood, basalt, and Gascony wines, nor on Eastland[7] for flax, pitch, tar, masts, etc. So we should not so exhaust our treasure and so exceedingly enrich our doubtful friends as we do, but should purchase the commodities that we want for half the treasure that now we do; but should by our own industries and the benefits of the soil there cheaply purchase oils, wines, salt, fruits, pitch, tar, flax, hemp, masts, boards, fish, gold, silver, copper, tallow, hides, and many commodities. Besides, if there be no flats to make salt on, if you have plenty of wood you may make it in sufficient quantity for common uses at home there.

If you can keep a safe haven, although you have not the friendship of the near neighbours, yet you may have traffic by sea upon one shore or other upon that firm, in time to come, if not present.

If you find plenty of timber on the shore-side or upon any portable river, you were best to cut down of the same the first winter to be seasoned for ships, barks, boats, and houses. If near such wood there be any river or brook upon the which a sawing-mill may be placed, it would do great service, and therefore consideration would be had of such place.

And if such port and chosen place of settling were in possession and after fortified by art, although by the land-side our Englishmen were kept in and might not enjoy any traffic with the next neighbours nor any victuals, yet might they victual themselves of fish to serve very necessity and enter into amity with the enemies of their next neighbours; and so have vent of their merchandise of England and also have victuals, or by means hereupon to be used to force the next neighbours to amity. And, keeping a navy at the settling place, they should find out where to have traffic along the tract of land and at divers islands also. And so this first seat might in time become a stapling place[8] of the commodities of many countries and territories, and in time this place might become of all the provinces round about the only governor. If the place first chosen should not so well please our people as some other more lately found out, there might be an easy remove, and that might be razed, or rather kept for others of our nation, to avoid an ill neighbour, etc.

If the soils adjoining to such convenient haven and settling places be found marshy and boggy, then men skilful in draining are to be carried thither. For art may work wonderful effects therein and make the soil rich for many uses.

To plant upon an island in the mouth of some notable river, or upon the point of the land entering into the river, if no such island be, were to great end. For if such river were navigable or portable far into the land, then would arise great hope of planting in fertile soils and traffic on the one or on the other side of the river, or on both, or the linking in amity with one or other petty king contending there for dominion.

Such rivers found, both barges and boats may be made for the safe passage of such as shall pierce the same. These are to be covered with doubles of coarse linen[9] artificially wrought, to defend the rower from the arrow or the dart of the savage.

Since every soil of the world by art may be made to yield things to feed and to clothe man, bring in your return a perfect note of the soil without and within, and we shall devise, if need require, to amend the same and to draw it to more perfection. And if you find not fruits in your planting place to your liking, we shall in five dryfats[10] furnish you with such kinds of plants to be carried thither the winter after your planting as shall the very next summer following yield you some fruit, and the year next following as much as shall suffice a town as big as Calais, and that shortly after shall be able to yield you great store of strong, durable, good cider to drink. These trees shall be able to increase you within less than seven years as many trees presently to bear as may suffice the people of divers parishes, which at the first settling may stand you in good stead if the soil have not the commodity of fruits of goodness already. Because you ought greedily to hunt after things that yield present relief without trouble of carriage thither, therefore I make mention of these thus especially, to the end you may have it especially in mind.

# 2

# England's Time Approaches for Appropriating Part of the New World
## (1582)

Richard Hakluyt the preacher believed in overseas expansion with the fervour of religion, and he sought to stir his fellow-countrymen to a realization of their obligation to seize a part of the New World before Spain pre-empted it all. In the dedication to Philip Sidney of *Divers Voyages touching the Discovery of America* (1582), his first compilation, he emphasized the opportunities now awaiting Englishmen overseas and the advantages that would accrue from colonization. The dedicatory preface to *Divers Voyages* has been reprinted by Taylor, *Original Writings . . . of the Two Richard Hakluyts*, I, 175–81.

To the right worshipful and most virtuous gentleman, Master Philip Sidney, Esquire

I marvel not a little (Right Worshipful) that since the first discovery of America (which is now full fourscore-and-ten years), after so great conquest and plantings of the Spaniards and Portugals there, that we of England could never have the grace to set fast footing in such fertile and temperate places as are left as yet unpossessed by them. But, again, when I consider that there is a time for all men, and see the Portugals' time to be out of date, and that the nakedness of the Spaniards and their long-hidden secrets are now at length espied, whereby they went about to delude the world, I conceive great hope that the time approacheth and now is that we of England may share and part stakes[1] (if we will ourselves) both with the Spaniard and the Portugal in part of America and other regions as yet undiscovered.

And surely, if there were in us that desire to advance the honour of our country which ought to be in every good man, we would not all this while have forslown[2] the possessing of those lands which of equity and right appertain unto us, as by the discourses that follow shall appear most plainly. Yea, if we would behold with the eye of pity how all our prisons are pestered[3] and filled with able men to serve their country, which for small robberies are daily hanged up in great numbers, some twenty at a clap out of one jail (as was seen at the last assizes at Rochester), we would hasten and further, every man to his power, the deducting of some colonies of our superfluous people into those temperate and fertile parts of America, which, being within six weeks' sailing of England, are yet unpossessed by any Christians and seem to offer themselves unto us, stretching nearer unto Her Majesty's dominions than to any other part of Europe.

We read that the bees, when they grow to be too many in their own hive at home, are wont to be led out by their captains to swarm abroad and seek themselves a new dwelling place. If the examples of the Grecians and Carthaginians of old time and the practice of our age may not move us, yet let us learn wisdom of these small, weak, and unreasonable creatures.

It chanced very lately that upon occasion I had great conference in matters of cosmography with an excellent learned man of Portugal,[4] most privy to all the discoveries of his nation, who wondered that those blessed countries from the point of Florida northward were all this while unplanted by Christians, protesting with great affection and zeal that if he were now as young as I (for at this present he is threescore years of age) he would sell all he had (being a man of no small wealth and honour) to furnish a convenient number of ships to sea for the inhabiting of those countries and reducing those gentile people to Christianity. Moreover, he added that John Barros, their chief cosmographer, being moved with the like desire, was the cause that Brasilia was first inhabited by the Portugals; where they have nine baronies or lordships, and thirty *engenhos* or sugar mills, two or three hundred slaves belonging to each mill, with a judge and other officers and a church; so that every mill is as it were a little commonwealth; and that the country was first planted by such men as for small offences were saved from the rope. This spake he, not only unto me and in my hearing, but also in the presence of a friend of mine, a man of great skill in the mathematics. If this man's desire might be executed, we might not only for the present time take possession of that good land, but also in short space by God's grace find out that short and easy passage by the north-west, which we have hitherto so long desired and whereof we have made many good and more than probable conjectures, a few whereof I think it not amiss here to set down, although Your Worship know them as well as myself.

First, therefore, it is not to be forgotten that Sebastian Cabot wrote to Master Baptista Ramusius that he verily believed that all the north part of America is divided into islands. Secondly, that Master John Verrazano, which had been thrice on that coast, in an old excellent map which he gave to Henry the Eighth and is yet in the custody of Master Lok,[5] doth so lay it out as it is to be seen in the map annexed to the end of this book, being made according to Verrazano's plat. Thirdly, the story of Gil Gonsalva, recorded by Franciscus Lopez de Gómara, which is said to have sought a passage by the north-west, seemeth to argue and prove the same. Fourthly, in the second relation of Jacques Cartier, the twelfth chapter, the people of Saguenay[6] do testify that upon their coasts westward there is a sea the end whereof is unknown unto them. Fifthly, in the end of that discourse is added this as a special remembrance: to wit, that they of Canada say that it is a month's space to sail to a land where cinnamon and cloves are growing. Sixthly, the people of Florida signified unto John Ribaut (as it is expressed in his discourse herewithal imprinted) that they might sail from the River of May unto Cibola and the South Sea through their country within twenty days. Seventhly, the experience of Captain Frobisher on the hither side, and Sir Francis Drake on the back side of America, with the testimony of Nicolaus and Anthony Zeni that Estotiland[7] is an island, doth yield no small hope thereof. Lastly, the judgement of the excellent geographer Gerardus Mercator, which his son Rumold Mercator, my friend, showed me in his letters and drew out for me in writing, is not of wise men lightly to be regarded. His words are these: *Magna tamet si pauca de nova Frobisheri navigatione scribis, quam miror ante multos annos non fuisse attentatam. Non enim dubium est, quin recta et brevis via pateat in occidentem Cathaium usque. In quod regnum si recte navigantium instituant nobilissimas totius mundi merces colligent, et multis Gentibus adhuc idololatris Christi nomen communicabant.* 'You write', saith he to his son, 'great matters, though very briefly, of the new discovery of Frobisher, which I wonder was never these many years heretofore attempted. For there is no doubt but that there is a straight and short way open into the west even unto Cathay. Into which kingdom, if they take their course aright, they shall gather the most noble merchandise of all the world and shall make the name of Christ to be known unto many idolatrous and heathen people.'

And here to conclude and shut up this matter, I have heard myself, of merchants of credit that have lived long in Spain, that King Philip hath made a law of late that none of his subjects shall discover to the northwards of five-and-forty degrees of America; which may be thought to proceed chiefly of two causes: the one, lest passing to the north they shall discover the open passage from the South Sea to our North Sea; the other because they have not people enough to possess and keep that passage but rather thereby should open a gap for other nations to pass that way. Certes, if hitherto in our own discoveries we had not been led with a preposterous desire of seeking rather gain than God's glory, I assure myself that our labours had taken far better effect. But we forgot that godliness is great riches, and that if we first seek the kingdom of God, all other things will be given unto us, and that as the light accompanieth the sun and the heat the fire, so lasting riches do wait upon them that are jealous[8] for the advancement of the kingdom of Christ and the enlargement of His glorious Gospel; as it is said, 'I will honour them that honour me.' I trust that now, being taught by their manifold losses, our men will take a more godly course and use some part of their goods to His glory; if not, He will turn even their covetousness to serve Him, as He hath done the pride and avarice of the Spaniards and Portugals, who, pretending in glorious words that they made their discoveries chiefly to convert infidels to our most holy faith (as they say) in deed and truth sought not them but their goods and riches.

Which thing that our nation may more speedily and happily perform, there is no better means in my simple judgement than the increase of knowledge in the art of navigation and breeding of skilfulness in seamen; which Charles the Emperor and the King of Spain that now is wisely considering have in their contractation house in Seville appointed a learned reader of the said art of navigation and joined with him certain examiners, and have distinguished the orders among the seamen, as the grummet, which is the basest degree, the mariner, which is the second, the master the third, and the pilot the fourth. Unto the which two last degrees none is admitted without he have heard the reader for a certain space (which is commonly an excellent mathematician, of which number were Pedro de Medina, which writ learnedly of the art of navigation, and Alonso de Chaves and Hieronymo de Chaves,[9] whose works likewise I have seen), and, being found fit by him and his assistants, which are to examine matters touching experience, they are admitted with as great solemnity and giving of presents to the ancient master and the pilots and the readers and examiners as the great doctors in the universities or our great sergeants at the law when they proceed, and so are admitted to take charge for the Indies.

And that Your Worship may know that this is true, Master Stephen

Borough, now one of the four masters of the Queen's Navy, told me that newly after his return from the discovery of Muscovy by the north in Queen Mary's day, the Spaniards, having intelligence that he was master in that discovery, took him into their contractation house at their making and admitting of masters and pilots, giving him great honour, and presented him with a pair of perfumed gloves worth five or six ducats.

I speak all this to the end that the like order of erecting such a lecturer[10] here in London or about Ratcliff in some convenient place were a matter of great consequence and importance for the saving of many men's lives and goods, which now through gross ignorance are daily in great hazard, to the no small detriment of the whole realm. For which cause I have dealt with the right worshipful Sir Francis Drake that, seeing God hath blessed him so wonderfully, he would do this honour to himself and benefit to his country to be at the cost to erect such a lecture. Whereunto in most bountiful manner at the very first he answered that he liked so well of the notion that he would give £20 by the year standing, and £20 more beforehand to a learned man, to furnish him with instruments and maps, that would take this thing upon him; yea, so ready he was that he earnestly requested me to help him to the notice of a fit man for that purpose, which I, for the zeal I bear to this good action, did presently and brought him one, who came unto him and conferred with him thereupon; but in fine he would not undertake the lecture unless he might have £40 a year standing, and so the matter ceased for that time. Howbeit the worthy and good knight remaineth still constant and will be, as he told me very lately, as good as his word. Now if God shall put into the head of any nobleman to contribute the £20 to make this lecture a competent living for a learned man, the whole realm no doubt might reap no small benefit thereby.

To leave this matter and to draw to an end, I have here, Right Worshipful, in this hasty work first put down the title which we have to that part of America which is from Florida to 67 degrees northward, by the letters patent granted to John Cabot and his three sons, Lewis, Sebastian, and Sancto, with Sebastian's own certificates to Baptista Ramusius of his discovery of America, and the testimony of Fabyan, our own chronicler. Next, I have caused to be added the letters of Master Robert Thorne to King Henry the Eighth, and his discourse to his ambassador, Doctor Ley, in Spain, of the like argument, with the King's setting-out of two ships for discovery in the nineteenth year of his reign. Then I have translated the voyage of John Verrazano from 30 degrees to Cape Breton; and the last year, at my charges and other of my friends' by my exhortation, I caused Jacques Cartier's two voyages of discovering the Grand Bay,[11] and Canada, Saguenay, and Hochelaga[12] to be translated out of my volumes, which are to be annexed to this present translation. Moreover, following the order of the map and not the course of time, I have put down the discourse of Nicolaus and Anthony Zeni. The last treatise of John Ribaut is a thing that hath been already printed but not now to be had, unless I had caused it to be printed again. The map is Master Michael Lok's, a man for his knowledge in divers languages, and especially in cosmography, able to do his country good, and worthy, in my judgement, for the manifold good parts in him, of good reputation and better fortune. This cursory pamphlet I am overbold to present unto Your Lordship; but I had rather want a little discretion than to be found unthankful to him which hath been always so ready to pleasure me and all my name.

Here I cease, craving pardon for my own boldness, trusting also that Your Worship will continue and increase your accustomed favour towards these godly and honourable discoveries.

Your Worship's humble always to command,

R.H.

[Richard Hakluyt]

3

# Reasons for Colonization (1585)

'Inducements to the Liking of the Voyage Intended towards Virginia in 40 and 42 Degrees of Latitude, Written 1585, by M. Richard Hakluyt the Elder, Sometime Student of the Middle Temple.' Printed in John Brereton's *Discovery of the North Part of Virginia* (1602) and reprinted by Taylor, *Original Writings . . . of the Two Richard Hakluyts*, II, 327–38. Miss Taylor points out that the title mentions 40–42 degrees north latitude but the text refers to the country in latitudes 36, 37, and 40 degrees, an indication that the material was prepared for Raleigh's colonial ventures and was adapted later for Brereton's expedition to the more northerly regions.

[REASONS for colonization:]

1. The glory of God by planting of religion among those infidels.

2. The increase of the force of the Christians.

3. The possibility of the enlarging of the dominions of the Queen's Most Excellent Majesty, and consequently of her honour, revenues, and of her power by this enterprise.

4. An ample vent in time to come of the woollen cloths of England, especially those of the coarsest sorts, to the maintenance of our poor, that else starve or become burdensome to the realm; and vent also of sundry our commodities upon the tract of that firm land, and possibly in other regions from the northern side of that main.

5. A great possibility of further discoveries of other regions from the north part of the same land by sea, and of unspeakable honour and benefit that may rise upon the same by the trades to ensue in Japan, China, and Cathay, etc.

6. By return thence, this realm shall receive (by reason of the situation of the climate, and by reason of the excellent soil) woad,[1] oil, wines, hops, salt, and most or all the commodities that we receive from the best parts of Europe, and we shall receive the same better cheap than now we receive them, as we may use the matter.

7. Receiving the same thence, the navy, the human strength of this realm, our merchants and their goods, shall not be subject to arrest of ancient enemies and doubtful friends as of late years they have been.

8. If our nation do not make any conquest there but only use traffic and change of commodities, yet, by means the country is not very mighty but divided into petty kingdoms, they shall not dare to offer us any great annoy but such as we may easily revenge with sufficient chastisement to the unarmed people there.

9. Whatsoever commodities we receive by the Steelyard Merchants, or by our own merchants from Eastland, be it flax, hemp, pitch, tar, masts, clapboard, wainscot, or such-like; the like good[s] may we receive from the north and north-east part of that country near unto Cape Breton, in return for our coarse woollen cloths, flannels, and rugs fit for those colder regions.

10. The passage to and fro is through the main ocean sea, so as we are not in danger of any enemy's coast.

11. In the voyage we are not to cross the burnt zone, nor to pass through frozen seas encumbered with ice and fogs, but in temperate climate at all times of the year; and it requireth not, as the East Indies voyage doth, the taking in of water in divers places, by reason that it is to be sailed in five or six weeks; and by the shortness the merchant

may yearly make two returns (a factory² once being erected there), a matter in trade of great moment.

12. In this trade by the way, in our pass to and fro, we have in tempests and other haps all the ports of Ireland to our aid and no near coast of any enemy.

13. By this ordinary trade we may annoy the enemies to Ireland and succour the Queen's Majesty's friends there, and in time we may from Virginia yield them whatsoever commodity they now receive from the Spaniard; and so the Spaniards shall want the ordinary victual that heretofore they received yearly from thence, and so they shall not continue trade, nor fall so aptly in practice against this government as now by their trade thither they may.

14. We shall, as it is thought, enjoy in this voyage either some small islands to settle on or some one place or other on the firm land to fortify for the safety of our ships, our men, and our goods, the like whereof we have not in any foreign place of our traffic, in which respect we may be in degree of more safety and more quiet.

15. The great plenty of buff hides and of many other sundry kinds of hides there now presently to be had, the trade of whale and seal fishing and of divers other fishings in the great rivers, great bays, and seas there, shall presently defray the charge in good part or in all of the first enterprise, and so we shall be in better case than our men were in Russia, where many years were spent and great sums of money consumed before gain was found.

16. The great broad rivers of that main that we are to enter into, so many leagues navigable or portable into the mainland, lying so long a tract with so excellent and so fertile a soil on both sides, do seem to promise all things that the life of man doth require and whatsoever men may wish that are to plant upon the same or to traffic in the same.

17. And whatsoever notable commodity the soil within or without doth yield in so long a tract, that is to be carried out from thence to England, the same rivers so great and deep do yield no small benefit for the sure, safe, easy, and cheap carriage of the same to shipboard, be it of great bulk or of great weight.

18. And in like sort whatsoever commodity of England the inland people there shall need, the same rivers do work the like effect in benefit for the incarriage of the same aptly, easily, and cheaply.

19. If we find the country populous and desirous to expel us and injuriously to offend us, that seek but just and lawful traffic, then, by reason that we are lords of navigation and they not so, we are the

better able to defend ourselves by reason of those great rivers and to annoy them in many places.

20. Where there be many petty kings or lords planted on the rivers' sides, and [who] by all likelihood maintain the frontiers of their several territories by wars, we may by the aid of this river join with this king here, or with that king there, at our pleasure, and may so with a few men be revenged of any wrong offered by any of them; or may, if we will proceed with extremity, conquer, fortify, and plant in soils most sweet, most pleasant, most strong, and most fertile, and in the end bring them all in subjection and to civility.

21. The known abundance of fresh fish in the rivers, and the known plenty of fish on the sea-coast there, may assure us of sufficient victual in spite of the people, if we will use salt and industry.

22. The known plenty and variety of flesh of divers kinds of beasts at land there may seem to say to us that we may cheaply victual our navies to England for our returns, which benefit everywhere is not found of merchants.

23. The practice of the people of the East Indies, when the Portugals came thither first, was to cut from the Portugals their lading of spice; and hereby they thought to overthrow their purposed trade. If these people shall practise the like, by not suffering us to have any commodity of theirs without conquest (which requireth some time), yet may we maintain our first voyage thither till our purpose come to effect by the sea-fishing on the coasts there and by dragging for pearls, which are said to be on those parts; and by return of those commodities the charges in part shall be defrayed: which is a matter of consideration in enterprises of charge.

24. If this realm shall abound too too much with youth, in the mines there of gold (as that of Chisca and Saguenay), of silver, copper, iron, etc., may be an employment to the benefit of this realm; in tilling of the rich soil there for grain and in planting of vines there for wine or dressing of those vines which grow there naturally in great abundance; olives for oil; orange trees, lemons, figs and almonds for fruit; woad, saffron, and madder for dyers; hops for brewers; hemp, flax; and in many such other things, by employment of the soil, our people void of sufficient trades may be honestly employed, that else may become hurtful at home.

25. The navigating of the seas in the voyage, and of the great rivers there, will breed many mariners for service and maintain much navigation.

26. The number of raw hides there of divers kinds of beasts, if we shall possess some island there or settle on the firm, may presently employ many of our idle people in divers several dressings of the same, and so we may return them to the people that cannot dress them so well, or into this realm, where the same are good merchandise, or to Flanders, etc., which present gain at the first raiseth great encouragement presently to the enterprise.

27. Since great waste woods be there of oak, cedar, pine, walnuts, and sundry other sorts, many of our waste people may be employed in making of ships, hoys,[3] busses,[4] and boats, and in making of rosin, pitch, and tar, the trees natural for the same being certainly known to be near Cape Breton and the Bay of Menan, and in many other places thereabout.

28. If mines of white or grey marble, jet, or other rich stone be found there, our idle people may be employed in the mines of the same and in preparing the same to shape, and, so shaped, they may be carried into this realm as good ballast for our ships and after serve for noble buildings.

29. Sugar-canes may be planted as well as they are now in the South of Spain, and besides the employment of our idle people, we may receive the commodity cheaper and not enrich infidels or our doubtful friends, of whom now we receive that commodity.

30. The daily great increase of wools in Spain, and the like in the West Indies, and the great employment of the same into cloth in both places, may move us to endeavour, for vent of our cloth, new discoveries of peopled regions where hope of sale may arise; otherwise in short time many inconveniences may possibly ensue.

31. This land that we purpose to direct our course to, lying in part in the 40th degree of latitude, being in like heat as Lisbon in Portugal doth, and in the more southerly part, as the most southerly coast of Spain doth, may by our diligence yield unto us, besides wines and oils and sugars, oranges, lemons, figs, raisins, almonds, pomegranates, rice, raw silks such as come from Granada, and divers commodities for dyers, as anil and cochineal, and sundry other colours and materials. Moreover, we shall not only receive many precious commodities besides from thence, but also shall in time find ample vent of the labour of our poor people at home, by sale of hats, bonnets, knives, fish-hooks, copper kettles, beads, looking-glasses, bugles, and a thousand kinds of other wrought wares that in short time may be brought in use among the people of that country, to the great relief of

the multitude of our poor people and to the wonderful enriching of this realm. And in time, such league and intercourse may arise between our stapling seats there, and other ports of our Northern America, and of the islands of the same, that incredible things, and by few as yet dreamed of, may speedily follow, tending to the impeachment of our mighty enemies and to the common good of this noble government.

The ends of this voyage are these:
1. To plant Christian religion.  ⎫
2. To traffic.                    ⎬  Or, to do all three.
3. To conquer.                    ⎭

To plant Christian religion without conquest will be hard. Traffic easily followeth conquest; conquest is not easy. Traffic without conquest seemeth possible and not uneasy. What is to be done is the question.

If the people be content to live naked and to content themselves with few things of mere necessity, then traffic is not. So then in vain seemeth our voyage, unless this nature may be altered, as by conquest and other good means it may be, but not on a sudden. The like whereof appeared in the East Indies, upon the Portugals seating there.

If the people in the inland be clothed, and desire to live in the abundance of all such things as Europe doth, and have at home all the same in plenty, yet we cannot have traffic with them, by means they want not anything that we can yield them.

Admit that they have desire to your commodities, and as yet have neither gold, silver, copper, iron, nor sufficient quantity of other present commodity to maintain the yearly trade, what is then to be done?

The soil and climate first is to be considered, and you are with Argus eyes to see what commodity by industry of man you are able to make it to yield that England doth want or both desire: as for the purpose, if you can make it to yield good wine or good oil, as it is like you may by the climate (where wild vines of sundry sorts do naturally grow already in great abundance), then your trade may be maintained. But admit the soil were in our disposition (as yet it is not), in what time may this be brought about?

For wine this is to be affirmed, that, first, the soil lying in 36 or 37 degrees, in the temperature of South Spain, in setting your vine plants this year you may have wine within three years. And it may be that the wild vines growing there already, by orderly pruning and dressing at your first arrival, may come to profit in shorter time.

And planting your olive trees this year, you may have oil within three years.

And if the sea-shores be flat and fit for receipt of salt water and for salt making, without any annoy of near freshes, then the trade of salt only may maintain a yearly navigation (as our men now trade to the isle of Maio and the Hollanders to *terra firma* near the west end of the Isle of Margarita).

But how the natural people of the country may be made skilful to plant vines and to know the use, or to set olive trees and to know the making of oil, and withal to use both the trades, that is a matter of small consideration; but to conquer a country or province in climate and soil of Italy, Spain, or the islands from whence we receive our wines and oils, and to man it, to plant it, and to keep it, and to continue the making of wines and oils able to serve England, were a matter of great importance both in respect of the saving at home of our great treasure now yearly going away, and in respect of the annoyance thereby growing to our enemies. The like consideration would be had touching a place for the making of salt, of temperature like those of France, not too cold, as the salts of the northern regions be, nor too too fiery, as those be that be made more southerly than France. In regard whereof, many circumstances are to be considered, and, principally, by what means the people of those parties may be drawn by all courtesy into love with our nation, that we become not hateful unto them as the Spaniard is in Italy and in the West Indies and elsewhere by their manner of usage: for a gentle course without cruelty and tyranny best answereth the profession of a Christian, best planteth Christian religion, maketh our seating most void of blood, most profitable in trade of merchandise, most firm and stable, and least subject to remove by practice of enemies. But that we may in seating there not be subject wholly to the malice of enemies, and may be more able to preserve our bodies, ships, and goods in more safety, and to be known to be more able to scourge the people there, civil or savage, than willing to offer any violence, and for the more quiet exercise of our manurance[5] of the soils where we shall seat and of our manual occupations, it is to be wished that some ancient[6] captains of mild disposition and great judgement be sent thither with men most skilful in the art of fortification, and that direction be taken that the mouths of great rivers and the islands in the same (as things of great moment) be taken, manned, and fortified, and that havens be cut out for safety of the navy, that we may be lords of the gates and entries to go out and come in at pleasure, and to lie in safety and be able to command and to control all within, and to force all foreign navigation to lie out in open road subject to all weathers, to be dispersed by tempests and flaws, if the force within be not able to give them the encounter abroad.

1. The red muscatel grape that Bishop Grindal procured out of Germany, the great white muscatel, the yellow grape: the cuts of these were wont yearly to be set at Fulham and after one year's rooting to be given by the Bishop and to be sold by his gardener. These presently provided and placed in earth, and many of these so rooted, with store of cuts unrooted besides, placed in tubs of earth shipped at the next voyage, to be planted in Virginia, may begin vineyards and bring wines out of hand.

2. Provision of great wild olive trees may be made out of this city so then to be carried to increase great store of stocks to graft the best olive on; and Virginia standing in the same degree that the Shroff,[7] the olive place, doth in Spain, we may win that merchandise, grafting the wild.

3. Sugar-canes, if you cannot procure them from the Spanish islands, yet may you by your Barbary merchants procure them.

4. There is an herb in Persia whereof anil is made, and it is also in Barbary; to procure that by seed or root were of importance for a trade of merchandise for our clothing country.

5. Woad by the seeds you may have, for you may have hundreds of bushels in England, as it is multiplied; and having soil and labour in Virginia cheap, and the woad in great value, lying in small room, it will be a trade of great gain to this clothing realm, and the thing cannot be destroyed by savages. The roots of this you may have in plenty and number coming in the trade; so this may grow in trade within a year ready for the merchant.

6. Fig trees of many good kinds may be had hence in barrel, if now presently they be provided; and they in that climate will yield noble fruit and feed your people presently, and will be brought in frails[8] home as merchandise, or in barrel, as raisins also may be.

7. Sawed boards of sassafras and cedar, to be turned into small boxes for ladies and gentlewomen, would become a present trade.

8. To the infinite natural increase of hogs, to add a device how the same may be fed by roots, acorns, etc., without spoiling your corn,

would be of great effect to feed the multitude continually employed in labour; and the same, cheaply bred and salted, and barrelled there and brought home, will be well sold for a good merchandise; and the barrels after will serve for our home herring fishing; and so you sell your woods and the labour of your cooper.

9. Receiving the savage women and their children of both sexes by courtesy into your protection, and employing the Englishwomen and the others in making of linen, you shall raise a wonderful trade of benefit, both to carry into England and also into the islands and into the main of the West Indies, victual and labour being so cheap there.

10. The trade of making cables and cordage there will be of great importance, in respect of a cheap maintenance of the navy that shall pass to and fro and in respect of such navy as may in those parties be used for the venting of the commodities of England to be brought thither. And poldavies,[9] etc., made for sails of the poor savages, yield to the navy a great help and a great gain in the traffic.

But if, seeking revenge on every injury of the savages, we seek blood and raise war, our vines, our olives, our fig trees, our sugar-canes, our oranges and lemons, corn, cattle, etc., will be destroyed and trade of merchandise in all things overthrown; and so the English nation there planted and to be planted shall be rooted out with sword and hunger.

Sorts of men which are to be passed in this voyage

1. Men skilful in all mineral causes.
2. Men skilful in all kind of drugs.
3. Fishermen, to consider of the sea-fishings there on the coasts, to be reduced to trade hereafter: and others for the freshwater fishings.
4. Salt-makers, to view the coast and to make trial how rich the sea-water there is, to advise for the trade.
5. Husbandmen, to view the soil, to resolve for tillage in all sorts.
6. Vineyard men bred, to see how the soil may serve for the planting of vines.
7. Men bred in the Shroff in South Spain, for discerning how olive trees may be planted there.
8. Others for planting of orange trees, fig trees, lemon trees, and almond trees, for judging how the soil may serve for the same.
9. Gardeners, to prove the several soils of the islands and of our settling places, to see how the same may serve for all herbs and roots for our victualling, since by rough seas sometimes we may want fish, and since we may want flesh to victual us, by the malice of the natural

people there; and gardeners for planting of our common trees of fruit, as pears, apples, plums, peaches, medlars, apricots, quinces for conserves, etc.

10. Lime-makers, to make lime for buildings.

11. Masons, carpenters, etc., for buildings there.

12. Brickmakers and tile-makers.

13. Men cunning in the art of fortification, that may choose out places strong by nature to be fortified, and that can plot out and direct workmen.

14. Choice spade-men, to trench cunningly and to raise bulwarks and rampires of earth for defence and offence.

15. Spade-makers that may out of the woods there make spades like those of Devonshire, and of other sorts, and shovels from time to time for common use.

16. Smiths, to forge the irons of the shovels and spades, and to make black bills and other weapons, and to mend many things.

17. Men that use to break ash trees for pikestaves, to be employed in the woods there.

18. Others, that finish up the same so rough hewed, such as in London are to be had.

19. Coopers, to make casks of all sorts.

20. Forgers of pikes'-heads and of arrow-heads, with forges, with Spanish iron, and with all manner of tools to be carried with them.

21. Fletchers, to renew arrows, since archery prevaileth much against unarmed people and gunpowder may soon perish by setting on fire.

22. Bowyers also, to make bows there for need.

23. Makers of oars, since for service upon those rivers it is to great purpose for the boats and barges they are to pass and enter with.

24. Shipwrights, to make barges and boats, and bigger vessels, if need be, to run along the coast and to pierce the great bays and inlets.

25. Turners, to turn targets of elm and tough wood for use against the darts and arrows of savages.

26. Such also as have knowledge to make targets of horn.

27. Such also as can make armour of hides upon moulds, such as were wont to be made in this realm about an hundred years since and were called Scottish Jacks: such armour is light and defensive enough against the force of savages.

28. Tanners, to tan hides of buffs, oxen, etc., in the isles where you shall plant.

29. Whittawers[10] of all other skins there.

30. Men skilful in burning of soap-ashes and in making of pitch and tar and rosin to be fetched out of Prussia and Poland, which are thence to be had for small wages, being there in manner of slaves.

The several sorts of trees, as pines, firs, spruces, birch and others, are to be bored with great augers a foot or half a yard above the ground, as they use in Vézelay towards Languedoc and near Bayonne in Gascony; and so you shall easily and quickly see what gums, rosin, turpentine, tar, or liquor is in them, which will quickly distil out clearly without any filthy mixture and will show what commodity may be made of them; their goodness and greatness for masts is also to be considered.

31. A skilful painter is also to be carried with you, which the Spaniards used commonly in all their discoveries to bring the descriptions of all beasts, birds, fishes, trees, towns, etc.

4

# John Hawkins Investigates the Coast of Florida (1565)

'The Voyage Made by Master John Hawkins . . . Begun in An. Dom. 1564' was written by John Sparke and first printed by Hakluyt, *Principal Navigations* (1589). A careful reprint was made by Clement R. Markham, *The Hawkins' Voyages*, The Hakluyt Society, No. 57 (London, 1878), pp. 8–64.

MASTER JOHN HAWKINS with the *Jesus of Lübeck*, a ship of seven hundred, and the *Solomon*, a ship of sevenscore, the *Tiger*, a bark of fifty, and the *Swallow* of thirty tons, being all well furnished with men to the number of one hundred threescore and ten, as also with ordnance and victual requisite for such a voyage, departed out of Plymouth the eighteenth day of October in the year of Our Lord 1564, with a prosperous wind. . . .

[Accounts of events on the coast of Africa, the hardships of the voyage, the difficulties encountered in trying to reach Havana, the separation of the fleet, and other mishaps are omitted.]

The fourteenth day [of July] the ship and barks came to the *Jesus*, bringing them news of the recovery of the men, which was not a little to the rejoicing of the captain and the whole company. And so then all together they kept on their way along the coast of Florida and the fifteenth day come to an anchor, and so from 26 degrees to 30½ degrees, where the Frenchmen are,* ranging all the coast along, seeking for fresh water, anchoring every night, because we would overshoot no place of fresh water; and in the day-time the captain in the ship's pinnace sailed along the shore, went into every creek, speaking with divers of the Floridians, because he would understand where the Frenchmen inhabited; and not finding them in 28 degrees, as it was declared unto him, marvelled thereat and never left sailing along the coast till he found them, who inhabited in a river by them called the River of May[1] and standing in 30 degrees and better.

In ranging this coast along, the captain found it to be all an island, and therefore it is all lowland and very scant of fresh water, but the country was marvellously sweet, with both marsh and meadow ground and goodly woods among. There they found sorrel to grow as abundantly as grass and, where their houses were, great store of maize and mill,[2] and grapes of great bigness but of taste much like our English grapes. Also deer great plenty, which came upon the sands before them.

Their houses are not many together, for in one house an hundred of them do lodge; they being made much like a great barn and in strength not inferior to ours, for they have stanchions and rafters of whole trees and are covered with palmetto leaves, having no place divided but one small room for their king and queen. In the midst of this house is a hearth, where they make great fires all night, and they sleep upon certain pieces of wood, hewn in for the bowing of their backs and another place made high for their heads, which they put one by another all along the walls on both sides. In their houses they remain only in the nights, and in the day they desire the fields, where they dress their meat and make provision for victuals, which they provide only for a meal from hand to mouth. There is one thing to be marvelled at, for the making of their fire, and not only they but also the Negroes do the same, which is made only by two sticks, rubbing them one against another; and this they may do in any place they come where they find sticks sufficient for the purpose.

In their apparel the men only use deerskins, wherewith some only cover their privy members, othersome use the same as garments to

cover them before and behind; which skins are painted, some yellow
and red, some black and russet, and every man according to his own
fancy. They do not omit to paint their bodies also with curious knots
or antic³ work, as every man in his own fancy deviseth, which painting,
to make it to continue the better, they use with a thorn to prick their
flesh and dent in the same, whereby the painting may have better hold.
In their wars they use a sleighter⁴ colour of painting their faces, thereby
to make themselves show the more fierce, which, after their wars ended,
they wash away again.

In their wars they use bows and arrows, whereof their bows are made
of a kind of yew, but blacker than ours, and for the most part passing
the strength of the Negroes' or Indians', for it is not greatly inferior to
ours. Their arrows are also of a great length but yet of reeds like other
Indians', but varying in two points, both in length and also for nocks
and feathers, which the other lack, whereby they shoot very steady.
The heads of the same are vipers' teeth, bones of fishes, flintstones,
piked points of knives, which they, having gotten of the Frenchmen,
broke the same, and put the points of them in their arrows' heads.
Some of them have their heads of silver, othersome, that have want
of these, put in a kind of hard wood, notched, which pierces as far as
any of the rest.

In their fight, being in the woods, they use a marvellous policy for
their own safeguard, which is by clasping a tree in their arms and yet
shooting notwithstanding; this policy they used with the Frenchmen
in their fight, whereby it appeareth that they are people of some policy;
and although they are called by the Spaniards *gente triste*, that is to
say, 'sad people', meaning thereby that they are not men of capacity,
yet have the Frenchmen found them so witty in their answers that, by
the captain's own report, a councillor with us could not give a more
profound reason.

The women also for their apparel use painted skins, but most of
them gowns of moss, somewhat longer than our moss, which they sew
together artificially and make the same surplice-wise, wearing their
hair down to their shoulders like the Indians.

In this River of May aforesaid, the captain, entering with his pinnace, found a French ship of fourscore ton and two pinnaces of fifteen
ton apiece by her, and, speaking with the keepers thereof, they told
him of a fort two leagues up which they had built, in which their
captain, Monsieur Laudonnière, was, with certain soldiers therein. To
whom our captain sending to understand of a watering-place where he

might conveniently take it in and to have licence for the same, he straight, because there was no convenient place but up the river five leagues, where the water was fresh, did send him a pilot for the more expedition thereof, to bring in one of his barks, which, going in with other boats provided for the same purpose, anchored before the fort, into the which our captain went; where he was, by the general with other captains and soldiers, very gently entertained, who declared unto him the time of their being there, which was fourteen months, with the extremity they were driven to for want of victuals, having brought very little with them. In which place they, being two hundred men at their first coming, had in short space eaten all the maize they could buy of the inhabitants about them and therefore were driven, certain of them, to serve a king of the Floridians against other his enemies for mill and other victuals; which, having gotten, could not serve them, being so many, so long a time, but want came upon them in such sort that they were fain to gather acorns, which, being stamped small and often washed to take away the bitterness of them, they did use for bread, eating withal sundry times roots, whereof they found many good and wholesome and such as serve rather for medicines than for meats alone.

But this hardness not contenting some of them, who would not take the pains so much as to fish in the river before their doors but would have all things put in their mouths, they did rebel against the captain, taking away first his armour and afterward imprisoning him; and so, to the number of fourscore of them, departed with a bark and a pinnace, spoiling their store of victual, and taking away a great part thereof with them, and so went to the islands of Hispaniola[5] and Jamaica a-roving, where they spoiled and pilled[6] the Spaniards; and, having taken two caravels laden with wine and cassava, which is a bread made of roots, and much other victuals and treasure, had not the grace to depart therewith but were of such haughty stomachs that they thought their force to be such that no man durst meddle with them, and so kept harbour in Jamaica, going daily ashore at their pleasure. But God, which would not suffer such evildoers unpunished, did indurate[7] their hearts in such sort that they lingered the time so long that a ship and galliass,[8] being made out of Santo Domingo, came thither into the harbour and took twenty of them, whereof the most part were hanged and the rest carried into Spain, and some (to the number of five-and-twenty) escaped in the pinnace and came to Florida, where at their landing they were put in prison, and, incontinent,[9] four of the chiefest, being condemned at the request of the soldiers, did pass the harquebusiers and then were hanged upon a gibbet.

This lack of threescore men was a great discourage[ment] and weakening to the rest, for they were the best soldiers that they had; for they had now made the inhabitants weary of them by their daily craving of maize, having no wares left to content them withal, and therefore were enforced to rob them and to take away their victual perforce; which was the occasion that the Floridians (not well contented therewith) did take certain of their company in the woods and slew them, whereby there grew great wars betwixt them and the Frenchmen. And therefore they, being but a few in number, durst not venture abroad but at such time as they were enforced thereunto for want of food to do the same; and, going twenty harquebusiers in a company, were set upon by eighteen kings, having seven or eight hundred men, which with one of their bows slew one of their men and hurt a dozen and drove them all down to their boats. Whose policy in fight was to be marvelled at, for, having shot at divers of their bodies which were armed, and perceiving that their arrows did not prevail against the same, they shot at their faces and legs, which were the places that the Frenchmen were hurt in. Thus the Frenchmen returned, being in ill case by the hurt of their men, having not above forty soldiers left unhurt, whereby they might ill make any more invasions upon the Floridians and keep their fort withal, which they must have been driven unto had not God sent us thither for their succour, for they had not above ten days' victual left before we came. In which perplexity our captain seeing them, [he] spared them out of his ship twenty barrels of meal and four pipes of beans, with divers other victuals and necessaries which he might conveniently spare; and to help them the better homewards, whither they were bound before our coming, at their request, we spared them one of our barks of fifty ton.

Notwithstanding the great want that the Frenchmen had, the ground doth yield victuals sufficient, if they would have taken pains to get the same, but they, being soldiers, desired to live by the sweat of other men's brows, for while they had peace with the Floridians they had fish sufficient, by weirs which they made to catch the same; but when they grew to wars the Floridians took away the same again, and then would not the Frenchmen take the pains to make any more.

The ground yieldeth naturally grapes in great store, for in the time that the Frenchmen were there they made twenty hogsheads of wine. Also it yieldeth roots passing good, deer marvellous store, with divers other beasts and fowl serviceable to the use of man. These be things wherewith a man may live, having corn or maize wherewith to make bread, for maize maketh good savoury bread and cakes as fine as flour. Also it maketh good meal, beaten and sodden[10] with water, and eateth like pap wherewith we feed children. It maketh also good beverage, sodden in water, and nourishable, which the Frenchmen did use to drink of in the morning, and it assuageth their thirst so that they had no need to drink all the day after. And this maize was the greatest lack they had, because they had no labourers to sow the same, and therefore to them that should inhabit the land it were requisite to have labourers to till and sow the ground, for they, having victuals of their own, whereby they neither rob nor spoil the inhabitants, may live not only quietly with them, who naturally are more desirous of peace than of wars, but also shall have abundance of victuals proffered them for nothing; for it is with them as it is with one of us: when we see another man ever taking away from us, although we have enough besides, yet then we think all too little for ourselves. For surely we have heard the Frenchmen report, and I know it by the Indians, that a very little contenteth them; for the Indians with the head of maize roasted will travail a whole day, and when they are at the Spaniards' finding[11] they give them nothing but sodden herbs and maize, and in this order I saw threescore of them feed, who were laden with wares and came fifty leagues off.

The Floridians when they travel have a kind of herb[12] dried, who, with a cane and an earthen cup in the end, with fire and the dried herbs put together, do suck through the cane the smoke thereof, which smoke satisfieth their hunger, and therewith they live four or five days without meat or drink. And this all the Frenchmen used for this purpose; yet do they hold opinion withal that it causeth water and phlegm to void from their stomachs.

The commodities of this land are more than are yet known to any man, for besides the land itself, whereof there is more than any king Christian is able to inhabit, it flourisheth with meadow, pasture ground, with woods of cedar and cypress and other sorts, as better cannot be in the world. They have for apothecary herbs, trees, roots, and gums great store, as *Storax liquida*,[13] turpentine, gum, myrrh, and frankincense, with many others whereof I know not the names. Colours both red, black, yellow, and russet, very perfect, wherewith they so paint their bodies and deerskins which they wear about them that with water it neither fadeth away nor altereth colour.

Gold and silver they want not; for at the Frenchmen's first coming thither they had the same offered them for little or nothing, for they received for a hatchet two pound weight of gold, because they knew not the estimation thereof; but the soldiers, being greedy of the same, did take it from them, giving them nothing for it, the which they, perceiving that both the Frenchmen did greatly esteem it and also did rigorously deal with them by taking the same away from them, at last would not be known they had any more, neither durst they wear the same for fear of being taken away; so that, saving at their first coming, they could get none of them. And how they came by this gold and silver the Frenchmen know not as yet but by guess, who, having travelled to the south-west of the cape, having found the same dangerous by means of sundry banks, as we also have found the same, and there finding masts which were wrecks of Spaniards coming from Mexico, judged that they had gotten treasure by them. For it is most true that divers wrecks have been made of Spaniards having much treasure; for the Frenchmen, having travelled to the capeward 150 miles, did find two Spaniards with the Floridians, which they brought afterward to their fort, whereof one was in a caravel coming from the Indies which was cast away fourteen years ago, and the other twelve years, of whose fellows some escaped, othersome were slain by the inhabitants. It seemeth they had estimation of[14] their gold and silver, for it is wrought flat and graven,[15] which they wear about their necks; othersome made round like a pancake, with a hole in the midst, to bolster up their breasts withal, because they think it a deformity to have great breasts. As for mines, either of gold or silver, the Frenchmen can hear of none they have upon the island but of copper, whereof as yet also they have not made the proof because they were but few men; but it is not unlike but that in the main where are high hills may be gold and silver as well as in Mexico, because it is all one main.

The Frenchmen obtained pearls of them of great bigness, but they were black by means of roasting of them, for they do not fish for them as the Spaniards do but for their meat; for the Spaniards used to keep daily a-fishing some two or three hundred Indians, some of them that be of choice a thousand; and their order is to go in canoes, or rather great pinnaces, with thirty men in a piece, whereof the one half or most part be divers, the rest do open the same for the pearls; for it is not suffered that they should use dragging, for that would bring them out of estimation[16] and mar the beds of them. The oysters which have the smallest sort of pearls are found in seven or eight fathom water but the greatest in eleven or twelve fathom.

The Floridians have pieces of unicorns' horns which they wear about their necks, whereof the Frenchmen obtained many pieces. Of those unicorns they have many, for that they do affirm it to be a beast with one horn, which, coming to the river to drink, putteth the same into the water before he drinketh. Of this unicorns' horn there are of our company that, having gotten the same of the Frenchmen, brought home thereof to show. It is therefore to be presupposed that there are more commodities as well as that, which for want of time and people sufficient to inhabit the same cannot yet come to light; but I trust God will reveal the same before it be long, to the great profit of them that shall take it in hand.

Of beasts in this country besides deer, foxes, hares, polecats, conies, ounces,[17] and leopards, I am not able certainly to say; but it is thought that there are lions and tigers as well as unicorns, lions especially, if it be true that is said of the enmity between them and the unicorns, for there is no beast but hath his enemy, as the cony the polecat, a sheep the wolf, the elephant the rhinoceros, and so of other beasts the like, insomuch that whereas[18] the one is the other cannot be missing. And seeing I have made mention of the beasts of this country, it shall not be from my purpose to speak also of the venomous beasts, as crocodiles, whereof there is great abundance, adders of great bigness, whereof our men killed some of a yard and a half long. Also I heard a miracle of one of these adders, upon the which a falcon seizing, the said adder did clasp her tail about her; which the French captain seeing, came to the rescue of the falcon and took her slaying the adder; and this falcon being wild, he did reclaim her and kept her for the space of two months, at which time for very want of meat he was fain to cast her off. On these adders the Frenchmen did feed, to no little admiration of us,[19] and affirmed the same to be a delicate meat. And the captain of the Frenchmen saw also a serpent with three heads and four feet, of the bigness of a great spaniel, which for want of a harquebus he durst not attempt to slay.

Of fish also they have in the river pike, rock, salmon, trout, and divers other small fishes, and of great fish some of the length of a man and longer, being of bigness accordingly, having a snout much like a sword of a yard long. There be also of sea fishes which we saw coming along the coast flying, which are of the bigness of a smelt, the biggest sort whereof have four wings but the other have but two; of these we saw coming out of Guinea a hundred in a company, which, being chased by the gilt-heads, otherwise called the bonitos, do to avoid them the better take their flight out of the water; but yet are they not able to fly far, because of the drying of their wings, which serve them not to fly but when they are moist, and therefore when they can fly no further they fall into the water and, having wet their wings, take a new flight again. These bonitos be of bigness like a carp and in colour like a mackerel, but it is the swiftest fish in swimming that is and followeth her prey very fiercely, not only in the water but also out of the water; for as the flying fish taketh her flight, so does this bonito leap after them and taketh them sometimes above the water. There were some of those bonitos which, being galled by a fish-gig, did follow our ship coming out of Guinea five hundred leagues. There is a sea-fowl also that chaseth this flying fish as well as the bonito; for as the flying fish taketh her flight, so doth this fowl pursue to take her, which to behold is a greater pleasure than hawking, for both the flights are as pleasant, and also more often than an hundred times; for the fowl can fly no way but one or other lighteth in her paws, the number of them are so abundant. There is an innumerable young fry of these flying fishes, which commonly keep about the ship and are not so big as butterflies and yet by flying do avoid the unsatiableness of the bonito. Of the bigger sort of these fishes we took many which both night and day flew into the sails of our ship, and there was not one of them which was not worth a bonito; for, being put upon a hook drabbling in the water, the bonito would leap thereat and so was taken. Also, we took many with a white cloth made fast to a hook, which being tied so short in the water that it might leap out and in, the greedy bonito, thinking it to be a flying fish, leapeth thereat and so is deceived. We took also dolphins, which are of very goodly colour and proportion to behold and no less delicate in taste.

Fowls also there be many, both upon land and upon sea; but, concerning them on the land, I am not able to name them because my abode was there so short. But for the fowl of the fresh rivers, these two I noted to be the chief, whereof the flamingo is one, having all red feathers and long red legs like a heron, a neck, according to the bill, red, whereof the upper neb hangeth an inch over the nether; and an egret, which is all white as the swan, with legs like to an heronshaw and of bigness accordingly, but it hath in her tail feathers of so fine a plume that it passeth[20] the ostrich his feather. Of the sea-fowl above all other not common in England I noted the pelican, which is feigned to be the lovingest bird that is; which, rather than her young should want, will spare her heart-blood out of her belly; but for all this lovingness she is very deformed to behold, for she is of colour russet, notwithstanding in Guinea I have seen of them as white as a swan, having legs like the same and a body like a heron, with a long neck and a thick, long beak, from the nether jaw whereof down to the breast passeth a skin of such a bigness as is able to receive a fish as big as one's thigh, and this her big throat and long bill doth make her seem so ugly.

Here I have declared the estate of Florida and the commodities therein to this day known, which although it may seem unto some, by the means that the plenty of gold and silver is not so abundant as in other places, that the cost bestowed upon the same will not be able to quit the charges; yet am I of the opinion that by that which I have seen in other islands of the Indians, where such increase of cattle hath been that of twelve head of beasts in five-and-twenty years did in the hides of them raise £1,000 profit yearly, that the increase of cattle only would raise profit sufficient for the same; for we may consider, if so small a portion did raise so much gains in such short time, what would a greater do in many years? And surely I may this affirm, that the ground of the Indians for the breed of cattle is not in any point to be compared to this of Florida, which all the year long is so green as any time in the summer with us; which surely is not to be marvelled at, seeing the country standeth in so watery a climate, for once a day without fail they have a shower of rain which, by means of the country itself, which is dry and more fervent hot than ours, doth make all things to flourish therein. And because there is not the thing we all seek for, being rather desirous of present gains, I do therefore affirm the attempt thereof to be more requisite for a prince, who is of power able to go through with the same, rather than for any subject. . . .

5

# Hawkins's and Drake's Slaving Expedition Comes to Grief at San Juan de Ulúa (1567–8)

From John Hawkins, 'The Third Troublesome Voyage Made with the *Jesus of Lübeck*, the *Minion*, and Four Other Ships to the Parts of Guinea and the West Indies in the Years 1567 and 1568'. First printed by Hakluyt, *Principal Navigations* (1589). Included in Markham, *Hawkins' Voyages*, pp. 70–81.

THE ships departed from Plymouth the second day of October, anno 1567, and had reasonable weather until the seventh day, at which time, forty leagues north from Cape Finisterre, there arose an extreme storm, which continued four days in such sort that the fleet was dispersed and all our great boats lost and the *Jesus*, our chief ship, in such case as not thought able to serve the voyage. Whereupon, in the same storm we set our course homeward, determining to give over the voyage; but the eleventh day of the same month the wind changed with fair weather, whereby we were animated to follow our enterprise and so did, directing our course with the islands of the Canaries, where, according to an order before prescribed, all our ships, before dispersed, met at one of those islands called Gomera, where we took water, and departed from thence the fourth day of November towards the coast of Guinea and arrived at Cape Verde the eighteenth of November, where we landed 150 men, hoping to obtain some Negroes: where we got but few and those with great hurt and damage to our men, which chiefly proceeded of their envenomed arrows, and although in the beginning they seemed to be but small hurts, yet there hardly escaped any that had blood drawn of them but died in strange sort, with their mouths shut some ten days before they died and after their wounds were whole; where I myself had one of the greatest wounds yet, thanks be to God, escaped.

From thence we passed the time upon the coast of Guinea, searching with all diligence the rivers from Rio Grande unto Sierra Leone till the twelfth of January, in which time we had not gotten together 150 Negroes; yet, notwithstanding, the sickness of our men and the late

46

time of the year commanded us away. And thus, having nothing wherewith to seek the coast of the West Indies, I was with the rest of our company in consultation to go to the coast of the Mine,[1] hoping there to have obtained some gold for our wares and thereby to have defrayed our charge. But even in that present instant there came to us a Negro, sent from a king oppressed by other kings, his neighbours, desiring our aid, with promise that as many Negroes as by these wars might be obtained, as well of his part as of ours, should be at our pleasure; whereupon we concluded[2] to give aid and sent 120 of our men, which the fifteenth of January assaulted a town of the Negroes of our ally's adversaries, which had in it 8,000 inhabitants, being very strongly impaled and fenced after their manner; but it was so well defended that our men prevailed not but lost six men and forty hurt, so that our men sent forthwith to me for more help. Whereupon, considering that the good success of this enterprise might highly further the commodity of our voyage, I went myself and with the help of the king of our side assaulted the town, both by land and sea, and very hardly with fire (their houses being covered with dry palm leaves) obtained the town and put the inhabitants to flight, where we took 250 persons, men, women, and children, and by our friend the king of our side there were taken six hundred prisoners, whereof we hoped to have had our choice; but the Negro (in which nation is seldom or never found truth) meant nothing less,[3] for that night he removed his camp and prisoners so that we were fain to content us with those few which we had gotten ourselves.

Now had we obtained between four and five hundred Negroes, wherewith we thought it somewhat reasonable to seek the coast of the West Indies, and there for our Negroes and other our merchandise we hoped to obtain whereof to countervail our charges with some gains, whereunto we proceeded with all diligence, furnished our watering, took fuel, and departed the coast of Guinea the third of February, continuing at the sea with a passage more hard than before hath been accustomed till the twenty-seventh day of March, which day we had sight of an island called Dominica upon the coast of the West Indies, in 14 degrees; from thence we coasted from place to place, making our traffic with the Spaniards as we might, somewhat hardly, because the King had straitly commanded all his governors in those parts by no means to suffer any trade to be made with us. Notwithstanding, we had reasonable trade and courteous entertainment from the Isle of Margarita unto Cartagena, without anything greatly worth the noting saving at

Capo de la Vela,[4] in a town called Rio de la Hacha,[5] from whence come all the pearls, the treasurer who had the charge there would by no means agree to any trade or suffer us to take water. He had fortified his town with divers bulwarks in all places where it might be entered and furnished himself with an hundred harquebusiers, so that he thought by famine to have enforced us to have put aland our Negroes; of which purpose he had not greatly failed unless we had by force entered the town, which (after we could by no means obtain his favour) we were enforced to do and so with two hundred men broke in upon their bulwarks and entered the town with the loss only of two men of our parts and no hurt done to the Spaniards, because after their volley of shot discharged they all fled.

Thus, having the town with some circumstance,[6] as partly by the Spaniards' desire of Negroes and partly by friendship of the treasurer, we obtained a secret trade whereupon the Spaniards resorted to us by night and bought of us to the number of two hundred Negroes; in all other places where we traded the Spaniard inhabitants were glad of us and traded willingly.

At Cartagena, the last town we thought to have seen on the coast, we could by no means obtain to deal with any Spaniard, the governor was so strait; and because our trade was so near finished we thought not good either to adventure any landing or to detract[7] further time but in peace departed from thence the twenty-fourth of July, hoping to have escaped the time of their storms, which then soon after began to rain, the which they called furicanos;[8] but, passing by the west end of Cuba towards the coast of Florida, there happened to us the twelfth day of August an extreme storm which continued by the space of four days, which so beat the *Jesus* that we cut down all her higher buildings; her rudder also was sore shaken and withal was in so extreme a leak that we were rather upon the point to leave her than to keep her any longer; yet, hoping to bring all to good pass, we sought the coast of Florida, where we found no place nor haven for our ships because of the shallowness of the coast. Thus, being in greater despair and taken with a new storm which continued other three days, we were enforced to take for our succour the port which serves the city of Mexico, called San Juan de Ulúa, which stands in 19 degrees; in seeking of which port we took in our way three ships which carried passengers to the number of an hundred, which passengers we hoped should be a mean to us the better to obtain victuals for our money and a quiet place for the repairing of our fleet.

Shortly after this, the sixteenth of September, we entered the port of San Juan de Ulúa and, in our entry, the Spaniards thinking us to be the fleet of Spain, the chief officers of the country came aboard us, which, being deceived of their expectation, were greatly dismayed, but immediately when they saw our demand was nothing but victuals were recomforted. I found also in the same port twelve ships which had in them, by report, £200,000 in gold and silver, all which (being in my possession, with the King's island, as also the passengers before in my way thitherward stayed) I set at liberty, without the taking from them the weight of a groat; only, because I would not be delayed of my dispatch, I stayed two men of estimation and sent post immediately to Mexico, which was two hundred miles from us, to the presidents and council there, showing them of our arrival there by the force of weather and the necessity of the repair of our ships and victuals, which wants we required as friends to King Philip to be furnished of for our money, and that the presidents and council there should with all convenient speed take order that at the arrival of the Spanish fleet, which was daily looked for, there might no cause of quarrel rise between us and them, but for the better maintenance of amity their commandment might be had in that behalf.

This message, being sent away the sixteenth day of September at night, being the very day of our arrival, in the next morning, which was the seventeenth day of the same month, we saw open of the haven thirteen great ships, and, understanding them to be the fleet of Spain, I sent immediately to advertise the general of the fleet of my being there, doing him to understand that before I would suffer them to enter the port there should some order of conditions pass between us for our safe being there and maintenance of peace.

Now it is to be understood that this port is made by a little island of stones not three foot above the water in the highest place and but a bowshot of length any way; this island standeth from the mainland two bowshots or more; also it is to be understood that there is not in all this coast any other place for ships to arrive in safety, because the north wind hath there such violence that unless the ships be very safely moored with their anchors fastened upon this island there is no remedy for these north winds but death; also the place of the haven was so little that of necessity the ships must ride one aboard the other, so that we could not give place to them nor they to us; and here I began to bewail that which after followed. For now, said I, I am in two dangers and forced to receive the one of them. That was, either I must have kept out the fleet from entering the port, the which with God's help I was very well able to do, or else suffer them to enter in with their accustomed treason, which they never fail to execute where they may have opportunity to compass it by any means. If I had kept them out, then had there been present shipwreck of all the fleet, which amounted in value to six millions, which was in value of our money £1,800,000, which I considered I was not able to answer, fearing the Queen's Majesty's indignation in so weighty a matter. Thus with myself revolving the doubts, I thought rather better to abide the jut[9] of the uncertainty than the certainty. The uncertain doubt I account was their treason, which by good policy I hoped might be prevented, and therefore, as choosing the least mischief, I proceeded to conditions.

Now was our first messenger come and returned from the fleet with report of the arrival of a viceroy,[10] so that he had authority, both in all this province of Mexico (otherwise called *Nueva Espana*) and in the sea, who sent us word that we should send our conditions, which of his part should (for the better maintenance of amity between the princes) be both favourably granted and faithfully performed, with many fair words how, passing the coast of the Indies, he had understood of our honest behaviour towards the inhabitants where we had to do, as well elsewhere as in the same port, the which I let pass. Thus following our demand, we required victuals for our money and licence to sell as much ware as might furnish our wants, and that there might be of either part twelve gentlemen as hostages for the maintenance of peace; and that the island for our better safety might be in our own possession during our abode there, and such ordnance as was planted in the same island, which were eleven pieces of brass; and that no Spaniard might land in the island with any kind of weapon.

These conditions at the first he somewhat misliked, chiefly the guard of the island to be in our own keeping, which if they had had, we had soon known our fare, for with the first north wind they had cut our cables and our ships had gone ashore; but in the end he concluded to our request, bringing the twelve hostages to ten, which with all speed of either part were received, with a writing from the viceroy signed with his hand and sealed with his seal of all the conditions concluded, and forthwith a trumpet blown with commandment that none of either part should bemean[11] to violate the peace upon pain of death; and further it was concluded that the two generals of the fleets should meet and give faith each to other for the performance of the premises, which was so done.

Thus, at the end of three days all was concluded and the fleet entered the port, saluting one another as the manner of the sea doth require. Thus, as I said before, Thursday we entered the port, Friday we saw the fleet, and on Monday at night they entered the port; then we laboured two days placing the English ships by themselves and the Spanish ships by themselves, the captains of each part and inferior men of their parts promising great amity of all sides; which even as with all fidelity it was meant on our part, so the Spaniards meant nothing less[12] on their parts, but from the mainland had furnished themselves with a supply of men to the number of one thousand and meant the next Thursday, being the twenty-third of September, at dinner-time, to set upon us on all sides.

The same Thursday in the morning, the treason being at hand, some appearance showed, as shifting of weapon from ship to ship, planting and bending of ordnance from the ship to the island where our men warded,[13] passing to and fro of companies of men more than required for their necessary business, and many other ill likelihoods, which caused us to have a vehement suspicion and therewithal sent to the viceroy to inquire what was meant by it, which sent immediately strait commandment to unplant all things suspicious, and also sent word that he in the faith of a viceroy would be our defence from all villainies. Yet we, being not satisfied with this answer, because we suspected a great number of men to be hid in a great ship of nine hundred tons, which was moored next unto the *Minion*, sent again to the viceroy the master of the *Jesus*, which had the Spanish tongue, and required to be satisfied if any such thing were or not. The viceroy, now seeing that the treason must be discovered, forthwith stayed our master, blew the trumpet, and of all sides set upon us. Our men which warded ashore, being stricken with sudden fear, gave place, fled, and sought to recover succour of the ships. The Spaniards, being before provided for the purpose, landed in all places in multitudes from their ships, which they might easily do without boats, and slew all our men ashore without mercy; a few of them escaped aboard the *Jesus*. The great ship, which had by the estimation three hundred men placed in her secretly, immediately fell aboard the *Minion*, but by God's appointment in the time of suspicion we had, which was only one half hour, the *Minion* was made ready to avoid; and so leesing[14] her head-fasts and haling away by the stern-fasts, she was gotten out: thus with God's help she defended the violence of the first brunt of these three hundred men.

The *Minion* being passed, they came aboard the *Jesus*, which also,

with very much ado and the loss of many of our men, was defended
and kept out. Then there were also two other ships that assaulted the
*Jesus* at the same instant, so that she had hard getting loose, but yet
with some time we had cut our head-fasts and gotten out by the stern-
fasts. Now when the *Jesus* and the *Minion* were gotten about two
ships' length from the Spanish fleet, the fight began so hot on all sides
that within one hour the admiral of the Spaniards was supposed to be
sunk, their vice-admiral burned, and one other of their principal ships
supposed to be sunk, so that the ships were little able to annoy[15] us.

Then it is to be understood that all the ordnance upon the island was
in the Spaniards' hands, which did us so great annoyance that it cut all
the masts and yards of the *Jesus*, in such sort that there was no hope to
carry her away; also it sunk our small ships, whereupon we determined
to place the *Jesus* on that side of the *Minion* that she might abide all
the battery from the land and so be a defence for the *Minion* till night,
and then to take such relief of victual and other necessaries from the
*Jesus* as the time would suffer us and to leave her. As we were thus
determining and had placed the *Minion* from the shot of the land,
suddenly the Spaniards had fired two great ships, which were coming
directly with us, and having no means to avoid the fire, it bred among
our men a marvellous fear, so that some said, 'Let us depart with the
*Minion*'; others said, 'Let us see whether the wind will carry the fire
from us.' But, to be short, the *Minion*'s men, which had always their
sails in a readiness, thought to make sure work, and so, without either
consent of the captain or master, cut their sail, so that very hardly I was
received into the *Minion*.

The most part of the men that were left alive in the *Jesus* made shift
and followed the *Minion* in a small boat; the rest, which the little boat
was not able to receive, were enforced to abide the mercy of the
Spaniards (which I doubt was very little). So with the *Minion* only
and the *Judith* (a small bark of fifty ton) we escaped, which bark the
same night forsook us in our great misery. We were now removed with
the *Minion* from the Spanish ships two bowshots and there rode all
that night. The next morning we recovered an island a mile from the
Spaniards, where there took us a north wind and, being left only with
two anchors and two cables (for in this conflict we lost three cables
and two anchors), we thought always upon death, which ever was
present, but God preserved us to a longer time.

The weather waxed reasonable, and the Saturday we set sail and,
having a great number of men and little victuals, our hope of life

waxed less and less. Some desired to yield to the Spaniards, some rather desired to obtain a place where they might give themselves to the infidels, and some had rather abide with a little pittance the mercy of God at sea. So thus, with many sorrowful hearts, we wandered in an unknown sea by the space of fourteen days, till hunger enforced us to seek the land, for hides were thought very good meat: rats, cats, mice, and dogs, none escaped that might be gotten. Parrots and monkeys, that were had in great price, were thought there very profitable if they served the turn one dinner. Thus in the end the eighth day of October we came to the land in the bottom of the same Bay of Mexico in $23\frac{1}{2}$ degrees, where we hoped to have found inhabitants of the Spaniards, relief of victuals, and place for the repair of our ship, which was so sore beaten with shot from our enemies and bruised with shooting off our own ordnance that our weary and weak arms were scarce able to defend and keep out water. But all things happened to the contrary, for we found neither people, victual, nor haven of relief, but a place where, having fair weather, with some peril we might land a boat. Our people, being forced with hunger, desired to be set on land, whereunto I consented.

And such as were willing to land I put them apart, and such as were desirous to go homewards I put apart, so that they were indifferently parted a hundred of one side and a hundred of the other side. These hundred men we set aland with all diligence in this little place before said, which, being landed, we determined there to take in fresh water and so with our little remain of victuals to take the sea.

The next day, having aland with me fifty of our hundred men that remained, for the speedier preparing of our water aboard, there arose an extreme storm, so that in three days we could by no means repair aboard our ship; the ship also was in such peril that every hour we looked for shipwreck.

But yet God again had mercy on us and sent fair weather. We had aboard our water and departed the sixteenth day of October, after which day we had fair and prosperous weather till the sixteenth day of November, which day, God be praised, we were clear from the coast of the Indies and out of the channel and gulf of Bahama, which is between the cape of Florida and the islands of Lucayo.[16] After this, growing near to the cold country, our men, being oppressed with famine, died continually, and they that were left grew into such weakness that we were scantly able to manage our ship, and, the wind being always ill for us to recover England, we determined to go with Galicia

E

in Spain with intent there to relieve our company and other extreme wants. And being arrived the last day of December in a place near unto Vigo called Pontevedra, our men with excess of fresh meat grew into miserable diseases and died, a great part of them.

This matter was borne out as long as it might be, but in the end, although there were none of our men suffered to go aland, yet, by access of the Spaniards, our feebleness was known to them. Whereupon they ceased not to seek by all means to betray us, but with all speed possible we departed to Vigo, where we had some help of certain English ships and twelve fresh men, wherewith we repaired our wants as we might and, departing the twentieth day of January 1568 [1569 new style], arrived in Mounts Bay in Cornwall the twenty-fifth of the same month, praised be God therefor.

If all the miseries and troublesome affairs of this sorrowful voyage should be perfectly and thoroughly written, there should need a painful[17] man with his pen and as great a time as he had that wrote the lives and deaths of the martyrs.

6

# David Ingram Reports an Incredible Journey on Foot from Mexico to Nova Scotia (1568–9)

David Ingram, Richard Browne, and Richard Twide, three from the ship's company that Drake and Hawkins put ashore in Mexico after the debacle at San Juan de Ulúa, near the site of modern Veracruz, made their way north-ward and claimed to have reached the vicinity of Cape Breton Island, where they were taken off by a French fishing vessel. Eventually they got back to England. In 1582 Ingram was questioned about the journey before Sir Francis Walsingham and others interested in colonization. His report was printed by Hakluyt, *Principal Navigations* (1589), but was omitted from the later edition because of 'certain incredibilities', Samuel Purchas asserted. Another version exists in Sloane MS. 1447 f. 1 in the British Museum. The Hakluyt and Sloane versions have been recently collated by David B. Quinn, *Voyages and Colonising Enterprises of Sir Humphrey Gilbert*, The Hakluyt Society, 2nd Ser., Nos. 83, 84 (London, 1938–9), II, 283–96. Whether Ingram and his colleagues actually walked the length of the North Atlantic coast or were rescued at some point nearer Mexico, they certainly made one of the most remarkable journeys of the sixteenth century.

*The relation of David Ingram of Barking, in the county of Essex, sailor, of sundry things which he with others did see, in travelling by land from the most northerly parts of the Bay of Mexico (where he with many others were set on shore by Master Hawkins) through a great part of America, until he came within fifty leagues or thereabouts of Cape Breton.*

About the beginning of October, anno 1568, David Ingram with the rest of his company, being a hundred persons in all, were set on land by Master John Hawkins about six leagues to the west of the river La Mina, or Rio de Minas,[1] which standeth about 140 leagues west and by north from the cape of Florida, who, travelling towards Cape Breton, spent about twelve months in the whole, and about seven months thereof in those countries which lie towards the north of the River of May, in which time (as the said Ingram thinketh) he travelled by land two thousand miles at the least and never continued in any one place above three or four days, saving only at the city of Balma, where he stayed six or seven days.

There are in those parts (saith he) very many kings, commonly within a hundred or a hundred and twenty miles one from another, who are at continual wars together. The first king that they came before dwelt in a country called Giricka, who caused them to be stripped naked and, wondering greatly at the whiteness of their skins, let them depart without further harm.

The kings in those countries are clothed with painted or coloured garments, and thereby you may know them. And they wear great precious stones, which commonly are rubies, being four inches long and two inches broad. And if the same be taken from them, either by force or sleight, they are presently deprived of their kingdoms.

When they mean to speak with any person publicly they are always carried by men in a sumptuous chair of silver or crystal garnished with divers sorts of precious stones. . . .

There is in some of those countries great abundance of pearl, for in every cottage be found pearl: in some houses a quart, in some a pottle, in some a peck, more or less, where he did see some as great as a bean. And Richard Browne, one of his companions, found one of these great pearls in one of their canoes or boats, which pearl he gave to

Monsieur Champagne, who took them aboard his ship and brought them to Newhaven[2] in France.

All the people generally do wear manilios, or bracelets, as big as a man's finger upon each of their arms, and the like on the small of each of their legs, whereof commonly one is gold and two silver. And many of the women also do wear plates of gold, covering their bodies in manner of a pair of curiets,[3] and many bracelets and chains of great pearl. The people commonly are of good favour, feature, and shape of body; of growth above five foot high, somewhat thick, with their faces and skins of colour like an olive, and toward the north somewhat tawny, but some of them are painted with divers colours. They are very swift of foot; the hair of their heads is shaven in sundry spots, and the rest of their head is traced. In the south parts of these countries they go all naked, saving that the noblemen's privities are covered with the neck of a gourd and the women's privities with the hair or leaf of the palm-tree. But in the north parts they are clothed with beasts' skins, the hairy side being next to their bodies in winter.

They are so brutish and beastly that they will not forbear the use of their wives in open presence. They are naturally very courteous if you do not abuse them, either in their persons or goods, but use them courteously. The killing or taking of their beasts, birds, fishes, or fruits cannot offend them, except it be of their cattle which they keep about their houses, as kine, guinea-hens, or such-like. If any of them do hold up both their hands at length together and kiss the backs of them on both sides, then you may undoubtedly trust them, for it is the greatest token of friendship that may be. . . .

If you will bargain for ware with them, leave the thing that you will sell upon the ground and go from it a pretty way off; then will they come and take it and set down such wares as they will give for it in the place. And if you think it not sufficient, leave the wares with signs that you like it not and they will bring more, until either they or you be satisfied or will give no more. Otherwise you may hang your wares upon a long pole's end and so put more or less on it until you have agreed on the bargain. . . .

The people in those countries are professed enemies to the cannibals or men-eaters. The cannibals do most inhabit between Norumbega[4] and Bariniah.* They have teeth like dogs' teeth, and thereby you may know them. In the wars they do pitch their camp as near as they may into some wood of palm-trees, which yield them meat, drink, and present remedy against poisonous arrows.

Their buildings are weak and of small force. Their houses are made round like dovehouses, and they do dwell together in towns and villages. And some of them have banqueting-houses in the top of them, made like the louver of a hall, builded with pillars of massy silver and crystal, framed square. Whereof many of them are as big as a boy's leg of fifteen years of age, and some less. . . .

They have in every house scoops, buckets, and divers other vessels of massy silver, wherewith they do throw out water and dust, and otherwise do employ them to their necessary uses in their houses. All which this Ingram did see common and usual in some of these countries, especially where he found the great pearls.

There are also great rivers, at the heads whereof this Ingram and his companions did find sundry pieces of gold, some as big as a man's fist, the earth being washed away with the water. And in other places they did see great rocks of crystal, which grew at the heads of great and many rivers, being in quantity to load ships. There are also in those parts plenty of fine furs unknown to this Ingram, dressed after the manner of the country.

The people there do burn a kind of white turf or earth, which they dig out of the marishes, a fathom deep in the ground. It burneth very clear and smelleth as sweet as musk, and that earth is as wholesome, sweet, and comfortable to smell unto as any pomander. They do make their fire of this earth for the sweetness thereof, having great abundance of wood. When they want fire they take briers and rub them very hard together between their fists, and so with hard and often rubbing they kindle and make fire.

They have great plenty of iron, and there is also great plenty of mineral salt in the marish ground, which looketh reddish, a thing necessary for the great fishings near the sea-shore, which are there abundant and the fish very large and huge.

The ground and country is most excellent, fertile and pleasant, and specially towards the River of May. For the grass of the rest is not so green as it is in these parts, for the other is burnt away with the heat of the sun. And as all the country is good and most delicate, having great plains, as large and as fair in many places as may be seen, being as plain as a board. And then great and huge woods of sundry kind of trees, as cedar, lignum vitae, bombax,[5] plants and bushes, bark that biteth like pepper (of which kind young Master Winter[6] brought home part from the Straits of Magellan), with the fruitful palm-tree and great plenty of other sweet trees to this Ingram unknown. And after that plains again and in other places great closes of pasture environed with most delicate trees instead of hedges, they being as it were set by the hands of men. Yet the best grass for the most part is in the high countries, somewhat far from the sea-side and great rivers, by reason that the low grounds there be so rank that the grass groweth faster than it can be eaten, whereby the old grass lieth withered thick and the new grass growing through it. Whereas in the upper parts the grass and ground is most excellent and green, the ground not being overcharged with any old withered grass, as is afore specified.

The palm-tree afore said carrieth hairs on the leaves thereof, which reach to the ground, whereof the Indians do make ropes and cords for their cotton beds and do use the same to many other purposes. The which tree, if you pick with your knife about two foot from the root, it will yield a wine in colour like whey but in taste strong and somewhat like bastard,[7] which is most excellent drink. But it will distemper both your head and body if you drink too much thereof, as our strong wines will do in these parts. The branches of the top of the tree are most excellent meat raw, after you have pared away the bark. Also there is a red oil that cometh out of the root of this tree, which is most excellent against poisoned arrows and weapons, for by it they do recover themselves of their poisoned wounds.

There is a tree called a plantain, with a fruit growing on it like a pudding, which is most excellent meat raw.

They have also a red berry like a peasecod called buyathos,* two or three inches long, which groweth on short bushes full of pricks like the sloe- or thorn-tree; and the fruit eateth like a green raisin but sharper somewhat. They stamp this berry and make wine thereof, which they keep in vessels made of wood.

They have also in many places vines which bear grapes as big as a man's thumb.

There is also great plenty of herbs and of all kinds of flowers, as roses and gillyflowers, like ours in England, and many others which he knew not.

Also, they have a kind of grain[8] the ear whereof is as big as the wrist of a man's arm; the grain is like a flat pea; it maketh very good bread and white.

They do also make bread of the root called cassava, which they do dry and beat it as small as they can and temper it with water, and so bake it in cakes on a stone.

There is also great plenty of buffs, bears, horses, kine, wolves, foxes, deer, goats, sheep, hares, and conies. Also other cattle like ours, [and very many unlike ours]* to this examinate unknown, the most part being wild; the hides and skins of them are good merchandise. There is very great store of those buffs, which are beasts as big as two oxen, in length almost twenty foot, having long ears like a bloodhound, with long hairs about their ears. Their horns be crooked like rams' horns, their eyes black, their hairs long, black, rough, and shagged as a goat. The hides of these beasts are sold very dear. This beast doth keep company only by couples, male and female, and doth always fight with others of the same kind when they do meet.

There is also great plenty of deer, both red, white, and speckled. This last sort this examinate knoweth not.

There is also great plenty of another kind of sheep which carry a kind of coarse wool. This sheep is very good meat, although the flesh be very red. They are exceeding fat and of nature loath to rise when they are laid, which is always from five o'clock at night until five o'clock in the morning, between which time you may easily kill them; but after they be on foot they are very wild and rest not in one place but live together in herds, in some five hundred, as it happeneth, more or less. And these red sheep are most about the Bay of Saint Marie,⁹ as this examinate guesseth.

There are bears both black and white. There are wolves. The foxes have their skins more grizzled than ours in England. There are conies both white and red and grey, in every place great plenty.

This examinate did also see in those countries a monstrous beast twice as big as an horse and in proportion like to an horse, both in mane, hoof and hair, and neighing, saving it was small towards the lower parts like a greyhound. These beasts hath two teeth or horns of a foot long growing straight forth by their nostrils; they are natural enemies to the horse.

He did also see in that country both elephants and ounces. He did also see one other strange beast bigger than a bear; he had neither head nor neck; his eyes and mouth were in his breast. This beast is very ugly to behold and cowardly of kind. It beareth a very fine skin like a rat, full of silver hairs.

There are in those countries abundance of russet parrots, but very few green. There are also birds of all sorts as we have, and many strange birds to this examinate unknown. There are great plenty of guinea-hens, which are tame birds and proper to the inhabitants,¹⁰ as big as geese, very black of colour, having feathers like down. There is also a bird called a flamingo, whose feathers are very red, and is bigger than a goose, billed like a shovel, and is very good meat.

There is also another kind of fowl in that country which hunteth the rivers near unto the islands. They are of the shape and bigness of a goose but their wings are covered with small yellow feathers and cannot fly. You may drive them before you like sheep. They are exceeding fat and very delicate meat. They have white heads, and therefore the countrymen call them penguins (which seemeth to be a Welsh name, and they have also in use divers other Welsh words,[11] a matter worthy the noting).

There is also a very strange bird thrice as big as an eagle, very beautiful to behold; his feathers are more orient than a peacock's feathers, his eyes are glittering as an hawk's eyes but as great as a man's eyes, his head and thigh as big as a man's head and thigh. It hath a crest and tuft of feathers of sundry colours on the top of the head like a lapwing hanging backwards, his beak and talons in proportion like eagles but very huge and large.

Touching tempests and other strange monstrous things in those parts, this examinate saith that he hath seen it lighten and thunder in summer season by the space of four-and-twenty hours together, the cause whereof he judgeth to be the heat of the climate.

He farther saith that there is a cloud sometime of the year seen in the air which commonly turneth to great tempests. And that sometimes of the year there are great winds in manner of whirlwinds. . . .

He saith further that he and his two fellows, namely, Richard Browne and Richard Twide, went into a poor man's house and there they did see the said Colluchio or devil with very great eyes like a black calf. Upon the sight whereof Browne said, 'There is the Devil', and thereupon he blessed himself in the name of the Father, and of the Son, and of the Holy Ghost. And Twide said very vehemently, 'I defy thee and all thy works.' And presently the Colluchio shrank away in a stealing manner forth of the doors and was seen no more unto them.

Also they passed over many great rivers in those countries in canoes or boats. Some four, some six, some eight, some ten miles over, whereof one was so large that they could scarce cross the same in four-and-twenty hours.

Also he saith that in the same country the people have instruments of music made of a piece of a cane almost a foot long, being open at both ends, which, sitting down, they smite upon their thighs and one of their hands, making a pleasant kind of sound. And they do use another kind of instrument like a tabor, covered with a white skin somewhat like parchment. This examinate can very well describe their gestures, dancing, and songs.

After long travail, the aforesaid David Ingram with his two companions, Browne and Twide, came to the head of a river called Garinda, which is sixty leagues west from Cape Breton, where they understood by the people of that country of the arrival of a Christian. Whereupon they made their repair to the sea-side and there found a French captain named Monsieur Champagne, who took them into his ship and brought them unto Newhaven, and from thence they were transported into England, anno Domini 1569.

This Monsieur Champagne, with divers of his company, was brought into that village of Bariniah about twenty miles up into the country of the said examinate and his two companions, by whose means he had a trade with the people of divers sorts of fine furs and of great red leaves of trees almost a yard long and about a foot broad, which he thinketh are good for dyeing.

Also the said Monsieur Champagne had there, for exchange of trifling wares, a good quantity of rude and wrought silver.

He saith further that divers of the said Frenchmen which were in the said ship called the *Gargarine* are yet living in Honfleur upon the coast of France, as he thinketh, for he did speak with some of them within these three years.

About a fortnight after their coming from Newhaven into England, this said examinate and his two companions came to Master John Hawkins, who had set them on shore upon the Bay of Mexico, and unto each of them he gave a reward.

Richard Browne, his companion, was slain about five years past in the *Elizabeth* of Master Cockins of London; and Richard Twide, his other companion, died at Ratcliff in John Sherwood's house there, about three years past. . . .

Also the said David Ingram, travelling towards the north, found the main sea upon the north side of America and travelled in the sight thereof the space of two whole days, where the people signified unto him that they had seen ships on that coast and did draw upon the ground the shape and figure of ships and of their sails and flags. Which thing especially proveth the passage of the north-west and is agreeable to the experience of Vásquez de Coronado, which found a ship of China or Cataia upon the north-west of America.

Also the said examinate saith that there is an island called Corrafau,[12] and there are in it five or six thousand Indians at the least, and all those are governed by one only Negro, who is but a slave to a Spaniard. And moreover, the Spaniards will send but one of their slaves with an hundred or two hundred of the Indians when they go to gather gold in the rivers descending from the mountains. And when they shall be absent by the space of twenty or thirty days at the least, every one of the Indians will nevertheless obey all the slave's commandments with as great reverence as if he were their natural king, although there be never a Christian near them by the space of an hundred or two hundred miles; which argueth the great obedience of those people and how easily they may be governed when they be once conquered.

7

# Henry Hawks Reveals the Rich Commodities of New Spain (1572)

Henry Hawks was one of a group of English traders who had settled in Spain and adopted Spanish ways. He was known to the Spaniards as Pero Sanchez. He sailed to New Spain via the Canaries in 1567. In Mexico he fell into the hands of the Inquisition but managed to escape to Spain and in 1571 returned to England, where he provided useful information to the expansionists. To Richard Hakluyt the lawyer in 1572 he made a valuable report on economic conditions in New Spain. This report, printed by Hakluyt, *Principal Navigations* (1589), has been reprinted by Taylor, *Original Writings . . . of the Two Richard Hakluyts*, II, 96–114.

SAN JUAN DE ULÚA is an island not high above the water, whereas now the Spaniards, upon Master John Hawkins's being there, are in making a strong fort. In this place all the ships that come out of Spain with goods for these parts do unlade. . . .

Five leagues from San Juan de Ulúa is a fair river; it lieth north-west from the port and goeth to a little town of the Spaniards called Veracruz, and with small vessels or barks, which they call frigates, they carry all their merchandise which cometh out of Spain to the said town and in like manner bring all the gold, silver, cochineal, hides, and all other things that the ships carry into Spain unto them. And the goods being in Veracruz, they carry it to Mexico and to Pueblo de los Angelos,

Zacatecas, and San Martín, and divers other places so far within the country that some of them are 700 miles off, and some more and some less, all upon horses, mules, and in wains drawn with oxen, and in cars drawn with mules.

In this town of Veracruz within these twenty years, when women were brought to bed, the children new-born incontinently died, which is not so now in these days, God be thanked.

This town is inclined to many kind of diseases, by reason of the great heat and a certain gnat or fly which they call a mosquito, which biteth both men and women in their sleep, and as soon as they are bitten, incontinently the flesh swelleth as though they had been bitten with some venomous worm. And this mosquito or gnat doth most follow such as are newly come into the country. Many there are that die of this annoyance.

This town is situated upon the river afore said and compassed with woods of divers manners and sorts and many fruits, as oranges and lemons, guavas, and divers others, and birds in them, popinjays both small and great, and some of them as big as a raven and their tails as long as the tail of a pheasant. There are also many other kind of birds of purple colour and small monkeys marvellous proper.

This hot or sick country continueth forty-five miles towards the city of Mexico, and the forty-five miles being passed, then there is a temperate country and full of tillage; but they water all their corn with rivers which they turn in upon it. And they gather their wheat twice a year. And if they should not water the ground whereas their corn is sown, the country is so hot it would burn all.

Before you come to Mexico there is a great town called Tlaxcala, which hath in it above 16,000 households. All the inhabitants thereof are free by the kings of Spain; for these were the occasion that Mexico was won in so short time and with so little loss of men. Wherefore they are all gentlemen and pay no tribute to the King. In this town is all the cochineal growing.

Mexico is a great city; it hath more than fifty thousand households, whereof there are not past five or six thousand houses of Spaniards; all the other are the people of the country, which live under the Spaniards' laws. There are in this city stately buildings and many monasteries of friars and nuns which the Spaniards have made. And the building of the Indians is somewhat beautiful outwardly, and within full of small chambers, with very small windows, which is not so comely as the building of the Spaniards. This city standeth in the midst of a great lake, and the water goeth through all or the most part of the streets, and there come small boats, which they call canoas, and in them they bring all things necessary, as wood and coals, and grass for their horses, stones and lime to build, and corn.

This city is subject to many earthquakes, which oftentimes cast down houses and kill people. This city is very well provided of water to drink and with all manner of victuals, as fruits, flesh and fish, bread, hens and capons, guinea-cocks and hens, and all other fowl. There are in this city every week three fairs or markets, which are frequented with many people, as well Spaniards as the people of the country. There are in these fairs or markets all manner of things that may be invented to sell, and in especial things of the country. . . .

Many rivers fall into this lake which the city standeth in; but there was never any place found whither it goeth out. The Indians know a way to drown the city, and within these three years they would have practised the same, but they which should have been the doers of it were hanged, and ever since the city hath been well watched both day and night for fear lest at some time they might be deceived; for the Indians love not the Spaniards. Round about the town there are very many gardens and orchards of the fruits of the country, marvellous fair, where the people have great recreation. The men of this city are marvellous vicious, and in like manner the women are dishonest of their bodies, more than they are in other cities or towns in this country.

There are near about this city of Mexico many rivers and standing waters, which have in them a monstrous kind of fish[1] which is marvellous ravening and a great devourer of men and cattle. He is wont to sleep upon the dry land many times, and if there come in the mean time any man or beast and wake or disquiet him, he speedeth well if he get from him. He is like unto a serpent saving that he doth not fly, neither hath he wings.

There is west out of Mexico a port town which is on the South Sea, called Puerto de Navidad,[2] whereas there are ships which they have ordinarily for the navigation of China, which they have newly found. This port is threescore leagues from Mexico.

There is another port town, which is called Culiacán, on the South Sea, which lieth west and by north out of Mexico and is 150 leagues from the same. And there the Spaniards made two ships to go seek the strait or gulf which as they say is between the Newfoundland and Greenland; and they call it the Englishmen's Strait, which as yet was never fully found. They say that strait lieth not far from the mainland of China, which the Spaniards accompt to be marvellous rich.

Toward the north from Mexico there are great store of silver mines. There is greater quantity of silver found in these mines toward the north than there is in any other parts, and as the most men of experience said always, they find the richer mines the more northerly. These mines are commonly upon great hills and stony ground, marvellous hard to be laboured and wrought.

Out of some of the mines the Indians find a certain kind of earth of divers colours, wherewith they paint themselves in times of their dances and other pastimes which they use.

In this country of Nova Hispania there are also mines of gold, although the gold be commonly found in rivers or very near unto rivers. And now in these days there is not so much gold found as there hath been heretofore.

There are many great rivers and great store of fish in them, not like unto our kinds of fish. And there are marvellous great woods and as fair trees as may be seen of divers sorts, and especially fir trees, that may mast any ship that goeth upon the sea, oaks and pineapples,[3] and another tree which they call mesquito; it beareth a fruit like unto a peasecod marvellous sweet, which the wild people gather and keep it all the year and eat it instead of bread.

The Spaniards have notice of seven cities which old men of the Indians show them should lie towards the north-west from Mexico. They have used and use daily much diligence in the seeking of them, but they cannot find any one of them. They say that the witchcraft of the Indians is such that when they come by these towns they cast a mist upon them so that they cannot see them.

They have understanding of another city which they call Copalla, and in like manner, at my being in the country, they have used much labour and diligence in the seeking of it. They have found the lake on which it should stand, and a canoa, the head whereof was wrought with copper curiously, and could not find nor see any man nor the town, which to their understanding should stand on the same water or very near the same.

There is a great number of beasts or kine[4] in the country of Cibola, which were never brought thither by the Spaniards but breed naturally in the country. They are like unto our oxen, saving that they have long hair like a lion and short horns, and they have upon their shoulders a bunch like a camel, which is higher than the rest of their body. They are marvellous wild and swift in running. They call them the beasts or kine of Cibola.

This Cibola is a city which the Spaniards found now of late, without any people in the same, goodly buildings, fair chimneys, windows made of stone and timber excellently wrought, fair wells with wheels to draw their water, and a place where they had buried their dead people, with many fair stones upon the graves. And the captain would not suffer his soldiers to break up any part of these graves, saying he would come another time to do it.

They asked certain people which they met whither the people of this city were gone; and they made answer they were gone down a river which was thereby very great and there had builded a city which was more for their commodity.

This captain, lacking things necessary for himself and his men, was fain to return back again without finding any treasure according to his expectation; neither found they but few people, although they found beaten ways which had been much haunted and frequented. The captain at his coming back again had a great check of the governor because he had not gone forwards and seen the end of that river.

They have in the country far from the sea-side standing waters which are salt; and in the months of April and May the water of them congealeth into salt, which salt is all taken for the King's use and profit.

Their dogs are all crooked-backed, as many as are of the country breed, and cannot run fast; their faces are like the face of a pig or an hog, with sharp noses.

In a certain province which is called Guatemala and Sacanusco there is growing great store of cacao, which is a berry like unto an almond. It is the best merchandise that is in all the Indies. The Indians make a drink of it and in like manner meat to eat. It goeth currently for money in any market or fair and may buy any flesh, fish, bread, or cheese or other things.

There are many kind of fruits of the country, which are very good, as plantains, sapotes, guavas, pinas, aluacatas, tunas,[5] mammees, lemons, oranges, walnuts very small and hard with little meat on them, grapes which the Spaniards brought into the country, and also wild grapes, which are of the country and are very small, quinces, peaches, figs, and but few apples and very small, and no pears, but there are melons and calabashes.

There is much honey, both of bees and also of a kind of tree which they call maguey. This honey of maguey is not so sweet as the other honey is, but it is better to be eaten only with bread than the other is; and the tree serveth for many things, as the leaves make thread to sew any kind of bags and are good to cover or thatch houses, and for divers other things.

They have in divers places of the country many hot springs of water. As, above all other, I have seen one in the province of Michoacán. In a plain field without any mountain there is a spring which hath much water, and it is so hot that if a whole quarter of beef be cast into it, within an half-hour it will be as well sodden as it will be over a fire in half a day. I have seen half a sheep cast in and immediately it hath been sodden, and I have eaten part of it.

There are many hares and some conies. There are no partridges, but abundance of quails.

They have great store of fish in the South Sea and many oysters and very great. The people do open the oysters and take out the meat of them and dry it, as they do any other kind of fish, and keep them all the year; and when the times serve they send them abroad into the country to sell, as all other fish. They have no salmon, nor trout, nor peal, nor carp, tench, nor pike, in all the country.

There are in the country mighty high mountains and hills, and snow upon them. They commonly burn, and twice every day they cast out much smoke and ashes at certain open places which are in the tops of them.

There is among the wild people much manna. I have gathered of the same and have eaten it, and it is good; for the apothecaries send their servants at certain times to gather of the same for purgations and other uses.

There are in the mountains many wild hogs, which all men may kill, and lions and tigers,[6] which tigers do much harm to men that travel in the wilderness.

In this country not long since there were two poor men that found a marvellous rich mine, and when these men went to make a register of the same, according to the law and custom, before the King's officers, they thought this mine not meet for such men as they were and violently took the said mine for the King and gave no part thereof unto the two poor men. And within certain days the King's officers resorted thither to labour in the mine and they found two great mighty hills were come together, so they found no place to work in. And in the time while I was among them, which was five years, there was a poor shepherd, who, keeping of his sheep, happened to find a well of quicksilver, and he went in like manner to manifest the same, as the custom and manner is. The King's officers dealt in like order as they did with the two poor men that found the rich mine, taking it quite from the shepherd; but when they went to fetch home the quicksilver, or part thereof, they could never find it again. So these things have been declared unto the King, who hath given commandment that nothing being found in the fields, as mines and such-like, shall be taken away from any man. And many other things have been done in this country which men might count for great marvels.

There is great abundance of sugar here, and they make divers conserves and very good and send them into Peru, whereas they sell them marvellous well, because they make none in those parts.

The people of the country are of a good stature, tawny-coloured, broad-faced, flat-nosed, and given much to drink both wine of Spain and also a certain kind of wine which they make with honey of maguey and roots and other things which they use to put into the same. They call the same wine pulco. They are soon drunk and given to much beastliness and void of all goodness. In their drunkenness they use and commit sodomy, and with their mothers and daughters they have their pleasures and pastimes. Whereupon they are defended[7] from the drinking of wines upon pains of money, as well he that selleth the wines as the Indian that drinketh the same. And if this commandment were not, all the wine in Spain and in France were not sufficient for the West Indies only.

They are of much simplicity and great cowards, void of all valour, and are great witches. They use divers times to talk with the Devil, to whom they do certain sacrifices and oblations;[8] many times they have been taken with the same, and I have seen them most cruelly punished for that offence.

The people are given to learn all manner of occupations and sciences, which for the most part they learned since the coming of the Spaniards. I say all manner of arts: they are very artificial in making of images with feathers, or the proportion or figure of any man, in all kind of manner as he is. The fineness and excellency of this is wonderful, that a barbarous people as they are should give themselves to so fine an art as this is. They are goldsmiths, blacksmiths and coppersmiths, carpenters, masons, shoemakers, tailors, saddlers, embroiderers, and of all other kind of sciences; and they will and do work so good cheap that poor young men that go out of Spain to get their living are not set on work. Which is the occasion there are many idle people in the country. For the Indian will live all the week with less than one groat, which the Spaniard cannot do, nor any man else.

They say that they came of the lineage of an old man which came thither in a boat of wood, which they call a canoa. But they cannot tell whether it were before the Flood or after, neither can they give any reason of the Flood nor from whence they came. And when the Spaniards came first among them, they did certain sacrifice to an image made in stone of their own invention. The stone was set upon a great hill, which they made of bricks of earth; they call it their *cowa*. And certain days in the year they did sacrifice certain old men and young children, and only believed in the sun and the moon, saying that from them they had all things that were needful for them.

They have in these parts great store of cotton wool, with which they make a manner of linen cloth, which the Indians wear, both men and women, and it serveth for shirts and smocks and all other kind of garments which they wear upon their bodies; and the Spaniards use it to all such purposes, especially such as cannot buy other. And if it were not for this kind of cloth, all manner of cloth that goeth out of Spain, I say linen cloth, would be sold out of all measure.

The wild people go naked, without anything upon them. The women wear the skin of a deer before their privities and nothing else upon all their bodies. They have no care for anything but only from day to day for that which they have need to eat. They are big men and likewise the women. They shoot in bows, which they make of a cherry tree, and their arrows are of cane, with a sharp flintstone in the end of the same; they will pierce any coat of mail, and they kill deer, and cranes, and wild geese, ducks, and other fowl, and worms, and snakes, and divers other vermin, which they eat. They live very long, for I have seen men that have been 100 years of age. They have but very little hair in their face, nor on their bodies.

The Indians have the friars in great reverence. The occasion is that by them and by their means they are free and out of bondage, which was so ordained by Charles the Emperor, which is the occasion that now there is not so much gold and silver coming into Europe as there was while the Indians were slaves. For when they were in bondage they could not choose but do their task every day and bring their masters so much metal out of their mines. But now they must be well paid and much entreated to have them work. So it hath been and is a great hindrance to the owners of the mines and to the King's *quinto*, or custom.

F

There are many mines of copper in great quantity, whereof they spend in the country as much as serveth their turns. There is some gold in it, but not so much as will pay the costs of the fining. The quantity of it is such, and the mines are so far from the sea, that it will not be worth the freight to carry it into Spain. On the other side, the King's officers will give no licence to make ordnance thereof; whereupon the mines lie unlaboured and of no valuation.

There is much lead in the country, so that with it they cover churches and other religious houses; wherefore they shall not need any of our lead, as they have had need thereof in times past.

The pomp and liberality of the owners of the mines is marvellous to behold. The apparel both of them and of their wives is more to be compared to the apparel of noble persons than otherwise. If their wives go out of their houses, as unto the church or any other place, they go out with great majesty and with as many men and maids as though she were the wife of some nobleman. I will assure you, I have seen a miner's wife go to the church with 100 men and 20 gentlewomen and maids. They keep open house; who will may come to eat their meat. They call men with a bell to come to dinner and supper. They are princes in keeping of their houses and bountiful in all manner of things.

A good owner of mines must have at the least an hundred slaves to carry and to stamp his metals; he must have many mules and men to keep the mines; he must have mills to stamp his metals; he must have many wains and oxen to bring home wood to fine the ore; he must have much quicksilver and a marvellous quantity of salt brine for the metals; and he must be at many other charges. And as for this charge of quicksilver, it is a new invention, which they find more profitable than to fine their ore with lead. Howbeit the same is very costly. For there is never a hundredth of quicksilver but costeth at the least £60 sterling. And the mines fall daily in decay and of less value, and the occasion is the few Indians that men have to labour their mines.

There is in New Spain a marvellous increase of cattle, which daily do increase, and they are of a greater growth than ours are. You may have a great steer that hath an hundredweight of tallow in his belly for sixteen shillings, and some one man hath 20,000 head of cattle of his own. They sell the hides unto the merchants, who lade into Spain as many as may be well spared. They spend many in the country in shoes and boots and in the mines; and as the country is great, so is the increase of the cattle wonderful. In the island of Santo Domingo they commonly kill the beasts for their hides and tallow and the fowls eat the carcasses; and so they do in Cuba and Puerto Rico, whereas there is much sugar and *cana fistula*, which daily they send into Spain. They have great increase of sheep in like manner, and daily do intend to increase them. They have much wool and as good as the wool of Spain. They make cloth as much as serveth the country for the common people and send much cloth into Peru. I have seen cloth made in the city of Mexico which hath been sold for ten pesos a vara, which is almost £4 English, and the vara is less than our yard. They have woad growing in the country, and alum and brazil and divers other things to dye withal, so that they make all colours. In Peru they make no cloth, but hereafter our cloth will be little set by in these parts, unless it be some fine cloth. The wools are commonly four shillings every row, which is five-and-twenty pounds; and in some places of the country, that are far from the places whereas they make cloth, it is worth nothing and doth serve but only to make beds for men to lie on.

They make hats, as many as do serve the country, as fine and good, and sell them better cheap, than they can be brought out of Spain, and in like manner send them into Peru.

Many people are set on work, both in the one and in the other. They spin their wool as we do, and instead of oil they have hogs' grease; they twist not their thread so much as we, neither work so fine a thread. They make no kerseys, but they make much cloth which is coarse and sell it for less than twelvepence the vara. It is called sayal.

They have much silk and make all manner of sorts thereof, as taffetas, satins, velvets of all colours, and they are as good as the silks of Spain, saving that the colours are not so perfect; but the blacks are better than the blacks that come out of Spain.

They have many horses and mares and mules, which the Spaniards brought thither. They have as good jennets as any are in Spain, and better cheap than they be in Spain. And with their mules they carry all their goods from place to place.

There is rain usually in this country from the month of May to the midst of October every day, which time they call their winter, by reason of the said waters. And if it were not for the waters which fall in these hot seasons, their maize, which is the greatest part of their sustenance, would be destroyed. This maize is the greatest maintenance which the Indian hath, and also all the common people of the Spaniards. And their horses and mules which labour cannot be without the same. This grain is substantial and increaseth much blood. If the miners should be without it, they could not labour their mines; for all their servants eat none other bread but only of this maize, and it is made in cakes, as they make oaten cakes in some places of England.

The Indians pay tribute, being of the age of twenty years, four shillings of money and a fanega of maize, which is worth four shillings more, unto the King every year. This is paid in all Nova Hispania of as many as be of the age of twenty years, saving the city of Tlaxcala, which was made free because the citizens thereof were the occasion that Cortés took Mexico in so little a time. And although at the first they were freed from payment of tribute, yet the Spaniards now begin to usurp upon them and make them to till a great field of maize at their own costs every year for the King, which is as beneficial unto him and as great cost unto them as though they paid their tribute as the others do.

The ships which go out of Spain with goods for Peru go to Nombre de Dios and there discharge the said goods; and from thence they be carried over the neck of a land unto a port town in the South Sea called Panama, which is seventeen leagues distant from Nombre de Dios. And there they do ship their goods again and so from thence go to Peru. They are in going thither three months and they come back again in twenty days. They have seldom foul weather and few ships are lost in the South Sea. Four years past, to wit, 1568, there was a ship made out of Peru to seek Solomon's Islands, and they came somewhat to the south of the equinoctial and found an island with many black people, in such number that the Spaniards durst not go on land among them. And because they had been long upon the voyage, their people were very weak and so went not on land to know what commodity was upon it. And for want of victuals they arrived in Nova Hispania in a port called Puerto de Navidad, and thence returned back again unto Peru, whereas they were evil entreated because they had not known more of the same island.

They have in this port of Navidad ordinarily their ships which go to the islands of China, which are certain islands which they have found within these seven years. They have brought from thence gold and much cinnamon, and dishes of earth, and cups of the same, so fine that every man that may have a piece of them will give the weight of silver for it. There was a mariner that brought a pearl as big as a dove's egg from thence, and a stone for which the viceroy would have given 3,000 ducats. Many things they bring from thence most excellent. There are many of these islands, and the Spaniards have not many of them as yet; for the Portugals disturb them much and combat with them every day, saying it is part of their conquest, and to the mainland they cannot come at any hand. There are goodly people in them, and they are great mariners, richly apparelled in cloth of gold and silver and silk of all sorts, and go apparelled after the manner of the Turks.

This report make such as come from thence. The men of the mainland have certain traffic with some of these islanders and come thither in a kind of ships which they have with one sail, and bring of such merchandise as they have need of. And of these things there have been brought into New Spain both cloth of gold and silver and divers manners of silks and works of gold and silver, marvellous to be seen. So by their saying there is not such a country in the whole world.

The mainland is from the islands 150 leagues; and the islands are not far from the Moluccas northwards. And the people of those islands which the Spaniards have say that if they would bring their wives and children, that then they should have among them what they would have. So there go women daily, and the King payeth all the charges of the married men and their wives that go to those islands. And there is no doubt but the trade will be marvellous rich in time to come.

It was my fortune to be in company with one Diego Gutierrez, who was the first pilot that ever went to that country of the Philippines. He maketh report of many strange things in that country, as well riches as others, and saith if there be any paradise upon earth it is in that country; and addeth that, sitting under a tree, you shall have such sweet smells, with such great content and pleasure, that you shall remember nothing, neither wife nor children, nor have any kind of appetite to eat or drink, the odoriferous smells will be so sweet. This man hath good livings in Nova Hispania, notwithstanding he will return thither with his wife and children, and as for treasure, there is abundance, as he maketh mention.

In this country of Nova Hispania there are many bucks and does, but they have not so long horns as they have here in England. The Spaniards kill them with handguns and with greyhounds, and the Indians kill them with their bows and arrows, and with the skins they make chamois, such as we in England make doublets and hose of, as good as the skins that are dressed in Flanders, and likewise they make marvellous good Spanish leather of them. There is a bird which is like unto a raven, but he hath some of his feathers white; there is such abundance of them that they eat all the corrupt and dead flesh which is in the country. Otherwise the abundance of carrion is so much that it would make a marvellous corrupt air in all the country and be so noisome that no man could abide it. Therefore it is commanded there shall none of them be killed. These birds are always about cities and towns, where there is much flesh killed.

The Indians are much favoured by the justices of the country, and they call them their orphans. And if any Spaniard should happen to do any of them harm or to wrong him in taking anything from him, as many times they do, or to strike any of them, being in any town whereas justice is, they are as well punished for the same as if they had done it one Spaniard to another. When a Spaniard is far from Mexico or any place of justice, thinking to do with the poor Indian what he list, considering he is so far from any place of remedy, he maketh the Indian do what he commandeth him, and if he will not do it he beateth and misuseth him, according to his own appetite. The Indian holdeth his peace until he find an opportunity and then taketh a neighbour with him and goeth to Mexico, although it be twenty leagues off, and maketh his complaint. This his complaint is immediately heard, and although it be a knight or a right good gentleman, he is forthwith sent for and punished, both by his goods and also his person is imprisoned, at the pleasure of the justice. This is the occasion that the Indians are so tame and civil as they are; and if they should not have this favour the Spaniards would soon dispatch all the Indians, or the Indians would kill them. But they may call them dogs and use other evil words as much as they will, and the Indian must needs put it up and go his way.

The poor Indians will go every day two or three leagues to a fair or market with a child upon their necks, with as much fruit or roots, or some kind of ware, as cotton wool or caddis[9] of all colours, as shall be not past worth a penny; and they will maintain themselves upon the same. For they live with a marvellous small matter.

They are in such poverty that if you need to ride into the country you shall have an Indian to go with you all the day with your bed upon his back for one rial of plate;[10] and this you shall have from one town to another. Here you are to understand that all men that travel by the way are always wont to carry their beds with them. They are great thieves and will steal all that they may, and you shall have no recompense at their hands.

The garments of the women are in this manner. The uppermost part is made almost like to a woman's smock, saving that it is as broad above as beneath and hath no sleeves but holes on each side to put out their arms. It is made of linen cloth, made of cotton wool, and filled full of flowers, of red caddis and blue, and other colours. This garment cometh down to the knees, and then they have another cloth made after the same manner and that goeth round about their waist and reacheth to their shoes, and over this a white fine sheet upon their heads, which goeth down half the leg. Their hair is made up round with an hair lace about their head. And the men have a small pair of breeches of the same cotton wool, and their shirts which hang over their breeches, and a broad girdle about their middles, and a sheet with flowers upon their backs and with a knot upon one shoulder, and an hat upon their heads, and a pair of shoes. And this is all their apparel, although it be a cacique,[11] which they use in all the country.

The walls of the houses of the Indians are but plain, but the stones are laid so close that you shall not well perceive the joints between one stone and another, they are so finely cut; and by the means that the stones are so workmanly done and finely joined together there is some beauty in their walls. They are marvellous small and light, as pumice-stones. They make their doors very little, so that there can go in but one man at a time. Their windows and rooms within their houses are small, and one room they have reserved for their friends when they come to talk one with another, and that is always fair matted and kept marvellous clean, and hanged full of images, and their chairs standing there to sit in. They eat their meat upon the ground and sleep on the ground upon a mat, without any bed, both the gentlemen and other.

The Indians strike their fire with one stick in another, as well the tame people as the wild; for they know not how to do it with an iron and a stone.

In Nova Hispania every ten or twelve leagues they have a contrary speech, saving only about Mexico; so there is a number of speeches in the country.

Montezuma, which was the last king of this country, was one of the richest princes which have been seen in our time, or long before. He had all kind of beasts which were then in the country, and all manner of birds and fishes, and all manner of worms which creep upon the earth, and all trees and flowers and herbs, all fashioned in silver and gold, which was the greatest part of his treasure, and in these things had he great joy, as the old Indians report. And unto this day they say that the treasure of Montezuma is hidden and that the Spaniards have it not.

This king would give none of his people freedom, nor forgive any of them that should pay him tribute, though he were never so poor. For if it had been told him that one of his tributaries was poor and that he was not able to pay his tribute according to the custom, then he would have him bound to bring at such times as tributes should be paid a quill full of lice, saying he would have none free but himself.

He had as many wives or concubines as he would have and such as liked him. Always, whensoever he went out of his court to pass the time, he was borne upon four of his noblemen's shoulders, set upon a table, some say, of gold, and very richly dressed with feathers, of divers and many colours, and flowers. He washed all his body every day, were it never so cold. And unto this day so do all the Indians, and especially the women.

The Spaniards keep the Indians in great subjection. They may have in their houses no sword nor dagger, nor knife with any point, nor may wear upon them any manner of arms; neither may they ride upon any horse nor mules in any saddle nor bridle; neither may they drink wine, which they take for the greatest pain of all. They have attempted divers times to make insurrections, but they have been overthrown immediately by their own great and beastly cowardliness.

There remain some among the wild people that unto this day eat one another. I have seen the bones of a Spaniard that have been as clean burnished as though it had been done by men that had no other occupation. And many times people are carried away by them, but they never come again, whether they be men or women.

They have in the sea islands of red salt in great abundance, whereas they lade it from place to place about the seacoast; and they spend very much salt with salting their hides and fish; and in their mines they occupy great quantity.

They have much alum and as good as any that is in all the Levant, so that they need none of that commodity.

They have also, of their own growing, much *cana fistula* and much sarsaparilla, which is marvellous good for many kind of diseases.

There are in Florida many gerfalcons and many other kind of hawks, which the gentlemen of Nova Hispania send for every year. The Spaniards have two forts there, chiefly to keep out the Frenchmen from planting there.

# 8

# Fish in Newfoundland Come at Command of Fisherman! (1578)

Anthony Parkhurst, a gentleman adventurer of Bristol, made several expeditions to the Newfoundland fishing banks and was an enthusiastic
advocate of the development of the fisheries there and the establishment of
salt works where salt could be evaporated cheaper than in England. During
the summer of 1578 he went on a fishing and exploring expedition to Newfoundland, made careful observations, and returned to write a report for
Richard Hakluyt the lawyer. This excerpt is taken from 'A Letter Written
to Mr Richard Hakluyt of the Middle Temple, Containing a Report of the
True State and Commodities of Newfoundland', dated from Bristol on
November 13, 1578. Printed by Hakluyt, *Principal Navigations* (1589) and
reprinted by Taylor, *Original Writings . . . of the Two Richard Hakluyts*, I,
127–34.

... Now to answer some part of your letter touching the sundry navies
that come to Newfoundland or Terra Nova for fish: you shall understand that some fish not near the other by two hundred leagues, and
therefore the certainty is not known. And some years come many more
than othersome, as I see the like among us, who since my first travail,
being but four years, are increased from thirty sail to fifty, which cometh
to pass chiefly by the imagination of the western men, who think their
neighbours have had greater gains than in very deed they have. For
that[1] they see me to take such pains yearly to go in proper person,[2] they
also suppose that I find some secret commodity, by reason that I do
search the harbours, creeks, and havens, and also the land, much more
than ever any Englishman hath done. Surely I am glad that it so increaseth, whereofsoever it springeth.

But to let this pass, you shall understand that I am informed that
there are above one hundred sails of Spaniards that come to take cod
(who make all wet and do dry it when they come home) besides twenty
or thirty more that come from Biscay to kill whale for train.[3] These be
better appointed for shipping and furniture of munition than any
nation, saving the Englishmen, who commonly are lords of the harbours where they fish and do use all strangers' help in fishing if need
require, according to an old custom of the country; which thing they do

willingly, so that you take nothing from them more than a boat or twain of salt, in respect of your protection of them against rovers or other violent intruders, who do often put them from good harbour, etc. As touching their tonnage, I think it may be near five or six thousand, but of Portugals there are not lightly[4] above fifty sail, and they make all wet in like sort, whose tonnage may amount to three thousand tons, and not upward; of the French nation and Bretons are about one hundred and fifty sails: the most of their shipping is very small, not past forty tons, among which some are great and reasonably well appointed, better than the Portugals, and not so well as the Spaniards, and the burden of them may be some seven thousand ton. Their shipping is from all parts of France and Brittany, and the Spaniards from most parts of Spain, the Portugals from Aviero and Viana and from two or three ports more. The trade that our nation hath to Island [Iceland] maketh that the English are not there in such numbers as other nations.

Now to certify you of the fertility and goodness of the country, you shall understand that I have in sundry places sown wheat, barley, rye, oats, beans, peas, and seeds of herbs, kernels, plum-stones, nuts, all which have prospered as in England. The country yieldeth many good trees of fruit, as filberts in some place[s], but in all places cherry-trees and a kind of pear-tree meet to graft on. As for roses, they are as common as brambles here; strawberries, dewberries, and raspis [raspberries], as common as grass. The timber is most fir, yet plenty of pineapple trees:[5] few of these two kinds meet[6] to mast a ship of threescore-and-ten, but near the Grand Bay or Cape Breton big and sufficient for any ship. There be also oaks and thorns. There is in all the country plenty of birch and alder, which be the meetest wood for coal, and also willow, which will serve for many other purposes.

As touching the kinds of fish, beside cod there are herrings, salmons, thornback, plaice (or rather we should call them flounders), dog-fish, and another most excellent of taste called of us a cat, oysters, and mussels, in which I have found pearls above forty in one mussel, and generally all have some, great or small. I heard of a Portugal that found one worth three hundred ducats. There are also other kinds of shell-fish, as limpets, cockles, whelks, lobsters, and crabs; also a fish like a smelt, which cometh on shore, and another that has the like property, called a squid. These be the fishes which (when I please to be merry with my old companions) I say do come on shore when I command them in the name of the Cinque Ports and conjure them by such-like words. These also be the fishes which I may sweep with brooms on a heap and never wet my foot, only pronouncing two or three words whatsoever they be appointed by any man, so they hear my voice. The virtue of the words be small but the nature of the fish great and strange. For the squid, whose nature is to come by night as well as by day, I tell them I set him a candle to see his way, with which he is much delighted, or else cometh to wonder at it, as do our fresh-water fish. The other cometh also in the night but chiefly in the day, being forced by the cod that would devour him, and therefore, for fear coming so near the shore, is driven dry by the surge of the sea on the pebble and sands. Of these, being as good as a smelt, you may take up with a shove-net, as plentifully as you do wheat in a shovel, sufficient in three or four hours for a whole city.

There be also other fishes which I tell those that are desirous of strange news that I take as fast as one would gather up stones, and them I take with a long pole and hook. 'Yea, marry', say they, 'we believe so, and that you catch all the rest you bring home in that sort, from Portugals and Frenchmen.' No, surely; but thus I do: with three hooks stretched forth in the end of a pole I make as it were an eel-spear, with which I prick those flounders as fast as you would take up fritters with a sharp pointed stick, and with that tool I may take up in less than half a day lobsters sufficient to find⁷ three hundred men for a day's meat.

This pastime ended, I show them that for my pleasure I take a great mastiff I have and say no more than thus: 'Go fetch me this rebellious fish that obeyeth not this gentleman that cometh from Kent and Christendom', bringing them to the high-water mark, and when he doubteth⁸ that any of those great cods, by reason of shelving ground, be like to tumble into the sea again, he will warily take heed and carry him up back to the heap of his fellows. This doth cause my friends to wonder and at the first hearing to judge them notorious lies, but they laugh and are merry when they hear the means how each tale is true.

I told you once I do remember how in my travel into Africa and America I found trees that bare oysters, which was strange to you till I told you that their boughs hung in the water, on which both oysters and mussels did stick fast, as their property is to stakes and timber.

Now to let these merry tales pass and to come to earnest matters again, you shall understand that Newfoundland is in a temperate climate and not so cold as foolish mariners do say, who find it cold sometimes when plenty of isles of ice lie near the shore; but up in the land they shall find it hotter than in England in many parts of the country toward the south. This cold cometh by an accidental means, as by the ice that cometh fleeting from the north parts of the world, and not by the situation of the country or nature of the climate.

The country is full of little small rivers all the year long, proceeding from the mountains, engendered both of snow and rain; few springs that ever I could find or hear of, except it be towards the south; in some places, or rather in most places, great lakes with plenty of fish, the country most covered with woods of fir, yet in many places indifferent good grass, and plenty of bears everywhere, so that you may kill them as oft as you list. Their flesh is as good as young beef, and hardly you may know the one from the other, if it be powdered but two days. Of otters we may take like store. There are sea-gulls, murres, ducks, wild geese, and many other kind of birds store, too long to write, especially at one island named Penguin, where we may drive them on a plank into our ship as many as shall lade her. These birds are also called penguins and cannot fly. There is more meat in one of these than in a goose. The Frenchmen that fish near the Great Bay do bring small store of flesh with them but victual themselves always with these birds.

Now again, for venison, plenty, especially to the north about the Grand Bay; and in the south near Cape Race and Pleasance there are many other kinds of beasts, as lucerns[9] and other mighty beasts like to camels[10] in greatness, and their feet cloven. I did see them far off, not able to discern them perfectly; but their steps showed that their feet were cloven and bigger than the feet of camels. I suppose them to be a kind of buffs, which I read to be in the countries adjacent and very many in the firm land. There be also to the northwards hares and foxes in all parts so plentifully that at noondays they take away our flesh before our faces, within less than half a pair of butts' length, where four-and-twenty persons were turning of dry fish and two dogs in sight. Yet stood they not in fear till we gave shot and set the dogs upon them. The bears also be as bold, which will not spare at midday to take your fish before your face, and I believe assuredly would not hurt anybody unless they be forced.

Now to show you my fancy what places I suppose meetest to inhabit in those parts discovered of late by our nation: there is near about the mouth of the Grand Bay an excellent harbour, called of the Frenchmen Château, and one island in the very entry of the strait called Belle Isle, which places if they be peopled and well fortified (as there are stones and things meet for it throughout all Newfoundland) we shall be lords of the whole fishing in small time, if it do so please the Queen's

Majesty, and from thence send wood and coal with all necessaries to Labrador lately discovered. But I am of opinion and do most stead- fastly believe that we shall find as rich mines in more temperate places and climates, and more profitable for fishing than any yet we have used, where we shall have not far from thence plenty of salt, made by fire un- doubtedly, and very likely by the heat of the sun, by reason I find salt kerned[11] on the rocks in nine-and-forty and better. These places may be found for salt in three-and-forty. I know more touching these two commodities last remembered than any man of our nation doth, for that I have some knowledge in such and have most desired the finding of them by painful travail and most diligent inquiry.

Now to be short, for I have been over-long by Master Butler's means, who cried on me to write at large and of as many things as I call to mind worthy of remembrance, wherefore this one thing more. I could wish the island[12] in the mouth of the river of Canada should be inhabited and the river searched, for that there are many things which may rise thereof, as I will show you hereafter. I could find in my heart to make proof whether it be true or no that I have read and heard of Frenchmen and Portugals to be in that river and about Cape Breton. I had almost forgot to speak of the plenty of wolves and to show you that there be foxes, black, white, and grey; other beasts I know none save those before remembered. I found also certain mines of iron and copper in St John's and in the Island of Iron, which things might turn to our great benefit if our men had desire to plant thereabout, for proof whereof I have brought home some of the ore of both sorts.

And thus I end, assuring you on my faith that if I had not been deceived by the vile Portugals, descending of the Jews and Judas kind, I had not failed to have searched this river and all the coast of Cape Breton what might have been found to have benefited our country; but they, breaking their bonds and falsifying their faith and promise, dis- appointed me of the salt they should have brought me in part of re- compense of my good service in defending them two years against French rovers, that had spoiled them if I had not defended them.

By means whereof they made me lose not only the searching of the country but also forced me to come home with great loss above £600. For recompense whereof I have sent my man into Portugal to demand justice at the King's hand; if not, I must put up my supplication to the Queen's Majesty and her honourable Council to grant me leave to stay here so much of their goods as they have damnified me, or else that I may take of them in Newfoundland as much fish as shall be worth £600 or as much as the salt might have made. I pray you advertise me what way I were best to take and what hope there may be of a recompense if I follow the suit. Many there are that do comfort me and do bid me proceed, for that Her Majesty and the Council do tender[13] poor fishermen, who with me have sustained £300 loss in that voyage. And to conclude, if you and your friend shall think me a man sufficient and of credit to seek the Isle of St John or the river of Canada, with any part of the firm land of Cape Breton, I shall give my diligence for the true and perfect discovery and leave some part of mine own business to further the same. And thus I end, committing you to God.

From Bristol the thirteenth of November, 1578.

Yours to use and command,

Anthony Parkhurst

9

# Sir Humphrey Gilbert's Tragic Adventure in Newfoundland (1583)

Edward Hayes, a West Country ship captain and adventurer, commanded his own vessel, the *Golden Hind*, in the voyage to Newfoundland in 1583 when Sir Humphrey Gilbert took possession of the island at St John's. On the return voyage, Gilbert was lost when his own little frigate, the *Squirrel*, foundered and sank. Hayes made a report of the voyage which Hakluyt printed in the *Principal Navigations* (1589) under the title 'A Report of the Voyage and Success Thereof, Attempted in the Year of Our Lord 1583 by Sir Humphrey Gilbert, Knight, with Other Gentlemen Assisting Him in That Action . . .' It has been reprinted by Quinn, *Voyages and Colonising Enterprises of Sir Humphrey Gilbert*, II, 385–423. Hayes begins his narrative with a long justification of English settlement in the North Atlantic region and then proceeds with an account of the departure of the fleet on the homeward voyage:

ORDERS thus determined, and promises mutually given to be observed, every man withdrew himself unto his charge; the anchors being already weighed and our ships under sail, having a soft gale of wind, we began our voyage upon Tuesday, the eleventh day of June, in the year of Our Lord 1583, having in our fleet (at our departure from Cawsand Bay) these ships, whose names and burdens, with the names of the captains and masters of them, I have also inserted as follows:

1. The *Delight*, alias the *George*, of burden 120 tons, was admiral, in which went the general, and William Winter, captain in her and part owner, and Richard Clarke, master.

2. The bark *Raleigh*, set forth by Master Walter Raleigh, of the burden of 200 tons, was then vice-admiral, in which went Master Butler, captain, and Robert Davis of Bristol, master.

3. The *Golden Hind*, of burden 40 tons, was then rear-admiral, in which went Edward Hayes, captain and owner, and William Cox of Limehouse, master.

4. The *Swallow*, of burden 40 tons; in her was Captain Maurice Browne.

5. The *Squirrel*, of burden 10 tons, in which went Captain William Andrewes and one Cade, master.

We were in number in all about 260 men, among whom we had of every faculty good choice, as shipwrights, masons, carpenters, smiths, and such-like, requisite to such an action; also mineral-men and refiners. Besides, for solace of our people and allurement of the savages, we were provided of music in good variety, not omitting the least toys, as Morris-dancers, hobby-horse, and May-like conceits to delight the savage people, whom we intended to win by all fair means possible. And to that end we were indifferently furnished of all petty haberdashery wares to barter with those simple people.

In this manner we set forward. . . .

Saturday the twenty-seventh of July we might descry not far from us as it were mountains of ice driven upon the sea, being then in 50 degrees, which were carried southward to the weather of us, whereby may be conjectured that some current does set that way from the north.

Before we come to Newfoundland, about fifty leagues on this side, we pass the Bank, which are high grounds rising within the sea and under water, yet deep enough and without danger, being commonly not less than twenty-five and thirty fathom water upon them: the same (as it were some vein of mountains within the sea) do run along and from the Newfoundland, beginning northward about 52 or 53 degrees of latitude, and do extend into the south infinitely. The breadth of this Bank is somewhere more and somewhere less, but we found the same about ten leagues over, having sounded both on this side thereof and the other toward Newfoundland, but found no ground with almost 200 fathom of line, both before and after we had passed the Bank. The

Portugals and French chiefly have a notable trade of fishing upon this bank, where are sometimes an hundred or more sails of ships, who commonly begin the fishing in April and have ended by July. That fish is large, always wet, having no land near to dry, and is called cor-fish.

During the time of fishing, a man shall know without sounding when he is upon the Bank by the incredible multitude of sea-fowl hovering over the same, to prey upon the offals and garbage of fish thrown out by fishermen and floating upon the sea.

Upon Tuesday the eleventh of June we forsook the coast of England. So again Tuesday the thirtieth of July (seven weeks after) we got sight of land, being immediately embayed in the Grand Bay, or some other great bay, the certainty whereof we could not judge: so great haze and fog did hang upon the coast as neither we might discern the land well nor take the sun's height. But by our best computation we were then in the 51 degrees of latitude.

Forsaking this bay and uncomfortable coast (nothing appearing unto us but hideous rocks and mountains, bare of trees and void of any green herb), we followed the coast to the south, with weather fair and clear.

We had sight of an island named Penguin of a fowl there breeding in abundance almost incredible, which cannot fly, their wings not able to carry their body, being very large (not much less than a goose) and exceeding fat; which the Frenchmen used to take without difficulty upon that island and to barrel them up with salt. But for lingering of time we had made us there the like provision.

Trending this coast, we came to the island called Baccalaos,[1] being not past two leagues from the main; to the south thereof lieth Cape St Francis,[2] five leagues distant from Baccalaos, between which goes in a great bay by the vulgar sort called the Bay of Conception. Here we met with the *Swallow* again, whom we had lost in the fog. . . .

Thus, after we had met with the *Swallow*, we held on our course southward until we came against the harbour called St John's, about five leagues from the former Cape of Saint Francis, where before the entrance into the harbour we found also the frigate or *Squirrel* lying at anchor, whom the English merchants (that were and always be admirals by turns interchangeable over the fleets of fishermen within the same harbour) would not permit to enter into the harbour. Glad of so happy meeting both of the *Swallow* and frigate in one day (being Saturday the third of August), we made ready our fights[3] and prepared to enter the harbour, any resistance to the contrary notwithstanding, there being within of all nations to the number of thirty-six sails. But first the general dispatched a boat to give them knowledge of his coming for no ill intent, having commission from Her Majesty for his voyage he had in hand. And immediately we followed with a slack gale, and in the very entrance (which is but narrow, not above two butts' length) the admiral fell upon a rock on the larboard side by great oversight, in that the weather was fair, the rock much above water fast by the shore, where neither went any sea-gate.[4] But we found such readiness in the English merchants to help us in that danger that without delay there were brought a number of boats which towed off the ship and cleared her of danger.

Having taken place convenient in the road, we let fall anchors, the captains and masters repairing aboard our admiral, whither also came immediately the masters and owners of the fishing fleet of Englishmen, to understand the general's intent and cause of our arrival there. They were all satisfied when the general had shown his commission and purpose to take possession of those lands to the behalf of the Crown of England and the advancement of Christian religion in those paganish regions, requiring but their lawful aid for repairing of his fleet and supply of some necessaries, so far as conveniently might be afforded him, both out of that and other harbours adjoining. In lieu whereof, he made offer to gratify[5] them with any favour and privilege which upon their better advice[6] they should demand, the like being not to be obtained hereafter for greater price. So, craving expedition[7] of his demand, minding to proceed further south without long detention in those parts, he dismissed them after promise given of their best endeavour to satisfy speedily his so reasonable request. The merchants with their masters departed, they caused forthwith to be discharged all the great ordnance of their fleet in token of our welcome.

It was further determined that every ship of our fleet should deliver unto the merchants and masters of that harbour a note of all their wants; which done, the ships as well English as strangers were taxed at an easy rate to make supply. And besides, commissioners were appointed, part of our own company and part of theirs, to go into other harbours adjoining (for our English merchants command all there) to levy our provision; whereunto the Portugals (above other nations) did most willingly and liberally contribute, insomuch as we were presented (above our allowance) with wines, marmalades, most fine rusk or biscuit, sweet oils, and sundry delicacies. Also we wanted not of fresh salmons, trouts, lobsters, and other fresh fish brought daily unto us. Moreover, as the manner is in their fishing every week to choose their

G

admiral anew, or rather they succeed in orderly course and have weekly their admiral's feast solemnized, even so the general, captains, and masters of our fleet were continually invited and feasted. To grow short, in our abundance at home the entertainment had been[8] delightful, but after our wants and tedious passage through the ocean it seemed more acceptable and of greater contentation by how much the same was unexpected in that desolate corner of the world, where at other times of the year wild beasts and birds have only the fruition of all those countries, which now seemed a place very populous and much frequented.

The next morning, being Sunday and the fourth of August, the general and his company were brought on land by English merchants, who showed unto us their accustomed walks unto a place they call 'the garden'. But nothing appeared more than Nature itself without art, who confusedly hath brought forth roses abundantly, wild, but odoriferous and to sense very comfortable. Also the like plenty of raspberries, which do grow in every place.

Monday following the general had his tent set up, who, being accompanied with his own followers, summoned the merchants and masters, both English and strangers, to be present at his taking possession of those countries. Before whom openly was read and interpreted unto the strangers his commission, by virtue whereof he took possession in the same harbour of St John's and 200 leagues every way, invested the Queen's Majesty with the title and dignity thereof, had delivered unto him (after the custom of England) a rod and a turf of the same soil, entering possession also for him, his heirs and assigns for ever; and signified unto all men that from that time forward they should take the same land as a territory appertaining to the Queen of England and himself authorized under Her Majesty to possess and enjoy it and to ordain laws for the government thereof, agreeable (so near as conveniently might be) unto the laws of England, under which all people coming thither hereafter, either to inhabit or by way of traffic, should be subjected and governed. And especially at the same time for a beginning he proposed and delivered three laws to be in force immediately, that is to say: the first for religion, which in public exercise should be according to the Church of England; the second for maintenance of Her Majesty's right and possession of those territories, against which if anything were attempted prejudicial, the party or parties offending should be adjudged and executed as in case of high treason according to the laws of England; the third, if any person should utter words sounding to the dishonour of Her Majesty he should lose his ears and have his ship and goods confiscate.

These contents published, obedience was promised by general voice and consent of the multitude, as well of Englishmen as strangers, praying for continuance of this possession and government begun. After this the assembly was dismissed. And afterward were erected not far from that place the arms of England engraven in lead and infixed upon a pillar of wood. Yet further and actually to establish this possession taken in the right of Her Majesty and to the behoof of Sir Humphrey Gilbert, Knight, his heirs and assigns for ever, the general granted in fee-farm divers parcels of land lying by the waterside, both in this harbour of St John's and elsewhere, which was to the owners a great commodity, being thereby assured (by their proper inheritance) of grounds convenient to dress and to dry their fish, whereof many times before they did fail, being prevented by them that came first into the harbour. For which grounds they did covenant to pay a certain rent and service unto Sir Humphrey Gilbert, his heirs or assigns for ever, and yearly to maintain possession of the same by themselves or their assigns.

Now remained only to take in provision granted according as every ship was taxed which did fish upon the coast adjoining. In the mean while the general appointed men unto their charge: some to repair and trim the ships; others to attend in gathering together our supply and provisions; others to search the commodities and singularities of the country to be found by sea or land and to make relation unto the general what either themselves could know by their own travel and experience or by good intelligence of Englishmen or strangers who had longest frequented the same coast. Also some observed the elevation of the Pole and drew plats of the country exactly graded. And by that I could gather by each man's several relation, I have drawn a brief description of the Newfoundland, with the commodities by sea or land already made, and such also as are in possibility and great likelihood to be made. Nevertheless, the cards and plats that were drawing, with the due gradation of the harbours, bays, and capes, did perish with the admiral; wherefore in the description following I must omit the particulars of such things.

### A Brief Relation of the Newfoundland and the Commodities Thereof

That which we do call the Newfoundland and the Frenchmen Baccalaos is an island, or rather (after the opinion of some) it consists of sundry islands and broken lands, situate in the north regions of America upon the gulf and entrance of the great river called St Lawrence in Canada. Into the which navigation may be made both on the south and north side of this island. The land lies south and north, containing in length between three and four hundred miles, accounting from Cape Race (which is in 46 degrees 25 minutes) unto the Grand Bay[9] in 52 degrees of septentrional latitude. The island round about has very many goodly bays and harbours, safe roads for ships, the like not to be found in any part of the known world. . . .

For amongst other charges given to inquire out the singularities of this country, the general was most curious in the search of metals, commanding the mineral-man and refiner especially to be diligent. The same was a Saxon born, honest and religious, named Daniel, who after search brought at first some sort of ore, seeming rather to be iron than other metal. The next time he found ore, which with no small show of contentment he delivered unto the general, using protestation that if silver were the thing which might satisfy the general and his followers, there it was, advising him to seek no further; the peril whereof he undertook upon his life (as dear unto him as the crown of England unto Her Majesty, that I may use his own words) if it fell not out accordingly.

Myself at this instant liker to die than to live, by a mischance, could not follow this confident opinion of our refiner to my own satisfaction, but afterward demanding our general's opinion therein, and to have some part of the ore, he replied: 'Content yourself, I have seen enough, and were it but to satisfy my private humour I would proceed no further. The promise unto my friends and necessity to bring also the south countries within compass of my patent near expired, as we have already done these north parts, do only persuade me further. And touching the ore, I have sent it aboard, whereof I would have no speech to be made so long as we remain within harbour, here being both Portugals, Biscayans, and Frenchmen not far off, from whom must be kept any bruit or muttering of such matter. When we are at sea, proof shall be made; if it be to our desire, we may return the sooner hither again.' Whose answer I judged reasonable and contenting me well, wherewith I will conclude this narration and description of the Newfoundland and proceed to the rest of our voyage, which ended tragically.

While the better sort of us were seriously occupied in repairing our wants and contriving of matters for the commodity of our voyage, others of another sort and disposition were plotting of mischief, some casting to steal away our shipping by night, watching opportunity by the general's and captain's lying on the shore: whose conspiracies discovered, they were prevented. Others drew together in company and carried away out of the harbours adjoining a ship laden with fish, setting the poor men on shore. A great many more of our people stole into the woods to hide themselves, attending time and means to return home by such shipping as daily departed from the coast. Some were sick of fluxes and many dead; and, in brief, by one means or other our company was diminished and many by the general licensed to return home. Insomuch as after we had reviewed our people, resolved to see an end of our voyage, we grew scant of men to furnish all our shipping. It seemed good, therefore, unto the general to leave the *Swallow* with such provision as might be spared for transporting home the sick people.

The captain of the *Delight*, or admiral, returned into England, in whose stead was appointed Captain Maurice Browne, before captain of the *Swallow*, who also brought with him into the *Delight* all his men of the *Swallow*, which before have been noted of outrage perpetrated and committed upon fishermen there met at sea.

The general made choice to go in his frigate, the *Squirrel* (whereof the captain also was among them that returned into England), the same frigate being most convenient to discover upon the coast and to search into every harbour or creek, which a great ship could not do. Therefore the frigate was prepared with her nettings and fights and overcharged with bases[10] and such small ordnance, more to give a show than with judgement to foresee unto the safety of her and the men, which afterward was an occasion also of their overthrow.

Now having made ready our shipping, that is to say, the *Delight*, the *Golden Hind*, and the *Squirrel*, and put aboard our provision, which was wines, bread or rusk, fish wet and dry, sweet oils, besides many other, as marmalades, figs, lemons barrelled, and such-like. Also we had other necessary provisions for trimming our ships, nets and lines to fish withal, boats or pinnaces fit for discovery. In brief, we were supplied of our wants commodiously, as if we had been in a country or some city populous and plentiful of all things.

We departed from this harbour of St John's upon Tuesday the twentieth of August, which we found by exact observation to be in 47 degrees 40 minutes. And the next day by night we were at Cape Race twenty-five leagues from the same harbour. . . .

### The Manner How Our Admiral Was Lost

Upon Tuesday, the twenty-seventh of August, toward the evening, our general caused them in his frigate to sound, who found white sand at thirty-five fathom, being then in latitude about 44 degrees.

Wednesday toward night the wind came south, and we bare with the land all the night west-north-west, contrary to the mind of Master Cox; nevertheless we followed the admiral, deprived of power to prevent a mischief, which by no contradiction could be brought to hold other course, alleging they could not make the ship to work better nor to lie otherways.

The evening was fair and pleasant, yet not without token of storm to ensue, and most part of this Wednesday night, like the swan that sings before death, they in the admiral, or *Delight*, continued in sounding of trumpets, with drums and fifes; also winding the cornets, hautboys and, in the end of their jollity, left with the battle and ringing of doleful knells.

Towards the evening also we caught in the *Golden Hind* a very mighty porpoise, with a harping-iron, having first stricken divers of them and brought away part of their flesh sticking upon the iron, but could recover only that one. These also, passing through the ocean in herds, did portend storm. I omit to recite frivolous reports by them in the frigate of strange voices the same night, which scared some from the helm.

Thursday the twenty-ninth of August the wind rose and blew vehemently at south and by east, bringing withal rain and thick mist, so that we could not see a cable-length before us. . . .

In this distress we had vigilant eye unto the admiral, whom we saw cast away without power to give the men succour; neither could we espy any of the men that leaped overboard to save themselves, either in the same pinnace or cock, or upon rafters and such-like means presenting themselves to men in those extremities, for we desired to save the men by every possible means. But all in vain, since God had determined their ruin; yet all that day and part of the next we beat up and down as near unto the wreck as was possible for us, looking out if by good hap we might espy any of them. . . .

Our people lost courage daily after this ill success; the weather continuing thick and blustering with increase of cold, winter drawing on, which took from them all hope of amendment, settling an assurance of worse weather to grow upon us every day. The lee side of us lay full of dangers and unto us unknown. But above all, provision waxed scant and hope of supply was gone with loss of our admiral. . . .

So upon Saturday in the afternoon the thirty-first of August we changed our course and returned back for England, at which very instant, even in the winding about, there passed along between us and towards the land which we now forsook a very lion to our seeming, in shape, hair, and colour, not swimming after the manner of a beast by moving of his feet, but rather sliding upon the water with his whole body (excepting the legs) in sight, neither yet diving under and again rising above the water as the manner is of whales, dolphins, tunny, porpoises, and all other fish, but confidently showing himself above water without hiding. Notwithstanding, we presented ourselves in open view and gesture to amaze him, as all creatures will be commonly at a sudden gaze and sight of men. Thus he passed along, turning his head to and fro, yawning and gaping wide, with ugly demonstration of long teeth and glaring eyes, and to bid us a farewell (coming right against the *Hind*) he sent forth a horrible voice, roaring or bellowing as doth a lion, which spectacle we all beheld so far as we were able to discern the same, as men prone to wonder at every strange thing, as this doubtless was, to see a lion in the ocean sea or fish in shape of a lion. What opinion others had thereof, and chiefly the general himself, I forbear to deliver. But he took it for *bonum omen*, rejoicing that he was to war against such an enemy, if it were the Devil. . . .

This Monday the general came aboard the *Hind* to have the surgeon of the *Hind* to dress his foot, which he hurt by treading upon a nail, at what time we comforted each other with hope of hard success[11] to be all past and of the good to come. So, agreeing to carry out lights always by night, that we might keep together, he departed into his frigate, being by no means to be entreated to tarry in the *Hind*, which had been more for his security. Immediately after followed a sharp storm, which we overpassed for that time, praised be God.

The weather fair, the general came aboard the *Hind* again to make merry together with the captain, master, and company, which was the last meeting and continued there from morning until night. During which time there passed sundry discourses touching affairs past and to come, lamenting greatly the loss of his great ship, more of the men, but most of all of his books and notes, and what else I know not, for which he was out of measure grieved, the same doubtless being some matter of more importance than his books, which I could not draw from him; yet by circumstance I gathered the same to be the ore which Daniel the

Saxon had brought unto him in the Newfoundland. Whatsoever it was, the remembrance touched him so deep as, not able to contain himself, he beat his boy in great rage, even at the same time, so long after the miscarrying of the great ship, because upon a fair day when we were calmed upon the coast of the Newfoundland near unto Cape Race he sent his boy aboard the admiral to fetch certain things, amongst which this, being chief, was yet forgotten and left behind. After which time he could never conveniently send again aboard the great ship, much less he doubted her ruin so near at hand.

Herein my opinion was better confirmed diversly and by sundry conjectures, which maketh me have the greater hope of this rich mine. For whereas the general had never before good conceit[12] of these north parts of the world, now his mind was wholly fixed upon the Newfoundland. . . .

Leaving the issue of this good hope unto God, Who knoweth the truth only and can at His good pleasure bring the same to light, I will hasten to the end of this tragedy, which must be knit up in the person of our general. And as it was God's ordinance upon him, even so the vehement persuasion and entreaty of his friends could nothing avail to divert him from a wilful resolution of going through in his frigate, which was overcharged upon their decks with fights, nettings, and small artillery too cumbersome for so small a boat that was to pass through the ocean sea at that season of the year, when by course we might expect much storm of foul weather, whereof indeed we had enough.

But when he was entreated by the captain, master, and other his well-willers of the *Hind* not to venture in the frigate, this was his answer: 'I will not forsake my little company going homeward, with whom I have passed so many storms and perils.' . . .

Seeing he would not bend to reason, he had provision out of the *Hind* such as was wanting aboard his frigate. And so we committed him to God's protection and set him aboard his pinnace, we being more than 300 leagues onward of our way home.

By that time we had brought the islands of Azores south of us; yet we then keeping much to the north until we had got into the height and elevation of England, we met with very foul weather and terrible seas, breaking short and high, pyramid-wise. . . . Howsoever it cometh to pass, men which all their life-time had occupied the sea never saw more outrageous seas. We had also upon our main-yard an apparition of a little fire by night, which seamen do call Castor and Pollux. But we had only one, which they take an evil sign of more tempest; the same is usual in storms.

Monday the ninth of September in the afternoon the frigate was near cast away, oppressed by waves, yet at that time recovered; and, giving forth signs of joy, the general, sitting abaft with a book in his hand, cried out unto us in the *Hind* (so oft as we did approach within hearing), 'We are as near to Heaven by sea as by land', reiterating the same speech, well beseeming a soldier resolute in Jesus Christ, as I can testify he was.

The same Monday night, about twelve of the clock or not long after, the frigate being ahead of us in the *Golden Hind*, suddenly her lights were out, whereof, as it were in a moment, we lost the sight, and withal our watch cried the general was cast away, which was too true. For in that moment the frigate was devoured and swallowed up of the sea. Yet still we looked out all that night, and ever after, until we arrived upon the coast of England, omitting no small sail at sea unto which we gave not the tokens between us agreed upon to have perfect knowledge of each other if we should at any time be separated.

In great torment of weather and peril of drowning, it pleased God to send safe home the *Golden Hind*, which arrived in Falmouth the twenty-second of September, being Sunday, not without as great danger escaped in a flaw,[13] coming from the south-east with such mist that we could not discern land to put in right with the haven.

From Falmouth we went to Dartmouth and lay there at anchor before the range while the captain went aland to inquire if there had been any news of the frigate, which sailing well might happily[14] have been before us. Also to certify Sir John Gilbert, brother unto the general, of our hard success, whom the captain desired (while his men were yet aboard him and were witnesses of all occurrences in that voyage) it might please him to take the examination of every person particularly in discharge of his and their faithful endeavour. Sir John Gilbert refused so to do, holding himself satisfied with report made by the captain, and, not altogether despairing of his brother's safety, offered friendship and courtesy to the captain and his company, requiring to have his bark brought into the harbour; in furtherance whereof a boat was sent to help to tow her in. . . .

Thus have I delivered the contents of the enterprise and last action of Sir Humphrey Gilbert, Knight, faithfully for so much as I thought meet to be published, wherein may always appear (though he be extinguished) some sparks of his virtues, he remaining firm and resolute in a purpose by all pretence honest and godly, as was this, to discover, possess, and to reduce unto the service of God and Christian piety those remote and heathen countries of America not actually possessed by Christians and most rightly appertaining unto the Crown of England. . . .

10

# Poetical Mariners Praise a Colonial Propagandist (1583)

Commendatory verses prefacing Sir George Peckham, *A True Report of the Late Discoveries of the New-Found Lands* (1583).

Sir Francis Drake, Knight, in Commendation of This Treatise

Who seeks by worthy deeds to gain renown for hire;
Whose heart, whose hand, whose purse is prest[1] to purchase[2] his
    desire:
If any such there be, that thirsteth after fame,
Lo! here a mean to win himself an everlasting name.

Who seeks by gain and wealth t'advance his house and blood;
Whose care is great, whose toil no less, whose hope is all for good:
If any one there be, that covets such a trade,
Lo! here the plot for common wealth and private gain is made.

He that for virtue's sake will venture far and near;
Whose zeal is strong, whose practice truth, whose faith is void of
    fear:
If any such there be, inflamed with holy care,
Here may he find a ready mean his purpose to declare.

So that, for each degree, this treatise doth unfold
The path to fame, the proof of zeal, and way to purchase gold.

                                                    Francis Drake

Mr John Hawkins His Opinion of This Intended Voyage

If zeal to God, or country's care, with private gain's access,
Might serve for spurs unto th' attempt, this pamphlet does express
One coast, one course, one toil might serve at full to make declar'd
A zeal to God, with country's good, and private gain's regard.
And, for the first, this enterprise the name of God shall found
Among a nation in whose ears the same did never sound.
Next, as an endless running stream her channels doth discharge,
That swell above their bounds into an ocean wide and large;
So England, that is pestered now and choked through want of ground,
Shall find a soil where room enough and profit doth abound.
The Romans, when the number of their people grew so great
As neither wars could waste nor Rome suffice them for a seat,
They led them forth by swarming troops to foreign lands amain,
And founded divers colonies unto the Roman reign.
Th' Athenians used the like device, the Argives thus have done,
And fierce Achilles' Myrmidons when Troy was overrun.
But Rome nor Athens nor the rest were never pestered so
As England, where no room remains her dwellers to bestow,
But shuffled in such pinching bonds that very breath doth lack,
And for the want of place they crawl one o'er another's back.
How nobly, then, shall they provide that for redress herein,
With ready hand and open purse this action doth begin;
Whence glory to the name of God and country's good shall spring,
And unto all that further it, a private gain shall bring.
Then, noble youths, courageously this enterprise discharge;
And age, that cannot manage arms, let them support the charge.
The issue of your good intent undoubted will appear
Both gracious in the sight of God and full of honour here.

John Hawkins

Master Captain Bingham His Commendation upon This Treatise

> If honour and reward may move the mind,
>    By noble actions, highly to aspire,
> The forward man in this discourse shall find
>    Reward and honour proposed for hire:
> Which meed no right renowned heart mislikes,
> Though gained by passing through ten thousand pikes.

The white³ whereat we level well is known,
  The plot and place with finger pointed out;
The name thereof through all the world is blown,
  To put the hard believers out of doubt.
Our foreign neighbours like it to their gain,
And suck the sweet while sleeping we remain.

The journey is but easy to be gone,
  The frozen Pole disjoined far doth lie:
We shape our course far from the Burning Zone;
  The soil is subject to a milder sky,
And, by proof of many records tried,
The Paradise of all the world beside.

Then launch, ye noble youths, into the main;
  No lurking perils lie amid the way;
Your travail shall return you treble gain,
  And make your names renowned another day.
For valiant minds through twenty seas will roam
And fish for luck, while sluggards lie at home.

                                        Richard Bingham

Master Anthony Parkhurst in Commendation of This Treatise

          Behold a work that doth reveal
          The ready way to wealth and fame;
          Commodious to the common weal,
          And just without impeach of blame;
              Which followed as the course doth lie
              May make all England thrive thereby.

          It is not fond surmised report,
          Nor fantasy vain heads to feed:
          The mention of the truth comes short,
          And lesser than the thing indeed.
              Of record many thousands are
              That can all this and more declare.

          How happy were our England then
          (Sith neither men nor shipping want),
          Some good and well-disposed men

Another England there would plant:
And so employ a number there,
Whose persons may be spared here.

Th' attempt could never fail his fame,
Nor proof return without effect:
For commonly all actions frame[4]
Where Christian cause hath chief respect.
And He that in the heavens above doth reign
(No doubt) will bless the sequel[5] of their pain.

Anthony Parkhurst

## II

# Francis Drake on the California Coast (1579)

Francis Drake's circumnavigation of the globe, performed in the years 1577–80, created great excitement when he returned in September 1580. The Queen's action in knighting him on the deck of his ship, the *Golden Hind* (the name with which he had rechristened the *Pelican* at sea), put the seal of her approval on his action and further stimulated public interest in his feat. But for all of the contemporary excitement over Drake's voyage, the most detailed account was not published until 1628, when Drake's nephew of the same name put together *The World Encompassed by Sir Francis Drake . . . Carefully Collected out of the Notes of Master Francis Fletcher, Preacher in This Employment and Divers Others His Followers in the Same*. There is some evidence that the compiler may have used some of Drake's own notes. *The World Encompassed* has been edited by W. S. W. Vaux, The Hakluyt Society, No. 16 (London, 1854) and by Sir Richard C. Temple (London, 1926).

The site of the harbour where Drake anchored on the coast of California has been a matter of controversy. It was either an inlet now called Drake's Bay, above the Golden Gate near San Francisco, or Bodega Bay, a little farther north. Drake nailed to a post a brass plate with an inscription naming the land Nova Albion and claiming it in the name of the Queen. In 1936 a brass plate bearing the inscription described in *The World Encompassed* was found by a travelling salesman in Marin County, California. Some historians in their first enthusiasm pronounced it genuine, but others are now convinced that the plate is a forgery. A year later another travelling salesman from California discovered an inscribed stone in North Carolina purporting to be a message to John White from his daughter, Eleanor Dare, one of the 'Lost Colony', who was being abducted by the Indians. The stone was an obvious forgery.

F ROM Guatulco we departed the day following, *viz.*, April 16 [1579], setting our course directly into the sea, whereon we sailed 500 leagues in longitude to get a wind, and between that and June 3, 1,400 leagues in all, till we came into 42 degrees of north latitude, where in the night following we found such alteration of heat into extreme and nipping cold that our men in general did grievously complain thereof. . . .

In 38 degrees 30 minutes we fell with a convenient and fit harbour and June 17 came to anchor therein, where we continued till the twenty-third day of July following. During all which time, notwithstanding it was in the height of summer and so near the sun, yet were we continually visited with like nipping colds as we had felt before; insomuch that if violent exercises of our bodies and busy employment about our necessary labours had not sometimes compelled us to the contrary, we could very well have been contented to have kept about us still our winter clothes; yea (had our necessities suffered us), to have kept our beds; neither could we at any time, in whole fourteen days together, find the air so clear as to be able to take the height of sun or star. . . .

The next day after our coming to anchor in the aforesaid harbour the people of the country[1] showed themselves, sending off a man with great expedition to us in a canoe who, being yet but a little from the shore and a great way from our ship, spake to us continually as he came rowing on. And at last, at a reasonable distance staying himself, he began more solemnly a long and tedious oration after his manner, using in the delivery thereof many gestures and signs, moving his hands, turning his head and body many ways, and after his oration ended, with great show of reverence and submission, returned back to shore again. He shortly came again the second time in like manner, and so the third time, when he brought with him (as a present from the rest) a bunch of feathers, much like the feathers of a black crow, very neatly and artificially[2] gathered upon a string and drawn together into a round bundle, being very clean and finely cut and bearing in length an equal proportion one with another, a special cognizance[3] (as we afterwards observed) which they that guard their king's person wear on their heads. With this also he brought a little basket made of rushes and filled with an herb which they called *tabáh*,[4] both which, being tied to a short rod, he cast into our boat. Our general intended to have recompensed him immediately with many good things he would have bestowed on him, but, entering into the boat to deliver the same, he could not be drawn to receive them by any means, save one hat which, being cast into the water out of the ship, he took up (refusing utterly to meddle with any other thing, though it were upon a board put off unto him) and so presently made his return. After which time our boat could row no way but, wondering at us as at gods,[5] they would follow the same with admiration.

The third day following, *viz.*, the twenty-first, our ship, having received a leak at sea, was brought to anchor nearer the shore that, her goods being landed, she might be repaired; but for that we were to prevent any danger that might chance against our safety, our general first of all landed his men with all necessary provision to build tents and make a fort for the defence of ourselves and goods and that we might under the shelter of it with more safety (whatever should befall) end our business. Which when the people of the country perceived us doing, as men set on fire to war in defence of their country, in great haste and companies with such weapons as they had they came down unto us, and yet with no hostile meaning or intent to hurt us, standing, when they drew near, as men ravished in their minds with the sight of such things as they never had seen or heard of before that time, their errand being rather with submission and fear to worship us as gods than to have any war with us as with mortal men. Which thing, as it did partly show itself at that instant, so did it more and more manifest itself afterwards during the whole time of our abode amongst them. At this time, being willed by signs to lay from them their bows and arrows, they did as they were directed, and so did all the rest, as they came more and more by companies unto them, growing in a little while to a great number, both of men and women.

To the intent, therefore, that this peace which they themselves so willingly sought might, without any cause of the breach thereof on our part given, be continued, and that we might with more safety and expedition end our business in quiet, our general with all his company used all means possible gently to entreat[6] them, bestowing upon each of them liberally good and necessary things to cover their nakedness, withal signifying unto them we were no gods but men and had need of such things to cover our own shame; teaching them to use them to the same ends, for which cause also we did eat and drink in their presence, giving them to understand that without that we could not live and therefore were but men as well as they.

Notwithstanding, nothing could persuade them nor remove that opinion which they had conceived of us that we should be gods.

In recompense of those things which they had received of us, as shirts, linen cloth, etc., they bestowed upon our general and divers of our company divers things, as feathers, cauls of network, the quivers of their arrows made of fawn-skins, and the very skins of beasts that their women wore upon their bodies. Having thus had their fill of this time's visiting and beholding of us, they departed with joy to their houses, which houses are digged round within the earth and have from the uppermost brims of the circle clefts of wood set up and joined close together at the top like our spires on the steeple of a church, which, being covered with earth, suffer no water to enter and are very warm. The door in the most part of them performs the office also of a chimney to let out the smoke; it's made in bigness and fashion like to any ordinary scuttle in a ship and standing slopewise. Their beds are the hard ground, only with rushes strewed upon it, and lying round about the house have their fire in the midst, which, by reason that the house is but low vaulted, round, and close, gives a marvellous reflection to their bodies to heat the same.

Their men for the most part go naked; the women take a kind of bulrushes and, combing it after the manner of hemp, make themselves thereof a loose garment which, being knit about their middles, hangs down about their hips and so affords to them a covering of that which Nature teaches should be hidden; about their shoulders they wear also the skin of a deer with the hair upon it. They are very obedient to their husbands and exceedingly ready in all service, yet of themselves offering to do nothing without the consents or being called of the men. . . .

Against the end of three days more (the news having the while spread itself farther and, as it seemed, a great way up into the country) were assembled the greatest number of people which we could reasonably imagine to dwell within any convenient distance round about. Amongst the rest, the king himself, a man of a goodly stature and comely personage, attended with his guard of about 100 tall and warlike men, this day, *viz.*, June 26, came down to see us. . . .

They made signs to our general to have him sit down, unto whom both the king and divers others made several orations, or rather, indeed, if we had understood them, supplications, that he would take the province and kingdom into his hand and become their king and patron, making signs that they would resign unto him their right and title to the whole land and become his vassals in themselves and their posterities; which that they might make us indeed believe that it was their true meaning and intent, the king himself, with all the rest, with one consent and with great reverence joyfully singing a song, set the crown upon his head, enriched his neck with all their chains, and offering unto him many other things, honoured him by the name of *hióh*.[7] Adding thereunto (as it might seem) a song and dance of triumph, because they were not only visited of the gods (for so they still judged us to be), but the great and chief God was now become their God, their king and patron, and themselves were become the only happy and blessed people in the world.

These things being so freely offered, our general thought not meet to reject or refuse the same, both for that he would not give them any cause of mistrust or disliking of him (that being the only place wherein at this present we were of necessity enforced to seek relief of many things), and chiefly for that he knew not to what good end God had brought this to pass or what honour and profit it might bring to our country in time to come.

Wherefore, in the name and to the use of Her Most Excellent Majesty, he took the sceptre, crown, and dignity of the said country into his hand, wishing nothing more than that it had lain so fitly for Her Majesty to enjoy as it was now her proper own, and that the riches and treasures thereof (wherewith in the upland countries it abounds) might with as great conveniency be transported, to the enriching of her kingdom here at home, as it is in plenty to be attained there; and especially that so tractable and loving a people as they showed themselves to be might have means to have manifested their most willing obedience the more unto her, and by her means, as a mother and nurse of the Church of Christ, might by the preaching of the Gospel be brought to the right knowledge and obedience of the true and everliving God.

The ceremonies of this resigning and receiving of the kingdom being thus performed, the common sort, both of men and women, leaving the king and his guard about him with our general, dispersed themselves among our people, taking a diligent view or survey of every man; and finding such as pleased their fancies (which commonly were the youngest of us), they, presently enclosing them about, offered their sacrifices unto them, crying out with lamentable shrieks and moans, weeping and scratching and tearing their very flesh off their faces with their nails; neither were it the women alone which did this, but even old men, roaring and crying out, were as violent as the women were. . . .

H

After that our necessary businesses were well dispatched, our general, with his gentlemen and many of his company, made a journey up into the land to see the manner of their dwelling and to be the better acquainted with the nature and commodities of the country. Their houses were all such as we have formerly described and, being many of them in one place, made several villages here and there. The inland we found to be far different from the shore, a goodly country and fruitful soil, stored with many blessings fit for the use of man. Infinite was the company of very large and fat deer which there we saw by thousands, as we supposed, in a herd; besides a multitude of a strange kind of conies by far exceeding them in number. Their heads and bodies, in which they resemble other conies, are but small, his tail, like the tail of a rat, exceeding long, and his feet like the paws of a want or mole. Under his chin, on either side, he hath a bag into which he gathereth his meat when he hath filled his belly abroad, that he may with it either feed his young or feed himself when he lists not to travel from his burrow. The people eat their bodies and make great account of their skins, for their king's holiday's coat was made of them.

This country our general named Albion, and that for two causes: the one in respect of the white banks and cliffs which lie toward the sea; the other that it might have some affinity, even in name also, with our own country, which was sometime so called.

Before we went from thence, our general caused to be set up a monument of our being there, as also of Her Majesty's and successors' right and title to that kingdom; namely, a plate of brass, fast nailed to a great and firm post, whereon is engraven Her Grace's name and the day and year of our arrival there and of the free giving-up of the province and kingdom, both by the king and people, into Her Majesty's hands, together with Her Highness' picture and arms in a piece of sixpence current English money, showing itself by a hole made of purpose through the plate. Underneath was likewise engraven the name of our general, etc.

The Spaniards never had any dealing or so much as set a foot in this country, the utmost of their discoveries reaching only to many degrees southward of this place. . . .

# 12

# A New Land Like unto That of the Golden Age (1584–5)

During the spring and summer of 1584, Sir Walter Raleigh sent two of his captains, Philip Amadas and Arthur Barlow, on a voyage of reconnaissance that took them along the coast of what is now North Carolina. On their return in September, Barlow made a report to Raleigh, from whom Richard Hakluyt obtained the account of their voyage of discovery. Hakluyt published the narrative in *Principal Navigations* (1589). It has been reprinted with copious annotations by David B. Quinn, *The Roanoke Voyages, 1584–1590*, The Hakluyt Society, 2nd Ser., No. 104 (London, 1952), I, 91–117.

*The first voyage made to the coasts of America with two barks, wherein were Captains Master Philip Amadas and Master Arthur Barlow, who discovered part of the country now called Virginia, anno 1584, written by one of the said captains and sent to Sir Walter Raleigh, Knight, at whose charge and direction the said voyage was set forth.*

The twenty-seventh day of April, in the year of our redemption 1584, we departed the west of England with two barks well furnished with men and victuals, having received our last and perfect directions by your letters, confirming the former instructions and commandments delivered by yourself at our leaving the river of Thames. And I think it a matter both unnecessary for the manifest discovery of the country, as also for tediousness sake, to remember unto you the diurnal of our course sailing thither and returning. Only I have presumed to present unto you this brief discourse by which you may judge how profitable this land is likely to succeed, as well to yourself (by whose direction and charge and by whose servants this our discovery hath been performed), as also to Her Highness and the commonwealth, in which we hope your wisdom will be satisfied, considering that as much by us hath been brought to light as by those small means and number of men we had could any way have been expected or hoped for.

The tenth of May we arrived at the Canaries and the tenth of June in this present year we were fallen with the islands of the West Indies, keeping a more south-easterly course than was needful, because we doubted that the current of the Bay of Mexico, disbogging[1] between the cape of Florida and the Havana, had been of greater force than afterwards we found it to be. At which islands we found the air very unwholesome, and our men grew for the most part ill-disposed, so that, having refreshed ourselves with sweet water and fresh victual, we departed the twelfth day after our arrival there. These islands, with the rest adjoining, are so well known to yourself and to many others as I will not trouble you with the remembrance of them.

The second of July we found shoal water, which smelt so sweetly and was so strong a smell as if we had been in the midst of some delicate garden, abounding with all kind of odoriferous flowers, by which we were assured that the land could not be far distant. And keeping good watch and bearing but slack sail the fourth of the same month, we arrived upon the coast, which we supposed to be a continent and firm land, and we sailed along the same 120 English miles before we could find any entrance or river issuing into the sea. The first that appeared unto us we entered, though not without some difficulty, and cast anchor about three harquebus shot within the haven's mouth[2] on the left hand of the same. And after thanks given to God for our safe arrival thither we manned our boats and went to view the land next adjoining and to 'take possession of the same in the right of the Queen's Most Excellent Majesty as rightful Queen and Princess of the same'; and after delivered the same over to your use, according to Her Majesty's grant and letters patents under Her Highness' Great Seal. Which being performed according to the ceremonies used in such enterprises, we viewed the land about us, being whereas we first landed very sandy and low towards the waterside, but so full of grapes as the very beating and surge of the sea overflowed them, of which we found such plenty, as well there as in all places else, both on the sand and on the green soil on the hills as in the plains, as well on every little shrub as also climbing towards the tops of the high cedars, that I think in all the world the like abundance is not to be found, and myself, having seen those parts of Europe that most abound, find such difference as were incredible to be written.

We passed from the sea-side towards the tops of those hills next adjoining, being but of mean height, and from thence we beheld the sea on both sides to the north and to the south, finding no end any of both ways. This land lay stretching itself to the west, which after we found to be but an island of twenty leagues long and not above six miles broad. Under the bank or hill whereon we stood we beheld the valleys replenished with goodly cedar trees and, having discharged our har-quebus shot, such a flock of cranes (the most part white) arose under us, with such a cry redoubled by many echoes, as if an army of men had shouted all together.

This island had many goodly woods full of deer, conies, hares, and fowl, even in the midst of summer, in incredible abundance. The woods are not such as you find in Bohemia, Muscovia, or Hyrcania, barren and fruitless, but the highest and reddest cedars of the world, far bettering the cedars of the Azores, of the Indies, or of Libanus, pines, cypress, sassafras, the lentisk,[3] or the tree that beareth the mastic, the tree that beareth the rind of black cinnamon of which Master Winter brought from the Straits of Magellan, and many other of excellent smell and quality.

We remained by the side of this island two whole days before we saw any people of the country. The third day we espied one small boat rowing towards us, having in it three persons. This boat came to the land's side, four harquebus shot from our ships, and there, two of the people remaining, the third came along the shore-side towards us, and, we being then all within-board, he walked up and down upon the point of the land next unto us. Then the master and the pilot of the admiral, Simon Ferdinando,[4] and the Captain, Philip Amadas, myself, and others rowed to the land, whose coming this fellow attended, never making any show of fear or doubt.

And after he had spoken of many things not understood by us, we brought him with his own good liking aboard the ships and gave him a shirt, a hat, and some other things and made him taste of our wine and our meat, which he liked very well. And after having viewed both barks he departed and went to his own boat again, which he had left in a little cove or creek adjoining. As soon as he was two bowshots into the water, he fell to fishing, and in less than half an hour he had laden his boat as deep as it could swim, with which he came again to the point of the land, and there he divided his fish into two parts, pointing[5] one part to the ship and the other to the pinnace, which, after he had (as much as he might) requited the former benefits received, he departed out of our sight.

The next day there came unto us divers boats and in one of them the king's brother, accompanied with forty or fifty men, very handsome and goodly people and in their behaviour as mannerly and civil as any of Europe. His name was Granganimo, and the king is called Wingina, the country Wingandacoa[6] (and now, by Her Majesty, Virginia).

The manner of his coming was in this sort: he left his boats altogether, as the first man did a little from the ships by the shore, and came along to the place over against the ships, followed with forty men. When he came to the place, his servants spread a long mat upon the ground on which he sat down, and at the other end of the mat four others of his company did the like; the rest of his men stood round about him, somewhat afar off. When we came to the shore to him with our weapons, he never moved from his place, nor any of the other four, nor never mistrusted any harm to be offered from us, but, sitting still, he beckoned us to come and sit by him, which we performed, and, being set, he makes all signs of joy and welcome, striking on his head and his breast and afterwards on ours, to show we were all one, smiling and making show the best he could of all love and familiarity. After he had made a long speech unto us, we presented him with divers things, which he received very joyfully and thankfully. None of his company durst to speak one word all the time, only the four which were at the other end spake one in the other's ear very softly.

The king is greatly obeyed and his brothers and children reverenced. The king himself in person was at our being there sore wounded in a fight which he had with the king of the next country called Wingina* and was shot in two places through the body and once clean through the thigh, but yet he recovered, by reason whereof and for that he lay at the chief town of the country, being six days' journey off, we saw him not at all.

After we had presented this his brother with such things as we thought he liked, we likewise gave somewhat to the other[s] that sat with him on the mat. But presently he arose and took all from them and put it into his own basket, making signs and tokens that all things ought to be delivered unto him and the rest were but his servants and followers.

A day or two after this, we fell to trading with them, exchanging some things that we had for chamois, buff, and deerskins. When we showed him all our packet of merchandise, of all things that he saw a bright tin dish most pleased him, which he presently took up and clapped it before his breast and after made a hole in the brim thereof and hung it about his neck, making signs that it would defend him against his enemies' arrows, for those people maintain a deadly and terrible war with the people and king adjoining. We exchanged our tin dish for twenty skins worth twenty crowns or twenty nobles and a copper kettle for fifty skins worth fifty crowns. They offered us very good exchange for our hatchets and axes and for knives, and would have given anything for swords, but we would not depart[7] with any.

After two or three days the king's brother came aboard the ships and drank wine and ate of our meat and of our bread and liked exceedingly thereof. And after a few days overpassed he brought his wife with him to the ships, his daughter, and two or three little children. His wife was very well favoured, of mean stature and very bashful. She had on her back a long cloak of leather with the fur side next to her body and before her a piece of the same. About her forehead she had a broad band of white coral and so had her husband many times. In her ears she had bracelets of pearls, hanging down to her middle (whereof we delivered Your Worship a little bracelet) and those were of the bigness of good peas.

The rest of her women of the better sort had pendants of copper hanging in every ear, and some of the children of the king's brother and other noblemen have five or six in every ear. He himself had upon his head a broad plate of gold or copper, for, being unpolished, we knew not what metal it should be, neither would he by any means suffer us to take it off his head, but, feeling it, it would bow very easily.

His apparel was as his wives, only the women wear their hair long on both sides and the men but on one. They are of colour yellowish, and their hair black for the most part, and yet we saw children that had very fine auburn and chestnut colour hair.

After that these women had been there, there came down from all parts great store of people, bringing with them leather, coral, divers kinds of dyes very excellent, and exchanged with us; but when Granganimo, the king's brother, was present none durst to trade but himself, except such as wear red pieces of copper on their heads like himself, for that is the difference between the noblemen and governors of countries and the meaner sort. And we both noted there, and you have understood since by these men[8] which we brought home, that no people in the world carry more respect to their king, nobility, and governors than these do. The king's brother's wife, when she came to us, as she did many times, she was followed with forty or fifty women always, and when she came into the ship, she left them all on land, saving her two daughters, her nurse, and one or two more. The king's brother always kept this order: as many boats as he would come withal to the ships, so many fires would he make on the shore afar off, to the end we might understand with what strength and company he approached.

Their boats are made of one tree, either of pine or of pitch trees, a wood not commonly known to our people nor found growing in England. They have no edge tools to make them withal. If they have any, they are very few and those it seems they had twenty years since, which as those two men declared was out of a wrack which happened upon their coast of some Christian ship, being beaten that way by some storm and outrageous weather, whereof none of the people were saved but only the ship or some part of her, being cast upon the sand, out of whose sides they drew the nails and spikes, and with those they made their best instruments. Their manner of making their boats is this: they burn down some great tree or take such as are wind-fallen, and, putting myrrh and rosin upon one side thereof, they set fire into it, and when it hath burnt it hollow, they cut out the coal with their shells, and everywhere they would burn it deeper or wider they lay on their gums, which burneth away the timber, and by this means they fashion very fine boats and such as will transport twenty men. Their oars are like scoops, and many times they set[9] with long poles, as the depth serveth.

The king's brother had great liking of our armour, a sword, and divers other things which we had, and offered to lay a great box of pearl in gage for them, but we refused it for this time, because we would not make them know that we esteemed thereof until we had understood in what places of the country the pearl grew, which now Your Worship doth very well understand.

He was very just of his promise, for many times we delivered him merchandise upon his word, but ever he came within the day and performed his promise. He sent us every day a brace or two of fat bucks, conies, hares, fish, the best of the world. He sent us divers kinds of fruits, melons, walnuts, cucumbers, gourds, peas, and divers roots and fruits very excellent good, and of their country corn, which is very white, fair, and well tasted, and groweth three times in five months. In May they sow, in July they reap; in June they sow, in August they reap; in July they sow, in September they reap. Only they cast the corn into the ground, breaking a little of the soft turf with a wooden mattock or pickaxe. Ourselves proved the soil and put some of our peas into the ground, and in ten days they were of fourteen inches high. They have also beans very fair, of divers colours and wonderful plenty, some growing naturally, and some in their gardens, and so have they both wheat and oats.

The soil is the most plentiful, sweet, fruitful, and wholesome of all the world. There are above fourteen several sweet-smelling timber trees, and the most part of their underwoods are bays and such-like. They have those oaks that we have, but far greater and better.

After they had been divers times aboard our ships, myself with seven more went twenty mile into the river that runneth toward the city of Skicoak, which river they call Occam, and the evening following we came to an island which they call Roanoke, distant from the harbour by which we entered seven leagues. And at the north end thereof was a village of nine houses built of cedar and fortified round about with sharp trees to keep out their enemies and the entrance into it made it like a turnpike very artificially.

When we came towards it, standing near unto the water's side, the wife of Granganimo, the king's brother, came running out to meet us very cheerfully and friendly. Her husband was not then in the village. Some of her people she commanded to draw our boat on the shore for[10] the beating of the billow. Others she appointed to carry us on their backs to the dry ground and others to bring our oars into the house for fear of stealing. When we were come into the utter room, having five rooms in her house, she caused us to sit down by a great fire and after took off our clothes and washed them and dried them again. Some of the women pulled off our stockings and washed them. Some washed our feet in warm water, and she herself took great pains to see all things ordered in the best manner she could, making great haste to dress some meat for us to eat.

After we had thus dried ourselves, she brought us into the inner room, where she set on the board standing along the house some wheat like frumenty,[11] sodden venison and roasted, fish sodden, boiled, and roasted, melons raw and sodden, roots of divers kinds, and divers fruits. Their drink is commonly water, but while the grape lasteth they drink wine, and for want of casks to keep it all the year after they drink water, but it is sodden with ginger in it and black cinnamon, and sometimes sassafras and divers other wholesome and medicinable herbs and trees.

We were entertained with all love and kindness and with as much bounty after their manner as they could possibly devise. We found the people most gentle, loving, and faithful, void of all guile and treason and such as lived after the manner of the Golden Age. The earth bringeth forth all things in abundance as in the first creation, without toil or labour. The people only care to defend themselves from the cold in their short winter and to feed themselves with such meat as the soil affordeth. Their meat is very well sodden, and they make broth very sweet and savoury. Their vessels are earthen pots, very large, white, and sweet; their dishes are wooden platters of sweet timber. Within the place where they feed was their lodging and within that their idol which they worship, of which they speak incredible things.

While we were at meat, there came in at the gates two or three men with their bows and arrows from hunting, whom when we espied, we began to look one towards another and offered to reach our weapons, but as soon as she espied our mistrust she was very much moved and caused some of her men to run out and take away their bows and arrows and break them and withal beat the poor fellows out of the gate again.

When we departed in the evening and would not tarry all night she was very sorry and gave us into our boat our supper half dressed, pots and all, and brought us to our boat's side, in which we lay all night, removing the same a pretty distance from the shore. She, perceiving our jealousy,[12] was much grieved and sent divers men and thirty women to sit all night on the bank's side by us, and sent us into our boats fine mats to cover us from the rain, using very many words to entreat us to rest in their houses; but because we were few men and if we had miscarried the voyage had been in very great danger, we durst not adventure anything, although there was no cause of doubt, for a more kind and loving people there cannot be found in the world, as far as we have hitherto had trial.

Beyond this island there is the mainland, and over against this island falleth into this spacious water the great river called Occam by the inhabitants, on which standeth a town called Pemeoke, and six days' journey further upon the same is situate their greatest city called Skicoak, which this people affirm to be very great. But the savages were never at it, only they speak of it by the report of their fathers and other men, whom they have heard affirm it to be above one day's* journey about.

Into this river falleth another great river called Cipo, in which there is found great store of the mussels in which there are pearls. Likewise there descendeth into this Occam another river called Nomopana, on the one side whereof standeth a great town called Chowanoake and the lord of that town and country is called Pooneno. This Pooneno is not subject to the king of Wingandacoa but is a free lord.

Beyond this country is there another king whom they call Menatonon, and these three kings are in league with each other. Towards the sunset* four days' journey is situate a town called Sequotan, which is the westernmost* town of Wingandacoa, near unto which, six-and-twenty years past, there was a ship cast away, whereof some of the people were saved, and those were white people whom the country people preserved.

And after ten days, remaining in an out-island uninhabited called Wococon, they, with the help of some of the dwellers of Sequotan, fastened two boats of the country together and made masts unto them and sails of their shirts, and, having taken into them such victuals as the country yielded, they departed after they had remained in this out-island three weeks. But shortly after, it seemed, they were cast away, for the boats were found upon the coast, cast aland in another island adjoining. Other than these, there was never any people apparelled or white of colour either seen or heard of amongst these people, and these afore said were seen only of the inhabitants of Sequotan; which appeared to be very true, for they wondered marvellously when we were amongst them at the whiteness of our skins, ever coveting to touch our breasts and to view the same. Besides they had our ships in marvellous admiration, and all things else was so strange unto them as it appeared that none of them had ever seen the like. When we discharged any piece, were it but a harquebus, they would tremble thereat for very fear and for the strangeness of the same, for the weapons which themselves use are bows and arrows.

The arrows are but of small canes, headed with a sharp shell or tooth of a fish sufficient enough to kill a naked man. Their swords are of wood hardened; likewise they use wooden breastplates for their defence. They have besides a kind of club in the end whereof they fasten the sharp horns of a stag or other beast. When they go to wars they carry with them their idol, of whom they ask counsel as the Romans were wont of the oracle of Apollo. They sing songs as they march towards the battle, instead of drums and trumpets. Their wars are very cruel and bloody, by reason whereof and of their civil dissensions, which have happened of late years amongst them, the people are marvellously wasted and in some places the country left desolate.

Adjoining unto this town afore said called Sequotan beginneth a country called Ponouike, belonging to another king whom they call Piemacum, and this king is in league with the next king adjoining towards the setting of the sun and the country Neiosioke, situate upon the side of a goodly river called Neuse. These kings have mortal war with Wingina, king of Wingandacoa, but about two years past there was a peace made between the king Piemacum and the lord of Sequotan, as these men which we have brought with us into England have made us understand. But there remaineth a mortal malice in the Sequotanes for many injuries and slaughters done upon them by this Piemacum. They invited divers men and thirty women of the best of his country to their town to a feast, and when they were altogether merry and praying before their idol, which is nothing else but a mere illusion of the Devil, the captain or lord of the town came suddenly upon them and slew them every one, reserving the women and children; and these two have oftentimes since persuaded us to surprise Piemacum his town, having promised and assured us that there will be found in it great store of commodities. But whether their persuasion be to the end they may be revenged of their enemies or for the love they bear to us, we leave that to the trial hereafter.

Beyond this island called Roanoke are many islands very plentiful of fruits and other natural increases, together with many towns and villages along the side of the continent, some bounding upon the islands and some stretching up further into the land.

When we first had sight of this country, some thought the first land we saw to be the continent, but after we entered into the haven we saw before us another mighty long sea, for there lieth along the coast a tract of islands two hundred miles in length, adjoining to the ocean sea, and between the islands two or three entrances. When you are entered between them (these islands being very narrow for the most part, as in most places six miles broad, in some places less, in few more) then there appeareth another great sea, containing in breadth in some places forty, and in some fifty, in some twenty miles over, before you come unto the continent, and in this enclosed sea there are about a hundred islands of divers bignesses, whereof one is sixteen miles long, at which we were, finding it to be a most pleasant and fertile ground, replenished with goodly cedars and divers other sweet woods full of currants, of flax, and many other notable commodities, which we at that time had no leisure to view. Besides this island, there are many, as I have said, some of two, of three, of four, of five miles, some more, some less, most beautiful and pleasant to behold, replenished with deer, conies, hares, and divers beasts, and about them the goodliest and best fish in the world and in greatest abundance.

Thus, sir, we have acquainted you with the particulars of our discovery, made this present voyage, as far north as the shortness of the time we there continued would afford us to take view of. And so con-

tenting ourselves with this service at this time, which we hope hereafter to enlarge as occasion and assistance shall be given, we resolved
to leave the country and to apply ourselves to return for England,
which we did accordingly and arrived safely in the west of England
about the midst of September.

And whereas we have above certified you of the country, taken in
possession by us to Her Majesty's use and so to yours by Her Majesty's
grant, we thought good for the better assurance thereof to record some
of the particular gentlemen and men of accompt who then were present
as witnesses of the same, that thereby all occasion of cavil to the title of
the country in Her Majesty's behalf may be prevented, which otherwise such as like not the action may use and pretend, whose names are:

Master Philip Amadas ⎫
Master Arthur Barlow ⎬ captains

William Greeneville ⎫
John Wood ⎪
James Browewich[13] ⎪
Henry Greene ⎬ of the company
Benjamin Wood ⎪
Simon Ferdinando ⎪
Nicholas Petman ⎪
John Hewes ⎭

## 13

# Glowing Prospects for Raleigh's Colony (1585)

In 1585 Raleigh sent out his first colony to Virginia, under the command of
Richard Grenville. When Grenville returned to England for supplies, he
left Ralph Lane, a cousin of Edward Dyer, on Roanoke Island as governor.
Within a year after Lane's optimistic report, the colonists had become discouraged and had begged Drake to take them home when his fleet put into
the sound. 'An Extract of M. Lane's Letter to M. Richard Hakluyt, Esquire,
and Another Gentlemen of the Middle Temple, from Virginia' was first
printed in Hakluyt's *Principal Navigations* (1589) and reprinted by Taylor,
*Original Writings . . . of the Two Richard Hakluyts*, II, 346–7.

In the mean while you shall understand that since Sir Richard Gren-ville's departure from us, as also before, we have discovered the main to be the goodliest soil under the cope of heaven, so abounding with sweet trees that bring such sundry rich and most pleasant gums, grapes of such greatness, yet wild, as France, Spain, nor Italy hath no greater, so many sorts of apothecary drugs, such several kinds of flax, and one kind like silk, the same gathered of a grass as common there as grass is here. And now within these few days we have found here a Guinea wheat, whose ear yieldeth corn for bread, 400 upon one ear, and the cane maketh very good and perfect sugar, also *terra samia*, otherwise *terra sigillata*.[1] Besides that, it is the goodliest and most pleasing terri-tory of the world (for the soil is of an huge and unknown greatness, and very well peopled and towned, though savagely) and the climate so wholesome that we have not had not one sick since we touched the land here. To conclude, if Virginia had but horses and kine in some reasonable proportion, I dare assure myself, being inhabited with English, no realm in Christendom were comparable to it. For this already we find, that what commodities soever Spain, France, Italy, or the East parts do yield unto us in wines of all sorts, in oils, in flax, in rosins, pitch, frankincense, currants, sugars, and such-like, these parts do abound with the growth of them all, but, being savages that possess the land, they know no use of the same. And sundry other rich com-modities that no parts of the world, be they West or East Indies, have, here we find great abundance of. The people naturally are most cour-teous and very desirous to have clothes, but especially of coarse cloth rather than silk; coarse canvas they also like well of, but copper car-rieth the price of all, so it be made red. Thus good M. Hakluyt and Master H., I have joined you both in one letter of remembrance, as two that I love dearly well; and, commending me most heartily to you both, I commit you to the tuition of the Almighty. From the new Fort in Virginia, this 3. September, 1585.

Your most assured friend

Rafe Lane

# 14

# Harriot Tells of the Goodness of Virginia (1588)

Thomas Harriot (or Hariot) was a mathematician and scientist attached to Raleigh's household who taught Raleigh and some of his captains navigation and astronomy. In the voyage to Virginia in 1585, Harriot and John White, a surveyor and painter, went along with the colonists to prepare a scientific account of the new land. White made the first paintings by an Englishman of natural objects and Indian life in North America. His water-colours have recently been published by the British Museum and the University of North Carolina Press. Harriot in 1588 published *A Brief and True Report of the New-Found Land of Virginia*, which Theodor de Bry reprinted in 1590 with engravings made from White's drawings. A facsimile reproduction of Harriot's book, with a bibliographical introduction by Randolph G. Adams, was issued by Edwards Brothers, Ann Arbor, Michigan, in 1931. Harriot's *Brief and True Report* is reprinted by Quinn, *Roanoke Voyages*, I, 317–87, with copious annotations.

To the adventurers, favourers, and well-willers of the enterprise for the inhabiting and planting in Virginia

Since the first undertaking by Sir Walter Raleigh to deal in the action of discovering of that country which is now called and known by the name of Virginia, many voyages having been thither made at sundry times to his great charge, as first in the year 1584, and afterwards in the years 1585, 1586, and now of late this last year of 1587, there have been divers and variable reports, with some slanderous and shameful speeches, bruited abroad by many that returned from thence. Especially of that discovery which was made by the colony transported by Sir Richard Grenville in the year 1585, being of all the others the most principal and as yet of most effect, the time of their abode in the country being a whole year, whenas in the other voyage before they stayed but six weeks, and the others after were only for supply and transportation, nothing more being discovered than had been before.

Which reports have not done a little wrong to many that otherwise would have also favoured and adventured in the action, to the honour and benefit of our nation, besides the particular profit and credit which would redound to themselves, the dealers therein, as I hope by the sequel of events, to the shame of those that have avouched the contrary, shall be manifest, if you, the adventurers, favourers, and wellwillers, do but either increase in number or in opinion continue, or, having been doubtful, renew your good liking and furtherance to deal therein according to the worthiness thereof already found and as you shall understand hereafter to be requisite. Touching which worthiness, through cause of the diversity of relations and reports, many of your opinions could not be firm nor the minds of some that are well disposed be settled in any certainty.

I have therefore thought it good, being one that have been in the discovery and in dealing with the natural inhabitants specially employed, and having therefore seen and known more than the ordinary, to impart so much unto you of the fruits of our labours as that you may know how injuriously the enterprise is slandered. And that in public manner at this present, chiefly for two respects.

First, that some of you which are yet ignorant or doubtful of the state thereof may see that there is sufficient cause why the chief enterpriser, with the favour of Her Majesty, notwithstanding such reports, hath not only since continued the action by sending into the country again and replanting this last year a new colony, but is also ready, according as the times and means will afford, to follow and prosecute the same.

Secondly, that you, seeing and knowing the continuance of the action by the view hereof, you may generally know and learn what the country is and thereupon consider how your dealing therein, if it proceed, may return you profit and gain, be it either by inhabiting and planting or otherwise in furthering thereof.

And lest that the substance of my relation should be [as] doubtful unto you as [those] of others, by reason of their diversity, I will first open the cause in a few words wherefore they are so different, referring myself to your favourable constructions and to be adjudged of as by good consideration you shall find cause.

Of our company that returned, some for their misdemeanour and ill dealing in the country have been there worthily punished, who by reason of their bad natures have maliciously not only spoken ill of their governors but for their sakes slandered the country itself. The like also have those done which were of their consort.

Some, being ignorant of the state thereof, notwithstanding since their return amongst their friends and acquaintance, and also others, especially if they were in company where they might not be gainsaid, would seem to know so much as no men more and make no men so great travailers as themselves. They stood so much, as it may seem, upon their credit and reputation that, having been a twelvemonth in the country, it would have been a great disgrace unto them, as they thought, if they could not have said much, whether it were true or false. Of which some have spoken of more than ever they saw or otherwise knew to be there; othersome have not been ashamed to make absolute denial of that which, although not by them yet by others, is most certainly and there plentifully known. And othersome make difficulties of those things they have no skill[1] of.

The cause of their ignorance was in that they were of the many that were never out of the island where we were seated, or not far, or at the leastwise in few places else, during the time of our abode in the country; or of that many that, after gold and silver was not so soon found as it was by them looked for, had little or no care of any other thing but to pamper their bellies; or of that many which had little understanding, less discretion, and more tongue than was needful or requisite.

Some, also, were of a nice bringing-up, only in cities or towns, or such as never (as I may say) had seen the world before. Because there were not to be found any English cities, nor such fair houses, nor at their own wish any of their old accustomed dainty food, nor any soft beds of down or feathers, the country was to them miserable and their reports thereof according.

Because my purpose was but in brief to open the cause of the variety of such speeches, the particularities of them and of many envious, malicious, and slanderous reports and devices else, by our own countrymen besides, as trifles that are not worthy of wise men to be thought upon, I mean not to trouble you withal but will pass to the commodities, the substance of that which I have to make relation of unto you. . . .

*The first part: Of merchantable commodities*

Silk of grass, or grass silk. There is a kind of grass in the country upon the blades whereof there groweth very good silk in form of a thin, glittering skin to be stripped off. It groweth two foot and an half high or better; the blades are about two foot in length and half inch broad. The like groweth in Persia, which is in the selfsame climate as Virginia, of which very many of the silk works that come from thence into Europe are made. . . . And by the means of sowing and planting it in good ground it will be far greater, better, and more plentiful than it is. Although, notwithstanding, there is great store thereof in many places of the country growing naturally and wild, which also by proof here in England, in making a piece of silk grogram, we found to be excellent good.

Worm silk. In many of our journeys we found silkworms fair and great, as big as our ordinary walnuts. Although it hath not been our hap to have found such plenty as elsewhere to be in the country we have heard of, yet, seeing that the country doth naturally breed and nourish them, there is no doubt but if art be added in planting of mulberry trees and others fit for them, in commodious places, for their feeding and nourishing, and some of them carefully gathered and husbanded in that sort as by men of skill is known to be necessary, there will rise as great profit in time to the Virginians as thereof doth now to the Persians, Turks, Italians, and Spaniards.

Flax and hemp. The truth is that of hemp and flax there is no great store in any one place together, by reason it is not planted but as the soil doth yield it of itself, and howsoever the leaf and stem or stalk do differ from ours, the stuff, by the judgement of men of skill, is altogether as good as ours. . . .

Alum. There is a vein of earth along the sea-coast for the space of forty or fifty miles whereof, by the judgement of some that have made trial here in England, is made good alum, of that kind which is called rock alum. . . . The same earth doth also yield white copperas, nitrum, and *alumen plumeum*, but nothing so plentifully as the common alum, which be also of price and profitable.

*Wapeih*, a kind of earth so called by the natural inhabitants, very like to *terra sigillata*, and, having been refined, it hath been found by some of our physicians and chirurgeons to be of the same kind of virtue and more effectual. The inhabitants use it very much for the cure of sores and wounds; there is in divers places great plenty and in some places of a blue sort.

Pitch, tar, rosin, and turpentine. There are those kinds of trees which yield them abundantly and great store. In the very same island where we were seated, being fifteen miles of length and five or six miles in breadth, there are few trees else but of the same kind, the whole island being full.

Sassafras, called by the inhabitants *winauk*, a kind of wood of most pleasant and sweet smell and of most rare virtues in physic for the cure of many diseases. It is found by experience to be far better and of more uses than the wood which is called guaiacum or lignum vitae. For the description, the manner of using, and the manifold virtues thereof, I refer you to the book of Monardes, translated and entitled in England 'The joyful news from the West Indies'.[2]

Cedar, a very sweet wood and fine timber, whereof if nests of chests be there made, or timber thereof fitted for sweet and fine bedsteads, tables, desks, lutes, virginals, and many things else (of which there hath been proof made already), to make up freight with other principal commodities, will yield profit.

Wine. There are two kinds of grapes that the soil doth yield naturally: the one is small and sour of the ordinary bigness as ours in England; the other far greater and of himself luscious sweet. When they are planted and husbanded as they ought, a principal commodity of wines by them may be raised.

Oil. There are two sorts of walnuts, both holding oil, but the one far more plentiful than the other. When there are mills and other devices for the purpose, a commodity of them may be raised, because there are infinite store. There are also three several kinds of berries in the form of oak acorns, which also by the experience and use of the inhabitants we find to yield very good and sweet oil. Furthermore, the bears of the country are commonly very fat and in some places there are many; their fatness, because it is so liquid, may well be termed oil and hath many special uses.

Furs. All along the sea-coast there are great store of otters, which, being taken by weirs and other engines made for the purpose, will yield good profit. We hope also of marten furs and make no doubt by the relation of the people but that in some places of the country there are store, although there were but two skins that came to our hands. Lucerns, also, we have understanding of, although for the time we saw none.

Deerskins, dressed after the manner of chamois, or undressed, are to be had of the natural inhabitants thousands yearly by way of traffic for trifles, and no more waste or spoil of deer than is and hath been ordiarily in time before.

Civet cats. In our travels there was found one to have been killed by a savage or inhabitant and in another place the smell where one or more had lately been before; whereby we gather besides than by the relation of the people that there are some in the country. Good profit will rise by them.

Iron. In two places of the country specially, one about fourscore and the other sixscore miles from the fort or place where we dwelt, we found near the waterside the ground to be rocky, which by the trial of a mineral-man was found to hold iron richly. It is found in many places of the country else. I know nothing to the contrary but that it may be allowed for a good merchantable commodity, considering there the small charge for the labour and feeding of men, the infinite store of wood, the want of wood and dearness thereof in England, and the necessity of ballasting of ships.

Copper. A hundred and fifty miles into the main, in two towns, we found with the inhabitants divers small plates of copper that had been made, as we understood, by the inhabitants that dwell farther into the country, whereas they say are mountains and rivers that yield also white grains of metal, which is to be deemed silver. For confirmation whereof at the time of our first arrival in the country, I saw with some others with me two small pieces of silver grossly beaten about the weight of a teston,[3] hanging in the ears of a werowance or chief lord that dwelt about fourscore miles from us, of whom, through inquiry, by the number of days and the way, I learned that it had come to his hands from the same place or near where I after understood the copper was made and the white grains of metal found. The aforesaid copper we also found by trial to hold silver.

Pearl. Sometimes, in feeding on mussels, we found some pearl; but it was our hap to meet with rags or of a pied colour, not having yet discovered those places where we heard of better and more plenty. One of our company, a man of skill in such matters, had gathered together from among the savage people about five thousand, of which number he chose so many as made a fair chain, which for their likeness and uniformity in roundness, orientness,[4] and piedness of many excellent colours, with equality in greatness, were very fair and rare and had therefore been presented to Her Majesty, had we not by casualty and through extremity of a storm lost them, with many things else, in coming away from the country.

Sweet gums of divers kinds and many other apothecary drugs, of which we will make special mention when we shall receive it from such men of skill in that kind that in taking reasonable pains shall discover them more particularly than we have done and than now I can make relation of, for want of the examples I had provided and gathered and are now lost, with other things, by casualty before mentioned.

Dyes of divers kinds. There is sumac, well known and used in

England for black, the seed of an herb called *wasewówr*, little small roots called *cháppacor*, and the bark of the tree called by the inhabitants *tangomockonomindge*, which dyes are for divers sorts of red; their goodness for our English clothes remain yet to be proved. The inhabitants use them only for the dyeing of hair and colouring of their faces and mantles made of deerskins, and also for the dyeing of rushes to make artificial works withal in their mats and baskets, having no other thing besides that they account of apt to use them for. If they will not prove merchantable there is no doubt but the planters there shall find apt uses for them, as also for other colours which we know to be there.

Woad, a thing of so great vent and use amongst English dyers, which cannot be yielded sufficiently in our own country for spare of ground, may be planted in Virginia, there being ground enough. The growth thereof need not be doubted, when as in the islands of the Azores it groweth plentifully, which is in the same climate. So likewise of madder.

We carried thither sugar-canes to plant, which being not so well preserved as was requisite, and besides, the time of the year being past for their setting when we arrived, we could not make that proof of them as we desired. Notwithstanding, seeing that they grow in the same climate in the south part of Spain and in Barbary, our hope in reason may yet continue. So likewise for oranges and lemons. There may be planted also quinces. Whereby may grow in reasonable time, if the action be diligently prosecuted, no small commodities in sugars, suckets, and marmalades.

Many other commodities by planting may there also be raised, which I leave to your discreet and gentle considerations, and many also may be there which yet we have not discovered. Two more commodities of great value, one of certainty and the other in hope, not to be planted but there to be raised and in short time to be provided and prepared, I might have specified. So likewise of those commodities already set down I might have said more, as of the particular places where they are found and best to be planted and prepared, by what means and in what reasonable space of time they might be raised to profit and in what proportion; but because others than well-willers might be therewithal acquainted, not to the good of the action, I have wittingly omitted them, knowing that to those that are well disposed I have uttered, according to my promise and purpose, for this part sufficient.

*The second part: Of such commodities as Virginia is known to yield for victual and sustenance of man's life, usually fed upon by the natural inhabitants, as also by us, during the time of our abode; and, first, of such as are sowed and husbanded.*

*Pagatowr,* a kind of grain so called by the inhabitants; the same in the West Indies is called maize. Englishmen call it Guinea wheat or Turkey wheat, according to the names of the countries from whence the like hath been brought. The grain is about the bigness of our ordinary English peas and not much different in form and shape but of divers colours: some white, some red, some yellow, and some blue. All of them yield a very white and sweet flour; being used according to his kind it maketh a very good bread. We made of the same in the country some malt, whereof was brewed as good ale as was to be desired. So likewise by the help of hops thereof may be made as good beer. It is a grain of marvellous great increase, of a thousand-, fifteen hundred-, and some two thousand-fold. There are three sorts, of which two are ripe in eleven and twelve weeks at the most—sometimes in ten—after the time they are set, and are then of height in stalk about six or seven foot. The other sort is ripe in fourteen and is about ten foot high; of the stalks some bear four heads, some three, some one, and some two, every head containing five, six, or seven hundred grains, within a few more or less. Of these grains besides bread the inhabitants make victual, either by parching them, or seething[5] them whole until they be broken, or boiling the flour with water into a pap.

*Okindgíer,* called by us beans, because in greatness and partly in shape they are like to the beans in England, saving that they are flatter, of more divers colours, and some pied. The leaf, also, of the stem is much different. In taste they are altogether as good as our English peas.

*Wickonzówr,* called by us peas, in respect of the beans, for distinction sake, because they are much less, although in form they little differ, but in goodness of taste much and are far better than our English peas. Both the beans and peas are ripe in ten weeks after they are set. They make them victual either by boiling them all to pieces into a broth or boiling them whole until they be soft and begin to break, as is used in England, either by themselves or mixtly together. Sometimes they mingle of the wheat with them. Sometime, also, being whole sodden, they bruise or pound them in a mortar and thereof make loaves or lumps of doughish bread, which they use to eat for variety.

*Macócqwer,* according to their several forms, called by us pompions,[6] melons, and gourds, because they are of the like forms as those kinds in England. In Virginia such of several forms are of one taste and very good and do also spring from one seed. There are of two sorts: one is ripe in the space of a month and the other in two months.

There is an herb which in Dutch is called *melden*. Some of those that I describe it unto take it to be a kind of orach; it groweth about four or five foot high. Of the seed thereof they make a thick broth and pottage of a very good taste; of the stalk, by burning into ashes, they make a kind of salt earth, wherewithal many use sometimes to season their broths: other salt they know not. We ourselves used the leaves also for pot-herbs.

There is also another great herb, in form of a marigold,[7] about six foot in height; the head with the flower is a span in breadth. Some take it to be *Planta solis*; of the seeds hereof they make both a kind of bread and broth.

All the aforesaid commodities for victual are set or sowed, sometimes in grounds apart and severally by themselves, but for the most part together in one ground mixtly: the manner thereof, with the dressing and preparing of the ground, because I will note unto you the fertility of the soil, I think good briefly to describe.

The ground they never fatten with muck, dung, or any other thing, neither plough nor dig it as we in England, but only prepare it in sort as followeth. A few days before they sow or set, the men with wooden instruments made almost in form of mattocks or hoes with long handles, the women with short peckers or parers, because they use them sitting, of a foot long and about five inches in breadth, do only break the upper part of the ground to raise up the weeds, grass, and old stubs of corn-stalks with their roots. The which, after a day or two's drying in the sun, being scraped up into many small heaps to save them labour for carrying them away, they burn into ashes. (And whereas some may think that they use the ashes for to better the ground, I say that then they would either disperse the ashes abroad, which we observed they do not, except the heaps be too great, or else would take special care to set their corn where the ashes lie, which also we find they are careless of.) And this is all the husbanding of their ground that they use.

Then their setting or sowing is after this manner. First, for their corn, beginning in one corner of the plot, with a pecker they make a hole, wherein they put four grains with that care they touch not one another (about an inch asunder) and cover them with the mould again; and so throughout the whole plot, making such holes and using them after such manner, but with this regard, that they be made in ranks, every rank differing from other half a fathom or a yard, and the holes also in every rank as much. By this means there is a yard spare ground between every hole, where, according to discretion, here and there they set as many beans and peas; in divers places also among the seeds of *macócqwer*, *melden*, and *Planta solis*.

The ground being thus set, according to the rate by us experimented, an English acre, containing forty perches in length and four in breadth, doth there yield in crop or offcome of corn, beans, and peas at the least two hundred London bushels, besides the *macócqwer*, *melden*, and *Planta solis*, whenas in England forty bushels of our wheat yielded out of such an acre is thought to be much.

I thought also good to note this unto you, that you which shall inhabit and plant there may know how specially that country corn is there to be preferred before ours. Besides the manifold ways in applying it to victual, the increase is so much that small labour and pains is needful in respect that must be used for ours. For this I can assure you, that, according to the rate we have made proof of, one may prepare and husband so much ground (having once borne corn before), with less than four-and-twenty hours' labour, as shall yield him victual in a large proportion for a twelvemonth, if he have nothing else but that which the same ground will yield and of that kind only which I have before spoken of, the said ground being also but of five-and-twenty yards square. And if need require but that there is ground enough, there might be raised out of one and the selfsame ground two harvests or offcomes; for they sow or set, and may at any time when they think good, from the midst of March until the end of June; so that they also set when they have eaten of their first crop. In some places of the country, notwithstanding, they have two harvests, as we have heard, out of one and the same ground. . . .

There is an herb which is sowed apart by itself and is called by the inhabitants *uppówoc*. In the West Indies it hath divers names, according to the several places and countries where it groweth and is used. The Spaniards generally call it tobacco. The leaves thereof, being dried and brought into powder, they use to take the fume or smoke thereof by sucking it through pipes made of clay into their stomach and head, from whence it purgeth superfluous phlegm and other gross humours, openeth all the pores and passages of the body: by which means the use thereof not only preserveth the body from obstructions but also, if any be, so that they have not been of too long continuance, in short time breaketh them, whereby their bodies are notably preserved in health and know not many grievous diseases wherewithal we in England are oftentimes afflicted.

This *uppówoc* is of so precious estimation amongst them that they think their gods are marvellously delighted therewith, whereupon sometime they make hallowed fires and cast some of the powder therein for a sacrifice; being in a storm upon the waters, to pacify their gods, they cast some up into the air and into the water; so, a weir for fish being newly set up, they cast some therein and into the air; also, after an escape of danger, they cast some into the air likewise: but all done with strange gestures, stamping, sometime dancing, clapping of hands, holding up of hands, and staring up into the heavens, uttering therewithal and chattering strange words and noises.

We ourselves during the time we were there used to suck it after their manner, as also since our return, and have found many rare and wonderful experiments of the virtues thereof, of which the relation would require a volume by itself; the use of it by so many of late, men and women of great calling as else, and some learned physicians also, is sufficient witness.

And these are the commodities for sustenance of life that I know and can remember they use to husband; all else that follow are found growing naturally or wild. . . .

[A section of various kinds of roots useful for food is omitted.]

### Of fruits

Chestnuts there are in divers places great store; some they use to eat raw, some they stamp and boil to make spoon-meat, and with some, being sodden, they make such a manner of doughbread as they use of their beans before mentioned.

Walnuts. There are two kinds of walnuts and of them infinite store. In many places where [are] very great woods for many miles together the third part of trees are walnut trees. The one kind is of the same taste and form, or little differing, from ours of England, but that they are harder and thicker-shelled; the other is greater and hath a very ragged and hard shell but the kernel great, very oily and sweet. Besides their eating of them after our ordinary manner, they break them with stones and pound them in mortars with water to make a milk, which they use to put into some sorts of their spoon-meat, also among their sod wheat, peas, beans, and pompions, which maketh them have a far more pleasant taste.

Medlars,[8] a kind of very good fruit, so called by us chiefly for these respects: first, in that they are not good until they be rotten; then, in that they open at the head as our medlars and are about the same bigness; otherwise in taste and colour they are far different, for they are as red as cherries and very sweet, but whereas the cherry is sharp-sweet, they are luscious-sweet.

*Metaquesúnnauk,*[9] a kind of pleasant fruit almost of the shape and bigness of English pears but that they are of a perfect red colour as well within as without. They grow on a plant whose leaves are very thick and full of prickles as sharp as needles. Some that have been in the Indies, where they have seen that kind of red dye of great price which is called cochineal to grow, do describe his plant right like unto this of *Metaquesúnnauk,* but whether it be the true cochineal or a bastard or wild kind, it cannot yet be certified, seeing that also, as I heard, cochineal is not of the fruit but found on the leaves of the plant, which leaves for such matter we have not so specially observed.

Grapes there are of two sorts, which I mentioned in the merchantable commodities.

Strawberries there are as good and as great as those which we have in our English gardens.

Mulberries, apple-crabs, hurts or hurtleberries, such as we have here in England. . . .

[Sections describing certain Indian berries, the use of acorns, deer, conies, squirrels, and other beasts are omitted.]

### Of fowl

Turkey cocks and turkey hens, stockdoves, partridges, cranes, herons, and in winter great store of swans and geese. Of all sorts of fowl I have the names in the country language of fourscore-and-six, of which number, besides those that be named, we have taken, eaten, and have the pictures as they were there drawn, with the names of the inhabitants, of several strange sorts of waterfowl eight, and seventeen kinds more of landfowl, although we have seen and eaten of many more, which for want of leisure there for the purpose could not be pictured; and after we are better furnished and stored upon further discovery with their strange beasts, fish, trees, plants, and herbs, they shall be also published.

There are also parrots,[10] falcons, and merlin hawks which, although with us they be not used for meat, yet for other causes I thought good to mention.

*Of fish*

For four months of the year—February, March, April, and May—
there are plenty of sturgeons. And also in the same months of herrings,
some of the ordinary bigness as ours in England, but the most part far
greater, of eighteen, twenty inches, and some two foot in length and
better. Both these kinds of fish in those months are most plentiful and
in best season, which we found to be most delicate and pleasant meat.

There are also trouts, porpoises, rays, oldwives, mullets, plaice, and
very many other sorts of excellent good fish, which we have taken and
eaten, whose names I know not but in the country language. We
have of twelve sorts more the pictures as they were drawn in the country, with their names.

The inhabitants use to take them two manner of ways. The one is
by a kind of weir made of reeds, which in that country are very strong.
The other way, which is more strange, is with poles made sharp at one
end, by shooting them into the fish after the manner as Irishmen cast
darts, either as they are rowing in their boats or else as they are wading
in the shallows for the purpose.

There are also in many places plenty of these kinds which follow:
Sea crabs, such as we have in England. Oysters, some very great and
some small; some round and some of a long shape. They are found both
in salt water and brackish, and those that we had out of salt water are
far better than the other, as in our own country. Also mussels, scallops,
periwinkles, and crayfish. . . .

And thus have I made relation of all sorts of victual that we fed upon
for the time we were in Virginia, as also the inhabitants themselves, as
far forth as I know and can remember, or that are specially worthy to
be remembered.

*The third and last part: Of such other things as is behoveful for those
which shall plant and inhabit to know of, with a description of the nature
and manners of the people of the country*

*Of commodities for building and other necessary uses*

Those other things which I am more to make rehearsal of are such as
concern building and other mechanical necessary uses, as, divers sorts
of trees for house and ship timber and other uses else, also lime, stone,
and brick, lest that, being not mentioned, some might have been
doubted of, or by some that are malicious reported the contrary. . . .

[Harriot describes various kinds of trees useful for buildings, ships, etc.: oak, fir, cedar, maple, holly, willow, beech, ash, elm, sassafras, and other varieties.]

Now for stone, brick, and lime, thus it is. Near unto the sea-coast where we dwelt there are no kind of stones to be found (except a few small pebbles about four miles off) but such as have been brought from farther out of the main. In some of our voyages we have seen divers hard, raggy stones, great pebbles, and a kind of grey stone like unto marble, of which the inhabitants make their hatchets to cleave wood. Upon inquiry we heard that a little further up into the country were of all sorts very many, although of quarries they are ignorant, neither have they use of any store whereupon they should have occasion to seek any. For if every household have one or two to crack nuts, grind shells, whet copper, and sometimes other stones for hatchets, they have enough; neither use they any digging but only for graves about three foot deep; and therefore no marvel that they know neither quarries nor limestones, which both may be in places nearer than they wot of.

In the mean time, until there be discovery of sufficient store in some place or other convenient, the want of you which are and shall be the planters therein may be as well supplied by brick, for the making whereof in divers places of the country there is clay both excellent good and plenty, and also by lime made of oyster shells and of others burnt after the manner as they use in the isles of Thanet and Sheppey and also in divers other places of England, which kind of lime is well known to be as good as any other. And of oyster shells there is plenty enough; for, besides divers other particular places where are abundance, there is one shallow sound along the coast where for the space of many miles together in length and two or three miles in breadth the ground is nothing else, being but half a foot or a foot under water for the most part. . . .

*Of the nature and manners of the people*

It resteth I speak a word or two of the natural inhabitants, their natures and manners, leaving large discourse thereof until time more convenient hereafter: now only so far forth as that you may know how that in respect of troubling our inhabiting and planting [they] are not to be feared, but that they shall have cause both to fear and love us that shall inhabit with them.

They are a people clothed with loose mantles made of deerskins and aprons of the same round about their middles, all else naked; of such a difference of statures only as we in England; having no edge tools or weapons of iron or steel to offend us withal, neither know they how to make any: those weapons that they have are only bows made of witch hazel and arrows of reeds, flat-edged truncheons, also of wood, about a yard long, neither have they anything to defend themselves but targets made of barks and some armours made of sticks wickered together with thread.

Their towns are but small and near the sea-coast but few, some containing but ten or twelve houses, some twenty; the greatest that we have seen have been but of thirty houses. If they be walled, it is only done with barks of trees made fast to stakes, or else with poles only fixed upright and close one by another.

Their houses are made of small poles made fast at the tops in round form after the manner as is used in many arbours in our gardens of England, in most towns covered with barks and in some with artificial mats, made of long rushes, from the tops of the houses down to the ground. The length of them is commonly double to the breadth; in some places they are but twelve and sixteen yards long, and in othersome we have seen of four-and-twenty.

In some places of the country one only town belongeth to the government of a werowance or chief lord; in othersome two or three; in some six, eight, and more. The greatest werowance that yet we had dealing with had but eighteen towns in his government and able to make not above seven or eight hundred fighting men at the most. The language of every government is different from any other, and the further they are distant the greater is the difference.

Their manner of wars amongst themselves is either by sudden surprising one another, most commonly about the dawning of the day or moonlight, or else by ambushes or some subtle devices. Set battles are very rare, except it fall out where there are many trees, where either part may have some hope of defence, after the delivery of every arrow, in leaping behind some or other.

If there fall out any wars between us and them, what their fight is likely to be, we having advantages against them so many manner of ways, as by our discipline, our strange weapons and devices else, especially by ordnance great and small, it may be easily imagined: by the experience we have had in some places, the turning up of their heels against us in running away was their best defence.

In respect of us they are a people poor, and for want of skill and judgement in the knowledge and use of our things do esteem our trifles before things of greater value. Notwithstanding, in their proper manner, considering the want of such means as we have, they seem very ingenious; for although they have no such tools, nor any such crafts, sciences, and arts as we, yet in those things they do they show excellency of wit. And by how much they upon due consideration shall find our manner of knowledges and crafts to exceed theirs in perfection and speed for doing or execution, by so much the more is it probable that they should desire our friendships and love and have the greater respect for pleasing and obeying us. Whereby may be hoped, if means of good government be used, that they may in short time be brought to civility and the embracing of true religion.

Some religion they have already, which although it be far from the truth, yet being as it is there is hope it may be the easier and sooner reformed.

They believe that there are many gods, which they call *mantóac*, but of different sorts and degrees, one only chief and great god, which hath been from all eternity. Who, as they affirm, when he purposed to make the world, made first other gods of a principal order to be as means and instruments to be used in the creation and government to follow, and after the sun, moon, and stars as petty gods and the instruments of the other order more principal. First, they say, were made waters, out of which by the gods was made all diversity of creatures that are visible or invisible.

For mankind, they say a woman was made first, which by the working of one of the gods conceived and brought forth children; and in such sort they say they had their beginning. . . .

They think that all the gods are of human shape, and therefore they represent them by images in the forms of men, which they call *kewasówok* —one alone is called *kewás*; them they place in houses appropriate, or temples, which they call *machicómuck*, where they worship, pray, sing, and make many times offerings unto them. In some *machicómuck* we have seen but one *kewás*, in some two, and in othersome three; the common sort think them to be also gods.

They believe also the immortality of the soul, that after this life, as soon as the soul is departed from the body, according to the works it hath done it is either carried to Heaven, the habitacle of gods, there to enjoy perpetual bliss and happiness, or else to a great pit or hole, which they think to be in the furthest parts of their part of the world toward the sunset, there to burn continually; the place they call *popogusso*. . . .

Most things they saw with us, as mathematical instruments, sea compasses, the virtue of the loadstone in drawing iron, a perspective glass, whereby was showed many strange sights, burning glasses, wild-

fire works, guns, books (writing and reading), spring clocks that seem
to go of themselves, and many other things that we had, were so
strange unto them and so far exceeded their capacities to comprehend
the reason and means how they should be made and done, that they
thought they were rather the works of gods than of men, or at the leastwise they had been given and taught us of the gods. . . .

Many times and in every town where I came, according as I was able,
I made declaration of the contents of the Bible: that therein was set
forth the true and only God and His mighty works; that therein was
contained the true doctrine of salvation through Christ; with many
particularities of miracles and chief points of religion, as I was able then
to utter and thought fit for the time. And although I told them the book
materially and of itself was not of any such virtue as I thought they did
conceive, but only the doctrine therein contained, yet would many be
glad to touch it, to embrace it, to kiss it, to hold it to their breasts and
heads and stroke over all their body with it, to show their hungry
desire of that knowledge which was spoken of.

The werowance with whom we dwelt, called Wingina, and many of
his people, would be glad many times to be with us at our prayers, and
many times call upon us both in his own town as also in others whither
he sometimes accompanied us, to pray and sing psalms, hoping thereby
to be partaker of the same effects which we by that means also expected. . . .

There was no town where we had any subtle device practised against
us, we leaving it unpunished or not revenged (because we sought by all
means possible to win them by gentleness), but that within a few days
after our departure from every such town the people began to die very
fast, and many in short space: in some towns about twenty, in some
forty, in some sixty, and in one sixscore, which in truth was very many
in respect of their numbers. This happened in no place that we could
learn but where we had been where they used some practice against
us, and after such time. The disease, also, was so strange that they
neither knew what it was nor how to cure it; the like, by report of the
oldest men in the country, never happened before, time out of mind—
a thing specially observed by us, as also by the natural inhabitants
themselves.

Insomuch that when some of the inhabitants which were our friends,
and especially the werowance Wingina, had observed such effects in
four or five towns to follow their wicked practices, they were persuaded
that it was the work of our God through our means, and that we by

Him might kill and slay whom we would, without weapons, and not come near them.

And thereupon, when it had happened that they had understanding that any of their enemies had abused us in our journeys, hearing that we had wrought no revenge with our weapons, and fearing upon some cause the matter should so rest, [they] did come and entreat us that we would be a means to our God that they as others that had dealt ill with us might in like sort die, alleging how much it would be for our credit and profit, as also theirs, and hoping, furthermore, that we would do so much at their requests in respect of the friendship we profess them.

Whose entreaties, although we showed that they were ungodly, affirming that our God would not subject Himself to any such prayers and requests of men; that indeed all things have been and were to be done according to His good pleasure as He had ordained; and that we, to show ourselves His true servants, ought rather to make petition for the contrary, that they with them might live together with us, be made partakers of His truth and serve Him in righteousness; but, notwithstanding, in such sort that we refer that, as all other things, to be done according to His divine will and pleasure and as by His wisdom He had ordained to be best.

Yet because the effect fell out so suddenly and shortly after according to their desires, they thought nevertheless it came to pass by our means, and that we in using such speeches unto them did but dissemble the matter, and therefore came unto us to give us thanks in their manner, that although we satisfied them not in promise, yet in deeds and effect we had fulfilled their desires.

This marvellous accident in all the country wrought so strange opinions of us that some people could not tell whether to think us gods or men, and the rather because that all the space of their sickness there was no man of ours known to die or that was specially sick; they noted also that we had no women amongst us, neither that we did care for any of theirs.

Some, therefore, were of opinion that we were not born of women and therefore not mortal, but that we were men of an old generation many years past, then risen again to immortality. . . .

These their opinions I have set down the more at large that it may appear unto you that there is good hope they may be brought through discreet dealing and government to the embracing of the truth and consequently to honour, obey, fear, and love us.

And although some of our company towards the end of the year showed themselves too fierce, in slaying some of the people in some towns upon causes that on our part might easily enough have been borne withal, yet notwithstanding, because it was on their part justly deserved, the alteration of their opinions generally and for the most part concerning us is the less to be doubted, and, whatsoever else they may be, by carefulness of ourselves need nothing at all to be feared.

The best, nevertheless, in this, as in all actions besides, is to be endeavoured and hoped, and of the worst that may happen notice to be taken with consideration and, as much as may be, eschewed. ....

## 15

# Return to Roanoke Island; the Birth of Virginia Dare (1587)

In 1587 Raleigh made a second attempt to establish a colony on Roanoke Island, where Grenville, returning with supplies from England, had left fifteen men to hold the land after he discovered that Lane's colonists had departed in Drake's fleet. John White went out as governor of the new colony. With him went his daughter, Eleanor, wife of Ananias Dare, and shortly after their arrival a child was born to the couple and christened Virginia. She was the first English child born in North America. John White returned to England to obtain additional supplies, but the Spanish war intervened and the colony mysteriously disappeared in the four years that passed before White could get back. The arrival of the colonists is described in White's 'The Fourth Voyage Made to Virginia in the Year 1587', first printed by Hakluyt, *Principal Navigations* (1589), and reprinted by Quinn, *Roanoke Voyages*, II, 515–38.

IN the year of Our Lord 1587, Sir Walter Raleigh, intending to persevere in the planting of his country of Virginia, prepared a new colony of 150 men to be sent thither under the charge of John White, whom he appointed Governor, and also appointed unto him twelve assistants, unto whom he gave a charter and incorporated them by the name of Governor and Assistants of the city of Raleigh in Virginia. ....

About the sixteenth of July we fell with the main of Virginia, which Simon Fernando took to be the island of Croatan, where we came to an anchor and rode there two or three days; but, finding himself deceived, he weighed and bare along the coast, where in the night, had not Captain Stafford been more careful in looking out than our Simon Fernando, we had been all cast away upon the beach called the Cape of Fear,[1] for we were come within two cables' length upon it, such was the carelessness and ignorance of our master.

The two-and-twentieth of July we arrived safe at Hatorask, where our ship and pinnace anchored. The Governor went aboard the pinnace, accompanied with forty of his best men, intending to pass up to Roanoke forthwith, hoping there to find those fifteen Englishmen which Sir Richard Grenville had left there the year before, with whom he meant to have conference concerning the state of the country and savages, meaning after he had so done to return again to the fleet and pass along the coast to the Bay of Chesapeake, where we intended to make our seat and fort, according to the charge given us among other directions in writing under the hand of Sir Walter Raleigh. But as soon as we were put with our pinnace from the ship, a gentleman by the name of Fernando, who was appointed to return for England, called to the sailors in the pinnace, charging them not to bring any of the planters back again but leave them in the island, except the Governor and two or three such as he approved, saying that the summer was far spent, wherefore he would land all the planters in no other place. Unto this were all the sailors, both in the pinnace and ship, persuaded by the master, wherefore it booted not the Governor to contend with them but passed to Roanoke and the same night at sunset went aland on the island in the place where our fifteen men were left, but we found none of them nor any signs that they had been there, saving only we found the bones of one of those fifteen which the savages had slain long before.

The twenty-third of July, the Governor with divers of his company walked to the north end of the island, where Master Ralph Lane had his fort, with sundry necessary and decent dwelling-houses, made by his men about it the year before, where we hoped to find some signs or certain knowledge of our fifteen men. When we came thither we found the fort razed down but all the houses standing unhurt, saving the nether rooms of them and also of the fort were overgrown with melons of divers sorts and deer within them, feeding on those melons; so we returned to our company without hope of ever seeing any of the fifteen men living.

The same day order was given that every man should be employed for the repairing of those houses which we found standing, and also to make other new cottages for such as should need. . . .

The eighth of August, the Governor, having long expected the coming of the werowances of Pomioake, Aquascoquos, Secota, and Dasamongueponke, seeing that the seven days were past within which they promised to come in or to send their answers by the men of Croatan and no tidings of them heard, being certainly also informed by those men of Croatan that the remnant of Wingina his men which were left alive, who dwelt at Dasamongueponke, were they which had slain George Howe and were also at the driving of our eleven Englishmen from Roanoke, he thought to defer the revenging thereof no longer. Wherefore the same night about midnight he passed over the water, accompanied with Captain Stafford and twenty-four men, whereof Manteo was one, whom we took with us to be our guide to the place where those savages dwelt, where he behaved himself toward us as a most faithful Englishman.

The next day, being the ninth of August, in the morning so early that it was yet dark, we landed near the dwelling-place of our enemies and very secretly conveyed ourselves through the woods to that side where we had their houses between us and the water; and, having espied their fire and some sitting about it, we presently set on them. The miserable souls, herewith amazed, fled into a place of thick reeds growing fast by, where our men, perceiving them, shot one of them through the body with a bullet, and therewith we entered the reeds, among which we hoped to acquit their evil doing towards us. But we were deceived, for those savages were our friends and were come from Croatan to gather the corn and fruit of that place, because they understood our enemies were fled immediately after they had slain George Howe and for haste had left all their corn, tobacco, and pompions standing, in such sort that all had been devoured of the birds and deer if it had not been gathered in time. But they had like to have paid dearly for it; for it was so dark that, they being naked and their men and women apparelled all so like others, we knew not but that they were all men; and if that one of them which was a werowance's wife had not had her child at her back, she had been slain instead of a man. And as hap was, another savage knew Master Stafford and ran to him, calling him by his name, whereby he was saved.

Finding ourselves thus disappointed of our purpose, we gathered all the corn, peas, pompions, and tobacco that we found ripe, leaving the rest unspoiled, and took Menatonon his wife,[2] with the young child, and the other savages, with us over the water to Roanoke.

Although the mistaking of these savages somewhat grieved Manteo, yet he imputed their harm to their own folly, saying to them that if their werowances had kept their promise in coming to the Governor at the day appointed, they had not known that mischance.

The thirteenth of August our savage Manteo, by the commandment of Sir Walter Raleigh, was christened in Roanoke and called Lord thereof and of Dasamongueponke, in reward of his faithful service.

The eighteenth, Eleanor, daughter to the Governor and wife to Ananias Dare, one of the Assistants, was delivered of a daughter in Roanoke, and the same was christened there the Sunday following; and because this child was the first Christian born in Virginia, she was named Virginia.

By this time our ships had unlanded the goods and victuals of the planters and began to take in wood and fresh water and to new caulk and trim them for England; the planters also prepared their letters and tokens to send back into England. . . .

The twenty-second of August, the whole company, both of the Assistants and planters, came to the Governor and with one voice requested him to return himself into England for the better and sooner obtaining of supplies and other necessaries for them; but he refused it and alleged many sufficient causes why he would not. The one was that he could not so suddenly return back again without his great discredit, leaving the action and so many whom he partly had procured through his persuasions to leave their native country and undertake that voyage, and that some enemies to him and the action at his return into England would not spare to slander falsely both him and the action by saying he went to Virginia but politicly and to no other end but to lead so many into a country in which he never meant to stay himself and there to leave them behind him. Also he alleged that, seeing they intended to remove fifty miles further up in the main presently, he being then absent, his stuff and goods might be both spoiled and most of it pilfered away in the carriage, so that at his return he should be either forced to provide himself of all such things again or else at his coming again to Virginia find himself utterly unfurnished, whereof already he had found some proof, being but once from them but three days. Wherefore he concluded that he would not go himself. . . .

The Governor, being at the last, through their extreme entreating, constrained to return into England, having then but half a day's respite to prepare himself for the same, departed from Roanoke the seven-and-twentieth of August in the morning. . . .

# 16

# A Promising Description of
# New England (1602)

The early efforts of Sir Walter Raleigh to found an English colony in North America failed, but interest in the new land did not diminish. In 1602 a group of twenty-four gentlemen and eight sailors left Falmouth in the small bark *Concord* on a voyage of exploration and intended settlement in the north parts of the continent. They were led by Captain Bartholomew Gosnold and had the permission of Raleigh, whose charter gave him jurisdiction as far as New England. They reached what is now Cape Cod about May 15, sailed around Nantucket and Martha's Vineyard, and made a temporary base on Cuttyhunk Island in Buzzard's Bay. There they traded with the Indians and loaded a cargo of furs and sassafras roots. The expedition planned to leave twelve of the gentlemen to hold land that they might choose, but after exploring the territory they decided that their number was too small and their supplies too limited for a settlement, and they sailed for home. Soon after the return of the explorers, John Brereton, 'one of the voyage', published *A Brief and True Relation of the Discovery of the North Part of Virginia . . . Made This Present Year 1602 by Captain Bartholomew Gosnold, Captain Bartholomew Gilbert, and Divers Other Gentlemen Their Associates by Permission of . . . Sir Walter Raleigh . . .* (1602), from which the selection below is taken. Brereton's tract was reprinted by Henry S. Burrage, *Early English and French Voyages*, Original Narratives of Early American History (New York, 1906), pp. 329–40. Brereton's narrative is the earliest of English eye-witness accounts of New England.

To the Honourable Sir Walter Raleigh, Knight: . . .

But on Friday the fourteenth of May, early in the morning, we made the land[1]—being full of fair trees, the land somewhat low, certain hummocks or hills lying into the land, the shore full of white sand but very stony or rocky. And, standing fair along by the shore, about twelve of the clock of the same day we came to an anchor, where six Indians in a Basque shallop with mast and sail, an iron grapple, and a kettle of copper, came boldly aboard us, one of them apparelled with a waistcoat and breeches of black serge, made after our sea fashion, hose and shoes on his feet. All the rest (saving one that had a pair of breeches of blue cloth) were all naked. These people are of tall stature, broad and grim visage, of a black swart complexion, their eyebrows painted white;

their weapons are bows and arrows. It seemed by some words and signs they made that some Basques or of Saint-Jean-de-Luz have fished or traded in this place, being in the latitude of 43 degrees.

But riding here in no very good harbour, and withal doubting the weather, about three of the clock the same day in the afternoon we weighed. Standing southerly off the sea the rest of that day and the night following with a fresh gale of wind, in the morning we found ourselves embayed with a mighty headland.[2] But coming to an anchor about nine of the clock the same day within a league of the shore, we hoisted out the one half of our shallop and Captain Bartholomew Gosnold, myself, and three others went ashore, being a white sandy and very bold shore. Marching all that afternoon with our muskets on our necks on the highest hills which we saw (the weather very hot), at length we perceived this headland to be a parcel of the main and sundry islands lying almost round about it. So returning towards evening to our shallop (for by that time the other part was brought ashore and set together), we espied an Indian, a young man of proper[3] stature and of a pleasing countenance. After some familiarity with him, we left him at the sea-side and returned to our ship, where in five or six hours' absence we had pestered our ship so with cod-fish that we threw numbers of them overboard again. Surely, I am persuaded that in the months of March, April, and May there is upon this coast better fishing and in as great plenty as in Newfoundland; for the schools of mackerel, herring, cod, and other fish that we daily saw as we went and came from the shore were wonderful; and besides, the places where we took these cod (and might in a few days have laden our ship) were but in seven fathom water and within less than a league of the shore, where in Newfoundland they fish in forty or fifty fathom water and far off.

From this place we sailed round about this headland almost all the points of the compass, the shore very bold, but as no coast is free from dangers, so I am persuaded this is as free as any—the land somewhat low, full of goodly woods, but in some places plain. At length we were come amongst many fair islands which we had partly discerned at our first landing, all lying within a league or two one of another and the outermost not above six or seven leagues from the main. But coming to an anchor under one of the[m][4] which was about three or four leagues from the main, Captain Gosnold, myself, and some others went ashore, and, going round about it, we found it to be four English miles in compass, without house or habitant, saving a little old house made of boughs, covered with bark, an old piece of a weir of the Indians to catch fish, and one or two places where they had made fires. The chiefest trees of this island are beeches and cedars, the outward parts all overgrown with low bushy trees three or four foot in height, which bear some kind of fruits, as appeared by their blossoms; strawberries, red and white, as sweet and much bigger than ours in England, raspberries, gooseberries, hurtleberries, and such an incredible store of vines, as well in the woody part of the island, where they run upon every tree, as on the outward parts, that we could not go for treading upon them; also, many springs of excellent sweet water, and a great standing lake of fresh water near the sea-side, an English mile in compass, which is maintained with the springs running exceeding pleasantly through the woody grounds, which are very rocky.

Here are also in this island great store of deer, which we saw, and other beasts, as appeared by their tracks, as also divers fowls, as cranes, heronshaws, bitterns, geese, mallards, teals, and other fowls, in great plenty, also, great store of peas, which grow in certain plots all the island over. On the north side of this island we found many huge bones and ribs of whales.

This island, as also all the rest of these islands, are full of all sorts of stones fit for building; the sea-sides all covered with stones, many of them glistering and shining like mineral stones, and very rocky. Also, the rest of these islands are replenished with these commodities and upon some of them inhabitants, as upon an island to the northward and within two leagues of this; yet we found no towns nor many of their houses, although we saw many Indians, which are tall, big-boned men, all naked, saving they cover their privy parts with a black, tewed skin, much like a blacksmith's apron, tied about their middle and between their legs behind. They gave us of their fish, ready boiled (which they carried in a basket made of twigs not unlike our osier), whereof we did eat and judged them to be freshwater fish. They gave us also of their tobacco, which they drink green but dried into powder, very strong and pleasant, and much better than any I have tasted in England. The necks of their pipes are made of clay hard dried (whereof in that island is great store both red and white); the other part is a piece of hollow copper very finely closed and cemented together. We gave unto them certain trifles, as knives, points, and such-like, which they much esteemed.

From thence we went to another island[5] to the northwest of this and within a league or two of the main, which we found to be greater than before we imagined, being sixteen English miles at the least in compass, for it contains many pieces or necks of land which differ nothing from several islands, saving that certain banks of small breadth do like bridges join them to this island. On the outsides of this island are many plain places of grass, abundance of strawberries and other berries before mentioned. In mid-May we did sow in this island (as for trial) in sundry places, wheat, barley, oats, and peas, which in fourteen days were sprung up nine inches and more. The soil is fat and lusty, the upper crust of grey colour, but a foot or less in depth, of the colour of our hemp lands in England, and being thus apt for these and the like grains. The sowing or setting (after the ground is cleansed) is no greater labour than if you should set or sow in one of our best prepared gardens in England.

This island is full of high-timbered oaks, their leaves thrice so broad as ours; cedars straight and tall; beech; elm; holly; walnut trees in abundance, the fruit as big as ours, as appeared by those we found under the trees, which had lain all the year ungathered; hazelnut trees; cherry trees, the leaf, bark, and bigness not differing from ours in England, but the stalk beareth the blossoms or fruit at the end thereof like a cluster of grapes, forty or fifty in a bunch; sassafras trees, plenty all the island over, a tree of high price and profit; also divers other fruit trees, some of them with strange barks of an orange colour, in feeling soft and smooth like velvet. In the thickest parts of the woods you may see a furlong or more round about.

On the north-west side of this island near to the sea-side is a standing lake of fresh water almost three English miles in compass, in the midst whereof stands a plot of woody ground an acre in quantity or not above. This lake is full of small tortoises and exceedingly frequented with all sorts of fowls before rehearsed, which breed, some low on the banks and other on low trees, about this lake in great abundance, whose young ones of all sorts we took and ate at our pleasure. But all these fowls are much bigger than ours in England. Also in every island, and almost in every part of every island, are great store of ground-nuts, forty together on a string, some of them as big as hen's eggs; they grow not two inches under ground—the which nuts we found to be as good as potatoes. Also, divers sorts of shell-fish, as scallops, mussels, cockles, lobsters, crabs, oysters, and whelks exceeding good and very great.

But, not to cloy you with particular rehearsal of such things as God and Nature hath bestowed on these places, in comparison whereof the most fertile part of all England is (of itself) but barren: we went in our light horseman[6] fro[m] this island to the main, right against this island some two leagues off, where, coming ashore, we stood a while like men ravished at the beauty and delicacy of this sweet soil. For besides divers clear lakes of fresh water (whereof we saw no end), meadows very large and full of green grass, even the most woody places (I speak only of such as I saw) do grow so distinct and apart, one tree from another, upon green, grassy ground somewhat higher than the plains, as if Nature would show herself above her power artificial.[7] Hard by we espied seven Indians, and, coming up to them, at first they expressed some fear, but, being emboldened by our courteous usage and some trifles which we gave them, they followed us to a neck of land which we imagined had been severed from the main, but, finding it otherwise, we perceived a broad harbour or river's mouth which ran up into the main; but because the day was far spent we were forced to return to the island from when[ce] we came, leaving the discovery of this harbour for a time of better leisure. Of the goodness of which harbour, as also of many others thereabouts, there is small doubt, considering that all the islands, as also the main (where we were), is all rocky grounds and broken lands.

Now the next day we determined to fortify ourselves in the little plot of ground in the midst of the lake above mentioned, where we built an house and covered it with sedge, which grew about this lake in great abundance; in building whereof we spent three weeks and more. But the second day after our coming from the main we espied nine canoes or boats with fifty Indians in them coming towards us from this part of the main where we, two days before, landed. Being loath they should discover our fortification, we went out on the sea-side to meet them; and, coming somewhat near them, they all sat down upon the stones, calling aloud to us (as we rightly guessed) to do the like a little distance from them. Having sat a while in this order, Captain Gosnold willed me to go unto them; one of them, to whom I had given a knife two days before in the main, knew me (whom I also very well remembered) and, smiling upon me, spake somewhat unto their lord or captain, which sat in the midst of them, who presently rose up and took a large beaver-skin from one that stood about him and gave it unto me, which I requited for that time the best I could. But I, pointing towards Captain Gosnold, made signs unto him that he was our captain and desirous to be his friend and enter league with him, which (as I perceived) he understood and made signs of joy. Whereupon Captain Gosnold with the rest of his company, being twenty in all, came up unto them and after many signs of gratulations[8] (Captain Gosnold

presenting their l[ord] with certain trifles which they wondered at
and highly esteemed), we became very great friends, and sent for meat
aboard our shallop and gave them such meats as we had then ready
dressed, whereof they misliked nothing but our mustard, whereat they
made many a sour face. While we were thus merry, one of them had
conveyed a target of ours into one of their canoes, which we suffered
only to try whether they were in subjection to this l[ord], to whom we
made signs (by showing him another of the same likeness and pointing
to the canoe) what one of his company had done, who suddenly expressed some fear and, speaking angrily to one about him (as we perceived by his countenance), caused it presently to be brought back
again. So the rest of the day we spent in trading with them for furs,
which are beavers, lucerns, martens, otters, wild-cat skins, very large
and deep fur, black foxes, cony skins of the colour of our hares but
somewhat less, deerskins very large, sealskins, and other beasts' skins
to us unknown.

They have also great store of copper, some very red and some of a
paler colour; none of them but have chains, earrings, or collars of this
metal. They head some of their arrows herewith much like our broad
arrow-heads, very workmanly made. Their chains are many hollow
pieces cemented together, each piece of the bigness of one of our reeds,
a finger in length, ten or twelve of them together on a string, which they
wear about their necks. Their collars they wear about their bodies like
bandoleers a handful broad, all hollow pieces like the other but somewhat shorter, four hundred pieces in a collar, very fine and evenly set
together. Besides these, they have large drinking-cups made like skulls
and other thin plates of copper made much like our boar-spear blades,
all which they so little esteem as they offered their fairest collars or
chains for a knife or such-like trifle, but we seemed little to regard it.
Yet I was desirous to understand where they had such store of this
metal and made signs to one of them (with whom I was very familiar),
who, taking a piece of copper in his hand, made a hole with his finger
in the ground and withal pointed to the main from whence they came.

They strike fire in this manner: every one carrieth about him in a
purse of tewed leather a mineral stone (which I take to be their copper),
and, with a flat emery-stone (wherewith glaziers cut glass and cutlers
glaze blades) tied fast to the end of a little stick, gently he striketh upon
the mineral stone. Within a stroke or two a spark falleth upon a piece of
touchwood (much like our sponge in England) and with the least spark
he maketh a fire presently. We had also of their flax, wherewith they

make many strings and cords, but it is not so bright of colour as ours in England. I am persuaded they have great store growing upon the main, as also mines and many other rich commodities, which we, wanting both time and means, could not possibly discover.

Thus they continued with us three days, every night retiring themselves to the furthermost part of our island two or three miles from our fort. But the fourth day they returned to the main, which we understood that within five or six days they would come from the main to us again. But, being in their canoes a little from the shore, they made huge cries and shouts of joy unto us, and we, with our trumpet and cornet and casting up our caps into the air, made them the best farewell we could. Yet six or seven of them remained with us behind, bearing us company every day into the woods, and helped us to cut and carry our sassafras, and some of them lay aboard our ship.

These people, as they are exceeding courteous, gentle of disposition, and well-conditioned, excelling all others that we have seen, so for shape of body and lovely favour I think they excel all the people of America: of stature much higher than we; of complexion or colour much like a dark olive; their eyebrows and hair black, which they wear long, tied up behind in knots, whereon they prick feathers of fowls in fashion of a crownet. Some of them are black, thin-bearded. They make beards of the hair of beasts, and one of them offered a beard of their making to one of our sailors for his that grew on his face, which, because it was of a red colour, they judged to be none of his own. They are quick-eyed and steadfast in their looks; fearless of others' harms, as intending none of themselves; some of the meaner sort given to filching, which the very name of savages (not weighing their ignorance in good or evil) may easily excuse. Their garments are of deerskins, and some of them wear furs round and close about their necks. They pronounce our language with great facility, for one of them one day sitting by me, upon occasion I spake smiling to him these words: 'How now, sirrah, are you so saucy with my tobacco?' Which words (without any further repetition) he suddenly spoke so plain and distinctly as if he had been a long scholar in the language. Many other such trials we had which are here needless to repeat.

Their women (such as we saw, which were but three in all) were but low of stature, their eyebrows, hair, apparel, and manner of wearing like to the men, fat and very well favoured and much delighted in our company. The men are very dutiful towards them. And truly, the wholesomeness and temperature of this climate doth not only argue this people to be answerable to this description but also of a perfect constitution of body, active, strong, healthful, and very witty, as the sundry toys of theirs cunningly wrought may easily witness.

For the agreeing of this climate with us (I speak of myself, and so I may justly do for the rest of our company), that we found our health and strength all the while we remained there so to renew and increase as, notwithstanding our diet and lodging was none of the best, yet not one of our company (God be thanked) felt the least grudging[9] or inclination to any disease or sickness but were much fatter and in better health than when we went out of England.

But after our bark had taken in so much sassafras, cedar, furs, skins, and other commodities as were thought convenient, some of our company that had promised Captain Gosnold to stay, having nothing but a saving voyage[10] in their minds, made our company of inhabitants (which was small enough before) much smaller; so as Captain Gosnold, seeing his whole strength to consist but of twelve men, and they but meanly provided, determined to return for England, leaving this island (which he called Elizabeth's Island) with as many true sorrowful eyes as were before desirous to see it. So the eighteenth of June, being Friday, we weighed and with indifferent fair wind and weather came to anchor the twenty-third of July, being also Friday (in all, bare five weeks) before Exmouth.

Your Lordship's to command,<br>John Brereton

17

# Captain Waymouth Explores the New England Coast (1605)

Captain George Waymouth (or Weymouth), an experienced sea-faring man from Devonshire, commanded an expedition in 1605 to explore the shoreline of New England to obtain information useful to a group projecting a colony there. The principal sponsors of the expedition were Henry Wriothesley, Earl of Southampton, and Sir Thomas Arundel. Waymouth made a successful reconnaissance and returned with five Indians, who were set to learning English in order that they might describe the wonders of the land that the promoters intended to settle. A narrative, written by James Rosier, 'a gentleman employed in the voyage', was published in 1605, soon after the expedition returned, with this title: *A True Relation of the Most Prosperous Voyage Made This Present Year 1605 by Captain George Waymouth in the Discovery of the Land of Virginia: Where He Discovered 60 Miles up a Most Excellent River, Together with a Most Fertile Land.* Rosier's narrative is reprinted by Burrage, *Early English and French Voyages,* pp. 357–94.

Upon Tuesday the fifth of March, about ten o'clock afore noon, we set sail from Ratcliff and came to an anchor that tide about two o'clock before Gravesend. . . .

Upon Easter Day, being the last of March, the wind coming at north-north-east, about five o'clock after noon we weighed anchor and put to sea in the name of God, being well victualled and furnished with munition and all necessaries, our whole company being but twenty-nine persons, of whom I may boldly say few voyages have been manned forth with better seamen generally in respect of our small number. . . .

Friday, the seventeenth of May, about six o'clock at night, we descried the land, which bare from us north-north-east; but because it blew a great gale of wind, the sea very high and near night, not fit to come upon an unknown coast, we stood off till two o'clock in the morning, being Saturday. Then, standing in with it again, we descried it by eight o'clock in the morning, bearing north-east from us. It appeared a mean highland,[1] as we after found it, being but an island of some six miles in compass, but I hope the most fortunate ever yet discovered. About twelve o'clock that day we came to an anchor on the north side of this island, about a league from the shore. About two o'clock our captain with twelve men rowed in his ship-boat to the shore, where we made no long stay but laded our boat with dry wood of old trees upon the shore-side and returned to our ship, where we rode that night.

This island is woody, grown with fir, birch, oak, and beech as far as we saw along the shore, and so likely to be within. On the verge grow gooseberries, strawberries, wild peas, and wild rose bushes. The water issued forth down the rocky cliffs in many places, and much fowl of divers kinds breed upon the shore and rocks.

While we were at shore, our men aboard with a few hooks got above thirty great cods and haddocks, which gave us a taste of the great plenty of fish which we found afterward wheresoever we went upon the coast.

From hence we might discern the mainland from the west-south-west to the east-north-east, and a great way (as it then seemed, and as

we after found it) up into the main we might discern very high mountains, though the main seemed but lowland, which gave us a hope it
would please God to direct us to the discovery of some good, although
we were driven by winds far from that place whither (both by our
direction and desire) we ever intended to shape the course of our
voyage.

The next day, being Whitsunday, because we rode too much open
to the sea and winds, we weighed anchor about twelve o'clock and
came along to the other islands[2] more adjoining to the main and in the
road directly with the mountains about three leagues from the first
island where we had anchored.

When we came near unto them (sounding all along in a good depth),
our captain manned his ship-boat and sent her before with Thomas
Cam, one of his mates, whom he knew to be of good experience, to
sound and search between the islands for a place safe for our ship to
ride in. In the mean while we kept aloof at sea, having given them in the
boat a token to waft[3] in the ship, if he found a convenient harbour,
which it pleased God to send us far beyond our expectation, in a most
safe berth defended from all winds, in an excellent depth of water for
ships of any burden in six, seven, eight, nine, and ten fathoms upon a
clay ooze very tough.

We all with great joy praised God for His unspeakable goodness,
Who had from so apparent danger delivered us and directed us upon
this day into so secure an harbour. In remembrance whereof we named
it Pentecost Harbour,[4] we arriving there that day out of our last harbour in England, from whence we set sail upon Easter Day.

About four o'clock, after we were anchored and well moored, our
captain with half a dozen of our company went on shore[5] to seek fresh
watering and a convenient place to set together a pinnace which we
brought in pieces out of England, both which we found very fitting.

Upon this island, as also upon the former, we found (at our first
coming to shore) where fire had been made, and about the place were
very great egg-shells bigger than goose eggs, fish-bones, and, as we
judged, the bones of some beast.

Here we espied cranes stalking on the shore of a little island adjoining,[6] where we after saw they used to breed.

Whitmonday, the twentieth day of May, very early in the morning,
our captain caused the pieces of the pinnace to be carried ashore, where,
while some were busied about her, others digged wells to receive the
fresh water which we found issuing down out of the land in many

places. Here I cannot omit (for foolish fear of imputation of flattery) the painful industry of our captain, who as at sea he is always most careful and vigilant, so at land he refused no pains, but his labour was ever as much or rather more than any man's, which not only encouraged others with better content but also effected much with great expedition.

In digging we found excellent clay for brick or tile.

The next day we finished a well of good and wholesome clear water in a great empty cask, which we left there. We cut yards, waste trees, and many necessaries for our ship, while our carpenter and cooper laboured to fit and furnish forth the shallop.

This day our boat went out about a mile from our ship, and in small time with two or three hooks was fished sufficiently for our whole company three days, with great cod, haddock, and thornback.

And towards night we drew with a small net of twenty fathoms very nigh the shore. We got about thirty very good and great lobsters, many rockfish, some plaice, and other small fishes, and fishes called lumps, very pleasant to the taste. And we generally observed that all the fish, of what kind soever we took, were well fed, fat, and sweet in taste.

Wednesday, the twenty-second of May, we felled and cut wood for our ship's use, cleansed and scoured our wells, and digged a plot of ground wherein, amongst some garden seeds, we sowed peas and barley, which in sixteen days grew eight inches above ground and so continued growing every day half an inch, although this was but the crust of the ground and much inferior to the mould we after found in the main.

Friday, the twenty-fourth of May, after we had made an end of cutting wood and carrying water aboard our ship, with fourteen shot and pikes we marched about and through part of two of the islands, the bigger of which we judged to be four or five miles in compass and a mile broad.

The profits and fruits which are naturally on these islands are these. All along the shore and some space within, where the wood hindereth not, grow plentifully raspberries, gooseberries, strawberries, roses, currants, wild vines, angelica. Within the islands grow wood of sundry sorts, some very great and all tall: birch, beech, ash, maple, spruce, cherry tree, yew, oak very great and good, fir tree (out of which issueth turpentine in so marvellous plenty and so sweet as our chirurgeon and others affirmed they never saw so good in England). We pulled off much gum congealed on the outside of the bark, which smelled like frankincense. This would be a great benefit for making tar and pitch.

We stayed the longer in this place, not only because of our good harbour (which is an excellent comfort), but because every day we did more and more discover the pleasant fruitfulness, insomuch as many of our company wished themselves settled here, not expecting any further hopes or better discovery to be made.

Here our men found abundance of great mussels among the rocks, and in some of them many pearls, and in one mussel (which we drew up in our net) was found fourteen pearls, whereof one of pretty bigness and orient, in another above fifty small pearls, and if we had had a drag, no doubt we had found some of great value, seeing these did certainly show that here they were bred, the shells all glistering with mother of pearl.

Wednesday, the twenty-ninth day, our shallop being now finished and our captain and men furnished to depart with her from the ship, we set up a cross on the shore-side upon the rocks.

Thursday, the thirtieth of May, about ten o'clock afore noon, our captain with thirteen men more, in the name of God and with all our prayers for their prosperous discovery and safe return, departed in the shallop, leaving the ship in a good harbour, which before I mentioned, well moored and manned with fourteen men.

This day, about five o'clock in the afternoon, we in the ship espied three canoes coming towards us, which went to the island adjoining, where they went ashore and very quickly had made a fire, about which they stood beholding our ships, to whom we made signs with our hands and hats, waving unto them to come unto us, because we had not seen any of the people yet. They sent one canoe with three men, one of which, when they came near unto us, spake in his language very loud and very boldly, seeming as though he would know why we were there, and, by pointing with his oar towards the sea, we conjectured he meant we should be gone. But when we showed them knives and their use by cutting of sticks, and other trifles, as combs and glasses, they came close aboard our ship, as desirous to entertain our friendship. To these we gave such things as we perceived they liked when we showed them the use: bracelets, rings, peacock-feathers, which they stuck in their hair, and tobacco pipes. After their departure to their company on the shore, presently came four other in another canoe, to whom we gave as to the former, using them with as much kindness as we could.

The shape of their body is very proportionable, they are well countenanced, not very tall nor big, but in stature like to us. They paint their bodies with black, their faces some with red, some with black, and some with blue.

Their clothing is beavers' skins, or deerskins, cast over them like a mantle and hanging down to their knees, made fast together upon the shoulder with leather. Some of them had sleeves, most had none. Some had buskins of such leather tewed. They have besides a piece of beaver's skin between their legs, made fast about their waist to cover their privities.

They suffered no hair to grow on their faces but on their head very long and very black, which those that have wives bind up behind with a leather string in a long round knot.

They seemed all very civil and merry, showing tokens of much thankfulness for those things we gave them. We found them then (as after) a people of exceeding good invention, quick understanding, and ready capacity.[7]

Their canoes are made, without any iron, of the bark of a birch tree, strengthened within with ribs and hoops of wood, in so good fashion, with such excellent ingenious art, as they are able to bear seven or eight persons, far exceeding any in the Indies. . . .

Our captain had in this small time discovered up a great river, trending alongst into the main about forty miles. The pleasantness whereof, with the safety of harbour for shipping, together with the fertility of ground and other fruits, which were generally by his whole company related, I omit till I report of the whole discovery therein after performed. For by the breadth, depth, and strong flood imagining it to run far up into the land, he with speed returned, intending to flank his light horseman[8] for arrows, lest it might happen that the further part of the river should be narrow and by that means subject to the volley of savages on either side out of the woods. . . .

Until his return our captain left on shore where he landed in a path (which seemed to be frequented) a pipe, a brooch, and a knife, thereby to know if the savages had recourse that way, because they could at that time see none of them, but they were taken away before our return thither.

I return now to our savages, who, according to their appointment, about one o'clock came with four canoes to the shore of the island right over against us, where they had lodged the last night, and sent one canoe to us with two of those savages who had been aboard and another, who then seemed to have command of them. . . . We victualled them and gave them aqua-vitae, which they tasted but would by no means

L

drink. Our beverage they liked well. We gave them sugar candy, which after they had tasted they liked and desired more, and raisins which were given them. And some of everything they would reserve to carry to their company. Wherefore, we pitying their being in the rain and therefore not able to get themselves victual (as we thought), we gave them bread and fish.

Thus, because we found the land a place answerable to the intent of our discovery, *viz.*, fit for any nation to inhabit, we used the people with as great kindness as we could devise or found them capable of. . . .

Owen Griffin, which lay on the shore, reported unto me their manner and (as I may term them) the ceremonies of their idolatry, which they perform thus: one among them (the eldest of the company, as he judged) riseth right up; the other, sitting still and looking about, suddenly cried with a loud voice, 'Baugh, waugh'.[9] Then the women fall down and lie upon the ground, and the men all together, answering the same, fall a-stamping round about the fire with both feet as hard as they can, making the ground shake, with sundry outcries and change of voice and sound. Many take the fire-sticks and thrust them into the earth, and then rest awhile. Of a sudden, beginning as before, they continue so stamping till the younger sort fetched from the shore many stones, of which every man took one and first beat upon them with their fire-sticks, then with the stones beat the earth with all their strength. And in this manner (as he reported) they continued above two hours.

After this ended, they which have wives take them apart and withdraw themselves severally into the wood all night. . . .

Saturday, the eighth of June, our captain, being desirous to finish all business about this harbour, very early in the morning, with the light horseman, coasted five or six leagues about the islands adjoining and sounded all along wheresoever we went. He likewise diligently searched the mouth of the harbour and about the rocks, which show themselves at all times and are an excellent breach of the water, so as no sea can come in to offend the harbour. This he did to instruct himself, and thereby [be] able to direct others that shall happen to come to this place. For everywhere, both near the rocks and in all soundings about the islands, we never found less water than four and five fathoms, which was seldom. But seven, eight, nine, and ten fathoms is the continual sounding by the shore. In some places much deeper upon clay ooze or soft sand, so that if any bound for this place should be either driven or scanted with winds he shall be able, with his directions, to

recover safely his harbour most securely in water enough by four
several passages, more than which I think no man of judgement will
desire as necessary.

Upon one of the islands (because it had a pleasant, sandy cove for
small barks to ride in) we landed and found hard by the shore a pond
of fresh water, which flowed over the banks, somewhat overgrown
with little shrub trees, and, searching up in the island, we saw it fed
with a strong run, which with small labour and little time might be
made to drive a mill. In this island, as in the other, were spruce trees of
excellent timber and height, able to mast ships of great burden.

While we thus sounded from one place to another in so good deeps,
our captain, to make some trial of the fishing himself, caused a hook or
two to be cast out at the mouth of the harbour, not above half a league
from our ship, where in small time only, with the baits which they cut
from the fish and three hooks, we got fish enough for our whole company (though now augmented) for three days. Which I omit not to
report, because it shows how great a profit the fishing would be, they
being so plentiful, so great, and so good, with such convenient drying
as can be wished near at hand upon the rocks. . . .

Tuesday, the eleventh of June, we passed up into the river with our
ship about six-and-twenty miles. Of which I had rather not write
than by my relation to detract from the worthiness thereof. For the
river, besides that it is subject by shipping to bring in all traffics of
merchandise—a benefit always accounted the richest treasury to any
land, for which cause our Thames hath that due denomination and
France by her navigable rivers receiveth her greatest wealth—yet this
place of itself from God and nature affordeth as much diversity of good
commodities as any reasonable man can wish for present habitation and
planting.

The first and chiefest thing required is a bold coast and fair land to
fall with; the next, a safe harbour for ships to ride in. The first is a
special attribute to this shore, being most free from sands or dangerous
rocks, in a continual good depth, with a most excellent landfall, which
is the first island we fell with, named by us St George's Island. For the
second, by judgement of our captain, who knoweth most of the coast
of England and most of other countries (having been experienced by
employments in discoveries and travels from his childhood), and by
opinion of others of good judgement in our ship, here are more good
harbours for ships of all burdens than England can afford and far more
secure from all winds and weathers than any in England, Scotland,

France, or Spain. For besides, without the river in the channel and sounds about the islands adjoining to the mouth thereof, no better riding can be desired for an infinite number of ships. The river itself, as it runneth up into the main very nigh forty miles toward the great mountains, beareth in breadth a mile, sometimes three quarters, and half a mile is the narrowest, where you shall never have under four and five fathoms water hard by the shore, but six, seven, eight, nine, and ten fathoms all along, and on both sides every half mile very gallant coves, some able to contain almost a hundred sail, where the ground is excellent soft ooze with a tough clay under for anchor-hold, and where ships may lie without either cable or anchor, only moored to the shore with a hauser.

It flows, by their judgement, eighteen or twenty feet at high water. Here are made by nature most excellent places as docks to grave or careen ships of all burdens, secured from all winds, which is such a necessary, incomparable benefit that in a few places in England or in any parts of Christendom art with great charges can make the like.

Besides, the bordering land is a most rich neighbour, trending all along on both sides in an equal plain, neither mountainous nor rocky but, verged with a green border of grass, doth make tender[10] unto the beholder of her pleasant fertility if by cleansing away the woods she were converted into meadow.

The wood she beareth is not shrubbish fit only for fuel but goodly tall fir, spruce, birch, beech, oak, which in many good places is not so thick but may with small labour be made feeding ground, being plentiful like the outward islands with fresh water which streams down in many places.

As we passed with a gentle wind up with our ship in this river, any man may conceive with what admiration we all consented[11] in joy. Many of our company who had been travellers in sundry countries and in the most famous rivers yet affirmed them not comparable to this they now beheld. Some that were with Sir Walter Raleigh in his voyage to Guiana, in the discovery of the river Orinoco, which echoed fame to the world's ears, gave reasons why it was not to be compared with this, which wanted the dangers of many shoals and broken ground wherewith that was encumbered, others[12] before that notable river in the West Indies called Rio Grande, some before the river of Loire, the river Seine, and of Bordeaux in France, which although they be great and goodly rivers, yet it is no detraction from them to be accounted inferior to this, which not only yieldeth all the aforesaid pleasant profits but also appeared infallibly to us free from all inconveniences.

I will not prefer it before our river of Thames, because it is England's richest treasure, but we all did wish those excellent harbours, good deeps in a continual convenient breadth, and small tide-gates, to be as well therein for our country's good as we found them here beyond our hopes in certain for those to whom it shall please God to grant this land for habitation, which if it had, with the other inseparable adherent commodities here to be found, then I would boldly affirm it to be the most rich, beautiful, large, and secure harbouring river that the world affords. . . .

The temperature of the climate (albeit a very important matter) I had almost passed without mentioning, because it afforded to us no great alteration from our disposition in England—somewhat hotter up into the main because it lieth open to the south, the air so wholesome as I suppose not any of us found ourselves at any time more healthful, more able to labour, nor with better stomachs to such good fare as we partly brought and partly found. . . .

Wherefore, our sails being down, Thomas King, boatswain, presently cast out a hook, and before he judged it at ground was fished and hauled up an exceeding great and well-fed cod. Then there was cast out three or four more, and the fish was so plentiful and so great as when our captain would have set sail we all desired him to suffer them to take fish a while, because we were so delighted to see them catch so great fish so fast as the hook came down. Some, with playing with the hook, they took by the back, and one of the mates, with two hooks at a lead at five draughts together, hauled up ten fishes. All were generally very great, some they measured to be five foot long and three foot about.

This caused our captain not to marvel at the shoaling, for he perceived it was a fish bank, which (for our farewell from the land) it pleased God in continuance of His blessings to give us knowledge of, the abundant profit whereof should be alone sufficient cause to draw men again if there were no other good both in present certain and in hope probable to be discovered. To amplify this with words were to add light to the sun, for every one in the ship could easily account this present commodity—much more those of judgement which knew what belonged to fishing—would warrant (by the help of God), in a short voyage with few good fishers, to make a more profitable return from hence than from Newfoundland, the fish being so much greater, better fed, and abundant with train, of which some they desired and did bring into England to bestow among their friends and to testify the true report.

After, we kept our course directly for England and, with ordinary winds and sometimes calms, upon Sunday the fourteenth of July, about six o'clock at night, we were come into sounding in our channel, but with dark weather and contrary winds we were constrained to beat up and down till Tuesday the sixteenth of July, when by five o'clock in the morning we made the Scilly Islands, from whence, hindered with calms and small winds, upon Thursday the eighteenth of July, about four o'clock after noon, we came into Dartmouth, which haven happily (with God's gracious assistance) we made our last and first harbour in England. . . .

## 18

# Seafarers' Tall Tales of Virginia (1605)

By the early years of the seventeenth century, many travellers had made the journey across the Atlantic and had come back with incredible stories. Many of these tales grew with the telling, and the tendency of travellers to exaggerate the wonders they had seen overseas was already a subject for satire. The play *Eastward Ho!* (1605), by George Chapman, Ben Jonson, and John Marston, utilizes this theme. Sir Petronel Flash, an adventurer in need of money, proposes to go to Virginia, where he believes he can recoup his fortune. In Act III, scene ii, Captain Seagull, commander of the ship that is to convey Sir Petronel, and some of his cronies are reporting on the wonders of the New World:

*Enter Seagull, Spendall, and Scapethrift,*
*in the tavern with a Drawer.*

*Sea.* Come, Drawer, pierce your neatest hogsheads and let's have cheer, not fit for your Billingsgate Tavern but for our Virginian colonel. He will be here instantly.

*Draw.* You shall have all things fit, sir. Please you have any more wine ?

*Spend.* More wine, slave ? Whether we drink it or no, spill it and draw more.

*Scape.* Fill all the pots in your house with all sorts of liquor, and let them wait on us here like soldiers in their pewter coats. And though we do not employ them now, yet we will maintain them till we do.

*Draw.* Said like an honourable captain. You shall have all you can command, sir.                                        *Exit Drawer.*

*Sea.* Come, boys; Virginia longs till we share the rest of her maidenhead.

*Spend.* Why, is she inhabited already with any English?

*Sea.* A whole country of English is there, man, bred of those that were left there in '79. They have married with the Indians and make 'hem bring forth as beautiful faces as any we have in England; and therefore the Indians are so in love with 'hem that all the treasure they have they lay at their feet.

*Scape.* But is there such treasure there, Captain, as I have heard?

*Sea.* I tell thee, gold is more plentiful there than copper is with us, and for as much red copper as I can bring, I'll have thrice the weight in gold. Why, man, all their dripping-pans and their chamber-pots are pure gold, and all the chains with which they chain up their streets are massy gold. All the prisoners they take are fettered in gold. And for rubies and diamonds, they go forth on holidays and gather them by the sea-shore to hang on their children's coats and stick in their caps, as commonly as our children wear saffron gilt brooches and groats with holes in them.

*Scape.* And is it a pleasant country withal?

*Sea.* As ever the sun shined on, temperate and full of all sorts of excellent viands. Wild boar is as common there as our tamest bacon is here, venison as mutton. And then you shall live freely there, without sergeants, or courtiers, or lawyers, or intelligencers,[1] only a few industrious Scots perhaps, who, indeed, are dispersed over the face of the whole earth. But as for them, there are no greater friends to Englishmen and England, when they are out on't, in the world, than they are. And for my part, I would a hundred thousand of them were there, for we are all one countrymen now, you know; and we should find ten times more comfort of them there than we do here. Then, for your means to advancement, there it is simple and not preposterously mixed. You may be an alderman there and never be scavenger. You may be a nobleman and never be a slave. You may come to preferment enough and never be a pander, to riches and fortune enough and have never the more villainy, nor the less wit.

*Spend.* Gods me![2] and how far is it thither?

*Sea.* Some six weeks' sail, no more, with any indifferent good wind. And if I get to any part of the coast of Africa, I'll sail thither with any wind. Or when I come to Cape Finisterre, there's a forthright wind continually wafts us till we come to Virginia. See, our colonel's come.

*Enter Sir Petronel.*

*Petr.* Well met, good Captain Seagull and my noble gentlemen! Now the sweet hour of our freedom is at hand. Come, Drawer, fill us some carouses and prepare us for the mirth that will be occasioned presently.

### 19

# Prudent Advice to Guide Settlers in Establishing Themselves (1606)

In 1607 another attempt was made to settle a colony on the Virginia coast. This expedition, sponsored by the newly formed Virginia Company, included among its members George Percy, Captain Bartholomew Gosnold, Captain Christopher Newport, and Captain John Smith. In preparation for the voyage, Richard Hakluyt drafted a set of instructions for the colonists entitled 'Instructions Given by Way of Advice by Us Whom It Has Pleased the King's Majesty to Appoint of the Council for the Intended Voyage to Virginia, to Be Observed by Those Captains and Company Which Are Sent at This Present to Plant There' (1606). The 'Instructions' were printed in Edward Arber, *Travels and Works of Captain John Smith* (Edinburgh, 1910), I, xxxiii–xxxvii, and included in Taylor, *Original Writings . . . of the Two Richard Hakluyts*, II, 492–6.

As we doubt not but you will have especial care to observe the ordinances set down by the King's Majesty and delivered unto you under the Privy Seal, so for your better directions upon your first landing we have thought good to recommend unto your care these instructions and articles following.

When it shall please God to send you on the coast of Virginia, you shall do your best endeavour to find out a safe port in the entrance of some navigable river, making choice of such a one as runneth farthest into the land. And if you happen to discover divers portable rivers, and amongst them any one that hath two main branches, if the difference be not great, make choice of that which bendeth most toward the north-west, for that way you shall soonest find the other sea.

When you have made choice of the river on which you mean to settle, be not hasty in landing your victuals and munitions, but first let Captain Newport discover how far that river may be found navigable, that you make election of the strongest, most wholesome, and fertile place, for if you make many removes, besides the loss of time, you shall greatly spoil your victuals and your cask and with great pain transport it in small boats.

But if you choose your place so far up as a bark of fifty tons will float, then you may lay all your provisions ashore with ease and the better receive the trade of all the countries about you in the land. Such a place you may perchance find a hundred miles from the river's mouth. The further up the better, for if you sit down near the entrance, except it be in some island that is strong by nature, an enemy that may approach you on even ground may easily pull you out. And if he be driven to seek you a hundred miles [in] the land in boats, you shall from both sides of the river where it is narrowest so beat them with your muskets as they shall never be able to prevail against you.

And to the end that you be not surprised, as the French were in Florida by Ménendez and the Spaniard in the same place by the French, you shall do well to make this double provision. First, erect a little stour[1] at the mouth of the river that may lodge some ten men, with whom you shall leave a light boat, that when any fleet shall be in sight, they may come with speed to give you warning. Secondly, you must in no case suffer any of the native people of the country to inhabit between you and the sea-coast, for you cannot carry yourselves so towards them but they will grow discontented with your habitation and be ready to guide and assist any nation that shall come to invade you. If you neglect this, you neglect your safety.

When you have discovered as far up the river as you mean to plant yourselves and landed your victuals and munitions, to the end that every man may know his charge you shall do well to divide your sixscore men into three parts, whereof one party of them you may appoint to fortify and build, of which your first work must be your storehouse for victuals. The other you may employ in preparing your ground and sowing your corn and roots. The other ten of these forty you must leave as sentinel at the haven's mouth. The other forty you may employ for two months in discovery of the river above you and on the country about you, which charge Captain Newport and Captain Gosnold may undertake of these forty discoverers. When they do espy any highlands or hills, Captain Gosnold may take twenty of the company to cross over the lands, and carrying a half dozen pickaxes to try if they can find any minerals. The other twenty may go on by river and pitch up boughs upon the bank's side, by which the other boats shall follow them by the same turnings. You may also take with them a wherry, such as is used here in the Thames, by which you may send back to the President for supply of munition or any other want, that you may not be driven to return for every small defect.

You must observe if you can whether the river on which you plant doth spring out of mountains or out of lakes. If it be out of any lake, the passage to the other sea will be more easy. And [it] is like enough that out of the same lake you shall find some spring which run[s] the contrary way towards the East India Sea, for the great and famous rivers of Volga, Tanais,[2] and Dvina have three heads near joined, and yet the one falleth into the Caspian Sea, the other into the Euxine[3] Sea, and the third into the Paelonian Sea.[4]

In all your passages you must have great care not to offend the naturals, if you can eschew it, and employ some few of your company to trade with them for corn and all other lasting victuals if you have any. And this you must do before that they perceive you mean to plant among them, for not being sure how your own seed corn will prosper the first year, to avoid the danger of famine, use and endeavour to store yourselves of the country corn.

Your discoverers that pass overland with hired guides must look well to them that they slip not from them, and for more assurance let them take a compass with them and write down how far they go upon every point of the compass, for that country, having no way nor path, if that your guides run from you in the great woods or desert, you shall hardly ever find a passage back.

And how weary soever your soldiers be, let them never trust the country people with the carriage of their weapons, for if they run from you with your shot, which they only fear, they will easily kill them all with their arrows. And whensoever any of yours shoots before them, be sure they may be chosen out of your best marksmen, for if they see your learners miss what they aim at, they will think the weapon not so terrible and thereby will be bold to assault you.

Above all things, do not advertise the killing of any of your men that the country people may know it. If they perceive that they are but common men and that with the loss of many of theirs they diminish any part of yours, they will make many adventures upon you. If the country be populous, you shall do well also not to let them see or know of your sick men, if you have any, which may also encourage them to many enterprises.

You must take especial care that you choose a seat for habitation that shall not be overburdened with woods near your town, for all the men you have shall not be able to cleanse twenty acres a year, besides that it may serve for a covert for your enemies round about.

Neither must you plant in a low or moist place, because it will prove unhealthful. You shall judge of the good air by the people, for some part of that coast where the lands are low have their people blear-eyed and with swollen bellies and legs. But if the naturals be strong and clean-made, it is a sign of a wholesome soil.

You must take order to draw up the pinnace that is left with you under the fort and take her sails and anchors ashore, all but a small kedge[5] to ride by, lest some ill-dispositioned persons slip away with her.

You must take care that your mariners that go for wages do not mar your trade, for those that mind not to inhabit for a little gain will debase the estimation of exchange and hinder the trade for ever after; and therefore you shall not admit or suffer any person whatsoever, other than such as shall be appointed by the President and Council there, to buy any merchandises or other things whatsoever.

It were necessary that all your carpenters and other such-like workmen about building do first build your storehouse and those other rooms of public and necessary use before any house be set up for any private person. And though the workmen may belong to any private persons, yet let them all work together first for the company and then for private men.

And seeing order is at the same price with confusion, it shall be advisably done to set your houses even and by a line that your street may have a good breadth and be carried square about your market place and every street's end opening into it, that from thence, with a few field-pieces, you may command every street throughout, which market place you may also fortify if you think it needful.

You shall do well to send a perfect relation by Captain Newport of all that is done, what height you are seated, how far into the land, what commodities you find, what soil, woods, and their several kinds, and so of all other things else to advertise particularly, and to suffer no man to return but by passport from the President and Council, nor to write any letter of anything that may discourage others.

Lastly and chiefly, the way to prosper and achieve good success is to make yourselves all of one mind for the good of your country and your own, and to serve and fear God, the giver of all goodness, for every plantation which our heavenly father hath not planted shall be rooted out.

20

# Michael Drayton's Ode, 'To the Virginian Voyage' (1606)

This poem, first printed in 1606, has been reprinted many times. It was inspired by the Virginia Company's projected expedition that resulted in the settlement of Jamestown.

> You brave heroic minds
> Worthy your country's name,
> 　　That honour still pursue,
> 　　Go and subdue,
> Whilst loit'ring hinds[1]
> Lurk here at home with shame.
>
> Britons, you stay too long;
> Quickly aboard bestow you,
> 　　And with a merry gale
> 　　Swell your stretched sail,
> With vows as strong
> As the winds that blow you.
>
> Your course securely steer,
> West and by south forth keep,
> 　　Rocks, lee shores, nor shoals,
> 　　When Aeolus scowls,
> You need not fear,
> So absolute the deep.

And cheerfully at sea,
Success you still entice,
   To get the pearl and gold
   And ours to hold,
Virginia,
Earth's only Paradise,

Where nature hath in store
Fowl, venison, and fish,
   And the fruitful'st soil
   Without your toil
Three harvests more,
All greater than your wish.

And the ambitious vine
Crowns with his purple mass
   The cedar reaching high
   To kiss the sky,
The cypress, pine,
And useful sassafras.

To whose the golden age
Still nature's laws doth give,
   No other cares that tend,
   But them to defend
From winter's age,
That long there doth not live.

Whenas the luscious smell
Of that delicious land
   Above the seas that flows,
   The clear wind throws,
Your hearts to swell
Approaching the dear strand,

In kenning of the shore,
Thanks to God first given,
   O you, the happi'st men,
   Be frolic then,
Let cannons roar,
Frighting the wide heaven.

And in regions far
Such heroes bring ye forth
   As those from whom we came,
   And plant our name
Under that star
Not known unto our north.

And as there plenty grows
Of laurel everywhere,
   Apollo's sacred tree,
   You it may see
A poet's brows
To crown, that may sing there.

Thy voyages attend,
Industrious Hakluÿt,
   Whose reading shall enflame
   Men to seek fame,
And much commend
To after times thy wit.

21

# George Percy Gives an Account of Jamestown and the Early Hardships (1607)

George Percy, spendthrift brother of the 'Wizard Earl' of Northumberland, was leader of a faction of 'gentlemen' who in September 1609 deposed Captain John Smith as President of the Council in Virginia. Percy succeeded Smith and later, because of his rank and not because of any demonstrated ability, was named deputy governor pending the arrival of Sir Thomas Dale in 1611. Percy was hostile to Smith and could find nothing good to say about Smith's administration. His 'Observations Gathered out of a Discourse of the Plantation of the Southern Colony in Virginia by the English, 1606, Written by That Honourable Gentleman, Master George Percy', was printed by Purchas, *Pilgrims* (1625), Bk. IX, Ch. 2.

O n Saturday the twentieth of December in the year 1606 the fleet fell from London, and the fifth of January we anchored in The Downs; but the winds continued contrary so long that we were forced to stay there some time, where we suffered great storms, but by the skilfulness of the captain we suffered no great loss or danger. . . .[1]

[The description of the voyage from England to the West Indies and thence to Virginia is omitted.]

The six-and-twentieth day of April, about four o'clock in the morning, we descried the land of Virginia. The same day we entered into the Bay of Chesapeake directly, without any let or hindrance. There we landed and discovered a little way, but we could find nothing worth the speaking of but fair meadows and goodly tall trees, with such fresh waters running through the woods as I was almost ravished at the first sight thereof.

At night, when we were going aboard, there came the savages, creeping upon all four from the hills like bears, with their bows in their mouths, [and] charged us very desperately in the faces, hurt Captain Gabriel Archer in both his hands, and a sailor in two places of the body very dangerous. After they had spent their arrows and felt the sharpness of our shot, they retired into the woods with a great noise and so left us.

The seven-and-twentieth day we began to build up our shallop. The gentlemen and soldiers marched eight miles up into the land. We could not see a savage in all that march. We came to a place where they had made a great fire and had been newly a-roasting oysters. When they perceived our coming, they fled away to the mountains and left many of the oysters in the fire. We eat some of the oysters, which were very large and delicate in taste.

The eighteenth[2] day we launched our shallop. The Captain and some gentlemen went in her and discovered up the bay. We found a river on the south side running into the main. We entered it and found it very shoal water, not for any boats to swim. We went further into the bay and saw a plain plot of ground, where we went on land and found the place five miles in compass, without either bush or tree. We saw nothing there but a canoe, which was made out of the whole tree, which was five-and-forty foot long by the rule. Upon this plot of ground we got good store of mussels and oysters, which lay on the ground as thick as stones; we opened some and found in many of them pearls. We marched some three or four miles further into the woods, where we saw great smokes of fire. We marched to those smokes and found that the savages had been there burning down the grass, as we thought, either to make their plantation there or else to give signs to bring their forces together and so to give us battle. We passed through excellent ground full of flowers of divers kinds and colours and as goodly trees as I have seen, as cedar, cypress, and other kinds. Going a little further, we came into a little plot of ground full of fine and beautiful straw-berries, four times bigger and better than ours in England. All this march we could neither see savage nor town. When it grew to be to-wards night, we stood back to our ships. We sounded and found it shallow water for a great way, which put us out of all hopes for getting any higher with our ships, which rode at the mouth of the river. We rowed over to a point of land, where we found a channel and sounded six, eight, ten, or twelve fathom, which put us in good comfort. Therefore we named that point of land Cape Comfort.[3]

The nine-and-twentieth day we set up a cross at Chesapeake Bay and named that place Cape Henry. [The] thirtieth day we came with our ships to Cape Comfort, where we saw five savages running on the shore. Presently the Captain caused the shallop to be manned; so, row-ing to the shore, the Captain called to them in sign of friendship, but they were at first timorsome until they saw the Captain lay his hand on his heart. Upon that, they laid down their bows and arrows and came very boldly to us, making signs to come ashore to their town, which is called by the savages Kecoughtan.[4] We coasted to their town, rowing over a river running into the main, where these savages swam over with their bows and arrows in their mouths.

When we came over to the other side, there was a many of other savages, which directed us to their town, where we were entertained by them very kindly. When we came first aland, they made a doleful noise, laying their faces to the ground, scratching the earth with their nails. We did think that they had been at their idolatry. When they had ended their ceremonies, they went into their houses and brought out mats and laid upon the ground. The chiefest of them sate all in a rank; the mean-est sort brought us such dainties as they had and of their bread, which they make of their maize or Guinea wheat. They would not suffer us to eat unless we sate down, which we did on a mat right against them. After we were well satisfied, they gave us of their tobacco, which they took in a pipe made artificially of earth, as ours are, but far bigger, with the bowl fashioned together with a piece of fine copper. After they had feasted us, they showed us, in welcome, their manner of dancing, which was in this fashion: one of the savages standing in the midst singing, beating one hand against another, all the rest dancing about him, shouting, howling, and stamping against the ground, with many antic tricks and faces, making noise like so many wolves or devils. One thing of them I observed: when they were in their dance they kept stroke with their feet just one with another, but with their hands, heads, faces, and bodies every one of them had a several gesture; so they continued for the space of half an hour. When they had ended their dance, the Captain gave them beads and other trifling jewels.

They hang through their ears fowls' legs; they shave the right side of their heads with a shell; the left side they wear of an ell long, tied up with an artificial[5] knot, with a many of fowls' feathers sticking in it. They go altogether naked, but their privities are covered with beasts' skins, beset commonly with little bones or beasts' teeth. Some paint their bodies black, some red, with artificial knots of sundry lively colours, very beautiful and pleasing to the eye, in a braver fashion than they in the West Indies.

The fourth of May we came to the king or werowance of Paspahegh, where they entertained us with much welcome. An old savage made a long oration, making a foul noise, uttering his speech with a vehement action, but we knew little what they meant. Whilst we were in company with the Paspaheghs, the werowance of Rappahannock came from the other side of the river[6] in his canoe. He seemed to take displeasure of our being with the Paspaheghs; he would fain have had us come to his town. The Captain was unwilling; seeing that the day was so far spent, he returned back to his ships for that night.

The next day, being the fifth of May, the werowance of Rappahannock sent a messenger to have us come to him. We entertained the said messenger and gave him trifles which pleased him. We manned our shallop with muskets and targeteers sufficiently. This said messenger guided us where our determination was to go. When we landed, the werowance of Rappahannock came down to the waterside with all his train, as goodly men as I have ever seen of savages or Christians, the werowance coming before them playing on a flute made of a reed, with a crown of deer's hair coloured red, in fashion of a rose, fastened about his knot of hair, and a great plate of copper on the other side of his head, with two long feathers in fashion of a pair of horns placed in the midst of his crown. His body was painted all with crimson, with a chain of beads about his neck, his face painted blue, besprinkled with silver ore, as we thought, his ears all behung with bracelets of pearl, and in

M

either ear a bird's claw through it, beset with fine copper or gold. He entertained us in so modest a proud fashion as though he had been a prince of civil government, holding his countenance without laughter or any such ill behaviour. He caused his mat to be spread on the ground, where he sate down with a great majesty, taking a pipe of tobacco, the rest of his company standing about him. After he had rested a while, he rose and made signs to us to come to his town. He went foremost, and all the rest of his people and ourselves followed him up a steep hill, where his palace was settled. We passed through the woods in fine paths, having most pleasant springs which issued from the mountains. We also went through the goodliest corn-fields that ever was seen in any country. When we came to Rappahannock's[7] town, he entertained us in good humanity.

The eighth day of May we discovered up the river. We landed in the country of Appomattox. At our landing there came many stout and able savages to resist us with their bows and arrows in a most warlike manner, with the swords at their backs beset with sharp stones and pieces of iron able to cleave a man in sunder. Amongst the rest, one of the chiefest, standing before them cross-legged, with his arrow ready in his bow in one hand, and taking a pipe of tobacco in the other, with a bold uttering of his speech, demanded of us our being there, willing us to be gone. We made signs of peace, which they perceived in the end and let us land in quietness.

The twelfth day we went back to our ships and discovered a point of land called Archer's Hope, which was sufficient with little labour to defend ourselves against any enemy. The soil was good and fruitful, with excellent good timber. There are also great store of vines in bigness of a man's thigh, running up to the tops of the trees in great abundance. We also did see many squirrels, conies, blackbirds with crimson wings, and divers other fowls and birds of divers and sundry colours, of crimson, watchet,[8] yellow, green, murrey,[9] and of divers other hues naturally, without any art using.

We found store of turkey nests and many eggs. If it had not been disliked, because the ship could not ride near the shore, we had settled there to all the colony's contentment.

The thirteenth day we came to our seating place in Paspahegh's country, some eight miles from the point of land [of] which I made mention before; where our ships do lie so near the shore that they are moored to the trees in six fathom water.

The fourteenth day we landed all our men, which were set to work about the fortification, and othersome to watch and ward as it was convenient. The first night of our landing, about midnight, there came some savages sailing close to our quarter. Presently there was an alarum given; upon that the savages ran away and we [were] not troubled anymore by them that night. Not long after there came two savages that seemed to be commanders, bravely dressed, with crowns of coloured hair upon their heads, which came as messengers from the werowance of Paspahegh, telling us that their werowance was coming and would be merry with us with a fat deer.

The eighteenth day the werowance of Paspahegh came himself to our quarter, with one hundred savages armed, which guarded him in a very warlike manner with bows and arrows, thinking at that time to execute their villainy. Paspahegh made great signs to us to lay our arms away. But we would not trust him so far. He, seeing he could not have convenient time to work his will, at length made signs that he would give us as much land as we would desire to take. As the savages were in a throng in the fort, one of them stole a hatchet from one of our company, which spied him doing the deed; whereupon he took it from him by force and also struck him over the arm. Presently another savage, seeing that, came fiercely at our man with a wooden sword, thinking to beat out his brains. The werowance of Paspahegh saw us take to our arms [and] went suddenly away with all his company in great anger.

The nineteenth day myself and three or four more walking into the woods by chance, we espied a pathway like to an Irish pace.[10] We were desirous to know whither it would bring us; we traced some four miles, all the way as we went having the pleasantest suckles, the ground all flowing over with fair flowers of sundry colours and kinds, as though it had been in any garden or orchard in England. There be many strawberries and other fruits unknown. We saw the woods full of cedar and cypress trees, with other trees which issues out sweet gums like to balsam. We kept on our way in this Paradise; at length we came to a savage town, where we found but few people. They told us the rest were gone a-hunting with the werowance of Paspahegh. We stayed there a while and had of them strawberries and other things. In the mean time, one of the savages came running out of his house with a bow and arrows and ran mainly[11] through the woods. Then I began to mistrust some villainy, that he went to call some company and so betray us. We made all the haste away we could. One of the savages brought us on the way to the woodside, where there was a garden of tobacco and other fruits and herbs; he gathered tobacco and distributed to every one of us; so we departed.

The twentieth day the werowance of Paspahegh sent forty of his men with a deer to our quarter; but they came more in villainy than any love they bare us. They fain would have lain in fort all night, but we would not suffer them for fear of their treachery. One of our gentlemen having a target which he trusted in, thinking it would bear out a slight shot, he set it up against a tree, willing one of the savages to shoot, who took from his back an arrow of an ell long, drew it strongly in his bow, shoots the target a foot through or better; which was strange, being that a pistol could not pierce it. We, seeing the force of his bow, afterwards set him up a steel target. He shot again and burst his arrow all to pieces. He presently pulled out another arrow and bit it in his teeth and seemed to be in a great rage; so he went away in great anger. Their bows are made of tough hazel, their strings of leather, their arrows of canes or hazel, headed with very sharp stones, and are made artificially like a broad arrow; othersome of their arrows are headed with the ends of deers' horns and are feathered very artificially. Paspahegh was as good as his word, for he sent venison, but the sauce came within few days after.

At Port Cottage, in our voyage up the river,[12] we saw a savage boy about the age of ten years, which had a head of hair of a perfect yellow and a reasonable white skin, which is a miracle amongst all savages.

This river which we have discovered is one of the famousest rivers that ever was found by any Christian; it ebbs and flows a hundred and threescore miles, where ships of great burden may harbour in safety. Wheresoever we landed upon this river we saw the goodliest woods, as beech, oak, cedar, cypress, walnuts, sassafras, and vines in great abundance, which hang in great clusters on many trees, and other trees unknown; and all the grounds bespread with many sweet and delicate flowers of divers colours and kinds. There are also many fruits, as strawberries, mulberries, raspberries, and fruits unknown. There are many branches of this river, which run flowing through the woods with great plenty of fish of all kinds; as for sturgeon, all the world cannot be compared to it. In this country I have seen many great and large meadows, having excellent good pasture for any cattle. There is also great store of deer both red and fallow. There are bears, foxes, otters, beavers, musk-cats, and wild beasts unknown.

The four-and-twentieth day we set up a cross at the head of this river, naming it King's River, where we proclaimed James, King of

England, to have the most right unto it. When we had finished and set up our cross, we shipped our men and made for James Fort. By the way we came to Powhatan's town, where the Captain went on shore, suffering none to go with him. He presented the commander of this place with a hatchet, which he took joyfully and was well pleased.

But yet the savages murmured at our planting in the country, whereupon this werowance made answer again very wisely of a savage, 'Why should you be offended with them, as long as they hurt you not nor take anything away by force. They take but a little waste ground which doth you nor any of us any good.'

I saw bread made by their women, which do all their drudgery. The men takes their pleasure in hunting and their wars, which they are in continually, one kingdom against another. The manner of baking of bread is thus: after they pound their wheat into flour with hot water, they make it into paste and work it into round balls and cakes; then they put it into a pot of seething water; when it is sod thoroughly, they lay it on a smooth stone; there they harden it as well as in an oven.

There is notice to be taken to know married women from maids. The maids you shall always see the forepart of their head and sides shaven close, the hinder part very long, which they tie in a plait hanging down to their hips. The married women wears their hair all of a length and is tied of that fashion that the maids are. The womenkind in this country doth pounce and race[13] their bodies, legs, thighs, arms, and faces with a sharp iron, which makes a stamp in curious knots, and draws the proportion of fowls, fish, or beasts; then with paintings of sundry lively colours they rub it into the stamp, which will never be taken away, because it is dried into the flesh where it is seared.

The savages bear their years well, for when we were at Pamunkey's we saw a savage by their report was above eightscore years of age. His eyes were sunk into his head, having never a tooth in his mouth; his hair all grey, with a reasonable big beard, which was as white as any snow. It is a miracle to see a savage have any hair on their faces; I never saw, read, nor heard any have the like before. This savage was as lusty and went as fast as any of us, which was strange to behold.

The fifteenth day of June we had built and finished our fort, which was triangle-wise, having three bulwarks at every corner, like a half-moon, and four or five pieces of artillery mounted in them. We had made ourselves sufficiently strong for these savages. We had also sown most of our corn on two mountains; it sprang a man's height from the ground. This country is a fruitful soil, bearing many goodly and fruitful trees, as mulberries, cherries, walnuts, cedars, cypress, sassafras, and vines in great abundance.

Monday the two-and-twentieth of June in the morning, Captain Newport in the admiral departed from James Fort for England.

Captain Newport being gone for England, leaving us (104 persons) very bare and scanty of victuals, furthermore in wars and in danger of the savages, we hoped after a supply, which Captain Newport promised within twenty weeks. But if the beginners of this action do carefully further us, the country being so fruitful, it would be as great a profit to the realm of England as the Indies to the King of Spain. If this river which we have found had been discovered in the time of war with Spain, it would have been a commodity to our realm and a great annoyance to our enemies.

The seven-and-twentieth of July the king of Rappahannock demanded a canoe, which was restored, lifted up his hand to the sun, which they worship as their god, besides he laid his hand on his heart, that he would be our special friend. It is a general rule of these people, when they swear by their god, which is the sun; no Christian will keep their oath better upon this promise. These people have a great reverence to the sun above all other things. At the rising and setting of the same they sit down, lifting up their hands and eyes to the sun, making a round circle on the ground with dried tobacco; then they began to pray, making many devilish gestures, with a hellish noise, foaming at the mouth, staring with their eyes, wagging their heads and hands in such a fashion and deformity as it was monstrous to behold. . . .

The two-and-twentieth day of August there died Captain Bartholomew Gosnold, one of our Council; he was honourably buried, having all the ordnance in the fort shot off, with many volleys of small shot.

After Captain Gosnold's death the Council could hardly agree, by the dissension of Captain Kendall, which afterward was committed about heinous matters which was proved against him. . . .

Our men were destroyed with cruel diseases, as swellings, fluxes, burning fevers, and by wars, and some departed suddenly, but for the most part they died of mere famine. There were never Englishmen left in a foreign country in such misery as we were in this new-discovered Virginia. We watched every three nights, lying on the bare, cold ground, what weather soever came, [and] warded all the next day, which brought our men to be most feeble wretches. Our food was but a small can of barley sod in water to five men a day; our drink cold water taken out of the river, which was at a flood very salt, at a low tide full of slime and filth, which was the destruction of many of our men. Thus we lived for the space of five months in this miserable distress, not having five able men to man our bulwarks upon any occasion. If it had not pleased God to have put a terror in the savages' hearts, we had all perished by those vile and cruel pagans, being in that weak estate as we were, our men night and day groaning in every corner of the fort most pitiful to hear. If there were any conscience in men, it would make their hearts to bleed to hear the pitiful murmurings and outcries of our sick men, without relief every night and day for the space of six weeks, some departing out of the world, many times three or four in a night, in the morning their bodies trailed out of their cabins like dogs to be buried: in this sort did I see the mortality of divers of our people.

It pleased God after a while to send those people which were our mortal enemies to relieve us with victuals, as bread, corn, fish, and flesh in great plenty, which was the setting-up of our feeble men, otherwise we had all perished. Also we were frequented by divers kings in the country, bringing us store of provision, to our great comfort. . . .

22

# Captain John Smith's Explorations and Troubles with the Indians (1607)

Captain John Smith, one of the leaders in the first colony at Jamestown, was a colourful and controversial figure. His own accounts of his adventures in Virginia were regarded by nineteenth-century critics as gross exaggerations, but more recent scholarship gives Smith a higher place among the early reporters on Virginian affairs. The following excerpts are from his *General History of Virginia* (1624). The Second Book of the *General History* describes the terrain of Virginia and relates some of Smith's explorations up the Virginia rivers. Much of the geographical detail is omitted. The Third Book also relates some of Smith's own observations. A new book by Philip L. Barbour, *The Three Worlds of Captain John Smith* (Boston, 1964), provides a definitive discussion of Smith and his works.

THE SECOND BOOK. [Chapter One]

. . . THE mountains are of divers natures: for at the head of the bay the rocks are of a composition like millstones; some of marble, etc.; and many pieces like crystal we found, as thrown down by water from those mountains. For in winter they are covered with much snow, and when it dissolveth the waters fall with such violence that it causeth great inundations in some narrow valleys, which is scarce perceived being once in the rivers. These waters wash from the rocks such glistering tinctures that the ground in some places seemeth as gilded, where both the rocks and the earth are so splendent to behold that better judgements than ours might have been persuaded they contained more than probabilities. The vesture of the earth in most places doth manifestly prove the nature of the soil to be lusty and very rich. The colour of the earth we found in divers places resembleth bole armeniac, *terra sigillata* and *lemnia*, fuller's earth, marl, and divers other such appearances. But generally for the most part it is a black sandy mould, in some places a fat slimy clay, in other places a very barren gravel. But the best ground is known by the vesture it beareth, as by the greatness of trees, or abundance of weeds, etc.

The country is not mountainous, nor yet low, but such pleasant plain hills and fertile valleys, one prettily crossing another, and watered so conveniently with fresh brooks and springs, no less commodious than delightsome. By the rivers are many plain marishes, containing some twenty, some a hundred, some two hundred acres, some more, some less. Other plains there are few, but only where the savages inhabit, but all overgrown with trees and weeds, being a plain wilderness as God first made it. On the west side of the bay we said were five fair and delightful navigable rivers. . . .

Thirty leagues northward is a river[1] not inhabited, yet navigable; for the red clay resembling bole armeniac we called it Bolus. At the end of the bay, where it is six or seven miles in breadth, it divides itself into four branches. The best cometh north-west from among the mountains; but, though canoes may go a day's journey or two up it, we could not get two miles up it with our boat for rocks. Upon it is seated the Susquehannas. Near it north and by west runneth a creek a mile and a half, at the head whereof the ebb left us on shore, where we found many trees cut with hatchets. The next tide, keeping the shore to seek for some savages (for within thirty leagues' sailing we saw not any, being a barren country), we went up another small river like a creek six or seven mile. From thence returning we met seven canoes of the Massawomecks,[2] with whom we had conference by signs, for we understood one another scarce a word. The next day we discovered the small river and people of Tockwhogh,[3] trending eastward.

Having lost our grapnel among the rocks of Susquehanna, we were then near two hundred miles from home and our barge about two tons, and had in it but twelve men to perform this discovery, wherein we lay above twelve weeks upon those great waters in those unknown countries, having nothing but a little meal, oatmeal, and water to feed us, and scarce half sufficient of that for half that time but what provision we got among the savages and such roots and fish as we caught by accident and God's direction; nor had we a mariner nor any had skill to trim the sails but two sailors and myself, the rest being gentlemen or them were as ignorant in such toil and labour. Yet necessity in a short time by good words and examples made them do that that caused them ever after to fear no colours.[4] What I did with this small means I leave to the reader to judge, and the map I made of the country, which is but a small matter in regard of the magnitude thereof.

But to proceed, sixty of those Susquehannas came to us with skins, bows, arrows, targets, beads, swords, and tobacco pipes for presents. Such great and well-proportioned men are seldom seen, for they seemed like giants to the English, yea and to the neighbours, yet seemed of an honest and simple disposition, with much ado restrained from adoring us as gods. Those are the strangest people of all those countries, both in language and attire. For their language it may well beseem their proportions, sounding from them as a voice in a vault. Their attire is the skins of bears and wolves; some have cassocks made of bears' heads and skins that a man's head goes through the skin's neck and the ears of the bear fastened to his shoulders, the nose and teeth hanging down his breast, another bear's face split behind them, and at the end of the nose hung a paw; the half sleeves coming to the elbows were the necks of bears and the arms through the mouth, with paws hanging at their noses. One had the head of a wolf hanging in a chain for a jewel, his tobacco pipe three quarters of a yard long, prettily carved with a bird, a deer, or some such device at the great end, sufficient to beat out one's brains; with bows, arrows, and clubs suitable to their greatness.

These are scarce known to Powhatan. They can make near six hundred able men and are palisadoed in their towns to defend them from the Massawomecks, their mortal enemies. Five of their chief werowances came aboard us and crossed the bay in the barge. The picture of the greatest of them is signified in the map, the calf of whose leg was three quarters of a yard about, and all the rest of his limbs so answerable to that proportion that he seemed the goodliest man we ever beheld. His hair the one side was long, the other shorn close with a ridge over his crown like a cock's-comb. His arrows were five quarters long, headed with the splinters of a white crystal-like stone, in form of a heart, an inch broad and an inch and a half or more long. These he wore in a wolf's skin at his back for his quiver, his bow in the one hand and his club in the other, as is described. . . .

Southward we went to some parts of Chawonock and the Mangoags to search for them left by Master White.

Amongst those people are thus many several nations of sundry languages that environ Powhatan's territories. The Chawonockes, the Mangoags, the Monacans, the Manahoacs, the Massawomecks, the Powhatans, the Susquehannas, the Atquanachukes, the Tockwoghs, and the Kuskarawoaks. All those not any one understandeth another but by interpreters. Their several habitations are more plainly described by this annexed map, which will present to the eye the way of the mountains and current of the rivers, with their several turnings, bays, shoals, isles, inlets, and creeks, the breadth of the waters, the distances of places, and such-like. In which map observe this, that as far as you see the little crosses on rivers, mountains, or other places have been discovered; the rest was had by information of the savages and are set down according to their instructions.

> Thus have I walkt a wayless way with uncouth pace,[5]
> Which yet no Christian man did ever trace:
> But yet I know this not affects the mind,
> Which ears doth hear, as that which eyes do find. . . .

John Smith writ this with his own hand. . . .

### THE THIRD BOOK. [Chapter Two]

. . . And now, the winter approaching, the rivers became so covered with swans, geese, ducks, and cranes that we daily feasted with good bread, Virginia peas, pompions, and putchamins,[6] fish, fowl, and divers sorts of wild beasts, as far as we could eat them: so that none of our tuftaffeta humorists[7] desired to go for England. But our comedies never endured long without a tragedy. Some idle exceptions being muttered against Captain Smith for not discovering the head of Chickahominy River, and taxed by the Council to be too slow in so worthy an attempt, the next voyage he proceeded so far that, with much labour by cutting of trees in sunder, he made his passage. But when his barge could pass no farther he left her in a broad bay out of danger of shot, commanding none should go ashore till his return. Himself with two English and two savages went up higher in a canoe, but he was not long absent.

But his men went ashore, whose want of government gave both occasion and opportunity to the savages to surprise one George Cassen, whom they slew, and much failed not[8] to have cut off the boat and all the rest. Smith, little dreaming of that accident, being got to the marshes at the river's head twenty miles in the desert, had his two men slain (as is supposed) sleeping by the canoe whilst himself by fowling sought them victual; who, finding he was beset with two hundred savages, two of them he slew, still defending himself with the aid of a savage his guide, whom he bound to his arm with his garters and used him as a buckler,[9] yet he was shot in his thigh a little and had many arrows that stuck in his clothes but no great hurt, till at last they took him prisoner.

When this news came to Jamestown, much was their sorrow for his loss, few expecting what ensued. Six or seven weeks those barbarians kept him prisoner; many strange triumphs and conjurations they made of him, yet he so demeaned[10] himself amongst them as he not only diverted them from surprising the fort but procured his own liberty and got himself and his company such estimation amongst them that those savages admired him more than their own quiyouckosucks.[11] The manner how they used and delivered him is as followeth.

The savages, having drawn from George Cassen whither Captain Smith was gone, prosecuting that opportunity, they followed him with three hundred bowmen conducted by the king of Pamunkey, who in divisions searching the turnings of the river found Robinson and Emry by the fire-side; those they shot full of arrows and slew. Then, finding the captain, as is said, that used the savage that was his guide as his shield (three of them being slain and divers other so galled), all the rest would not come near him. Thinking thus to have returned to his boat, regarding them as he marched more than his way, [he] slipped up to the middle in an oozy creek and his savage with him; yet durst they not come to him till, being near dead with cold, he threw away his arms.

Then according to their composition they drew him forth and led him to the fire where his men were, slain. Diligently they chafed his benumbed limbs. He demanding for their captain, they showed him Opechancanough,[12] king of Pamunkey, to whom he gave a round ivory double compass dial. Much they marvelled at the playing of the fly and needle, which they could see so plainly and yet not touch it, because of the glass that covered them. But when he demonstrated by that globe-like jewel the roundness of the earth and skies, the sphere of the sun, moon, and stars, and how the sun did chase the night round about the world continually, the greatness of the land and sea, the diversity of nations, variety of complexions, and how we were to them antipodes, and many other such-like matters, they all stood as amazed with admiration. Notwithstanding, within an hour after they tied him to a tree and as many as could stand about him prepared to shoot him; but the king holding up the compass in hand, they all laid down their bows and arrows and in a triumphant manner led him to Orapaks,[13] where he was after their manner kindly feasted and well used.

Their order in conducting him was thus: drawing themselves all in file, the king in the midst had all their pieces[14] and swords borne before him. Captain Smith was led after him by three great savages, holding him fast by each arm, and on each side six went in file with their arrows nocked. But, arriving at the town (which was but only thirty or forty hunting-houses made of mats, which they remove as they please, as we our tents), all the women and children staring to behold him, the soldiers first all in file performed the form of a besom[15] so well as could be, and on each flank officers as sergeants to see them keep their orders. A good time they continued this exercise and then cast them-selves in a ring, dancing in such several postures and singing and yelling out such hellish notes and screeches; being strangely painted, every one his quiver of arrows and at his back a club; on his arm a fox or an otter's skin, or some such matter for his vambrace;[16] their heads and shoulders painted red, with oil and puccoon[17] mingled together, which scarlet-like colour made an exceeding handsome show; his bow in his hand, and the skin of a bird, with her wings abroad, dried, tied on his head, a piece of copper, a white shell, a long feather, with a small rattle growing at the tails of their snakes tied to it, or some such-like toy. All this while Smith and the king stood in the midst guarded, as before is said, and after three dances they all departed.

Smith they conducted to a long house, where thirty or forty tall fellows did guard him, and ere long more bread and venison was brought him than would have served twenty men; I think his stomach at that time was not very good. What he left they put in baskets and tied over his head. About midnight they set the meat again before him. All this time not one of them would eat a bit with him, till the next morning they brought him as much more, and then did they eat all the old and reserved the new as they had done the other, which made him think they would fat him to eat him. Yet in this desperate estate, to defend him from the cold, one Maocassater brought him his gown in requital of some beads and toys Smith had given him at his first arrival in Virginia.

Two days after, a man would have slain him (but that the guard prevented it) for the death of his son, to whom they conducted him to recover the poor man, then breathing his last. Smith told them that at Jamestown he had a water would do it if they would let him fetch it; but they would not permit that but made all the preparations they could to assault Jamestown, craving his advice, and for recompense he should have life, liberty, land, and women. In part of a table-book he writ his mind to them at the fort, what was intended, how they should follow that direction to affright the messengers, and without fail send him such things as he writ for, and an inventory with them. The difficulty and danger he told the savages of the mines, great guns, and other engines exceedingly affrighted them; yet according to his request they went to Jamestown, in as bitter weather as could be of frost and snow, and within three days returned with an answer.

But when they came to Jamestown, seeing men sally out as he had told them they would, they fled; yet in the night they came again to the same place where he had told them they should receive an answer and such things as he had promised them, which they found accordingly and with which they returned with no small expedition, to the wonder of them all that heard it, that he could either divine or the paper could speak. Then they led him to the Youghtanunds, the Mattapanients, the Payankatanks, the Nantaughtacunds, and Onawmanients upon the rivers of Rapphannock and Potomac, over all those rivers and back again by divers other several nations to the king's habitation at Pamunkey, where they entertained him with most strange and fearful conjurations;

> As if near led to hell,
> Amongst the devils to dwell.

Not long after, early in a morning, a great fire was made in a long house and a mat spread on the one side, as on the other. On the one they caused him to sit, and all the guard went out of the house, and presently came skipping in a great grim fellow, all painted over with coal mingled with oil; and many snakes and weasels' skins stuffed with moss and all their tails tied together, so as they met on the crown of his head in a tassel; and round about the tassel was as a coronet of feathers, the skins hanging round about his head, back, and shoulders, and in a manner covered his face. With a hellish voice and a rattle in his hand, with most strange gestures and passions, he began his invocation and environed the fire with a circle of meal; which done, three more such-like devils came rushing in with the like antic tricks, painted half black, half red, but all their eyes were painted white and some red strokes like mustachios along their cheeks.

Round about him those fiends danced a pretty while, and then came in three more as ugly as the rest, with red eyes and white strokes over their black faces; at last they all sat down right against him, three of them on the one hand of the chief priest and three on the other. Then all with their rattles began a song, which ended, the chief priest laid down five wheat corns, then, straining his arms and hands with such violence that he sweat and his veins swelled, he began a short oration. At the conclusion they all gave a short groan and then laid down three grains more. After that began their song again and then another oration, ever laying down so many corns as before, till they had twice encircled the fire. That done, they took a bunch of little sticks prepared for that purpose, continuing still their devotion, and at the end of every song and oration they laid down a stick betwixt the divisions of corn. Till night, neither he nor they did either eat or drink, and then they feasted merrily, with the best provisions they could make. Three days they used this ceremony, the meaning whereof they told him was to know if he intended them well or no. The circle of meal signified their country, the circles of corn the bounds of the sea, and the sticks his country. They imagined the world to be flat and round, like a trencher, and they in the midst. After this they brought him a bag of gunpowder, which they carefully preserved till the next spring to plant as they did their corn, because they would be acquainted with the nature of that seed.

Opitchapam, the king's brother, invited him to his house, where, with as many platters of bread, fowl, and wild beasts as did environ him, he bid him welcome; but not any of them would eat a bit with him but put up all the remainder in baskets. At his return to Opechancanough's, all the king's women and their children flocked about him for their parts, as a due by custom to be merry with such fragments.

But his waking mind in hideous dreams did oft see wondrous shapes, Of bodies strange, and huge in growth, and of stupendous makes.

At last they brought him to Meronocomo,[18] where was Powhatan their emperor. Here more than two hundred of those grim courtiers stood wondering at him, as he had been a monster, till Powhatan and his train had put themselves in their greatest braveries. Before a fire, upon a seat like a bedstead, he sat covered with a great robe, made of raccoon skins and all the tails hanging by. On either hand did sit a young wench of sixteen or eighteen years, and along on each side the house two rows of men, and behind them as many women, with all their heads and shoulders painted red; many of their heads bedecked with the white down of birds, but every one with something, and a great chain of white beads about their necks.

At his entrance before the king, all the people gave a great shout. The queen of Appomattox was appointed to bring him water to wash his hands, and another brought him a bunch of feathers, instead of a towel, to dry them. Having feasted him after their best barbarous manner they could, a long consultation was held, but the conclusion was, two great stones were brought before Powhatan.

Then as many as could laid hands on him, dragged him to them and thereon laid his head, and being ready with their clubs to beat out his brains, Pocahontas, the king's dearest daughter, when no entreaty could prevail, got his head in her arms and laid her own upon his to save him from death. Whereat the emperor was contented he should live to make him hatchets and her bells, beads, and copper; for they thought him as well of all occupations as themselves. For the king himself will make his own robes, shoes, bows, arrows, pots; plant, hunt, or do anything so well as the rest.

> They say he bore a pleasant show,
> But sure his heart was sad.
> For who can pleasant be, and rest,
> That lives in fear and dread:
> And, having life suspected,[19] doth
> It still suspected lead.

Two days after, Powhatan, having disguised himself in the most fearful manner he could, caused Captain Smith to be brought forth to a great house in the woods and there upon a mat by the fire to be left alone. Not long after, from behind a mat that divided the house, was made the most dolefullest noise he ever heard; then Powhatan, more like a devil than a man, with some two hundred more as black as himself, came unto him and told him how they were friends and presently he should go to Jamestown to send him two great guns and a grindstone, for which he would give him the country of Capahowosick and for ever esteem him as his son, Nantaquoud.

So, to Jamestown with twelve guides Powhatan sent him. That night they quartered in the woods, he still expecting (as he had done all this long time of his imprisonment) every hour to be put to one death or other, for all their feasting. But Almighty God (by His divine providence) had mollified the hearts of those stern barbarians with compassion.

The next morning betimes they came to the fort, where Smith, having used the savages with what kindness he could, he showed Rawhunt, Powhatan's trusty servant, two demi-culverins[20] and a mill-stone to carry Powhatan. They found them somewhat too heavy; but when they did see him discharge them, being loaded with stones, among the boughs of a great tree loaded with icicles, the ice and branches came so tumbling down that the poor savages ran away half dead with fear. But at last we regained some conference with them and gave them such toys and sent to Powhatan, his women and children, such presents as gave them in general full content.

Now in Jamestown they were all in combustion, the strongest pre-paring once more to run away with the pinnace, which with the hazard of his life with saker,[21] falcon,[22] and musket shot Smith forced now the third time to stay or sink. Some no better than they should be had plotted with the President the next day to have put him to death by the Levitical law for the lives of Robinson and Emry, pretending the fault was his that had led them to their ends. But he quickly took such order with such lawyers that he laid them by the heels till he sent some of them prisoners for England.

Now, ever once in four or five days, Pocahontas with her attendants brought him so much provision that saved many of their lives that else for all this had starved with hunger.

Thus from numb death our good God sent relief,
The sweet assuager of all other grief.

His relation of the plenty he had seen, especially at Werowocomoco, and of the state and bounty of Powhatan (which till that time was un-known), so revived their dead spirits (especially the love of Pocahontas) as all men's fear was abandoned. Thus you may see what difficulties still crossed any good endeavour, and the good success of the business being thus oft brought to the very period of destruction, yet you see by what strange means God hath still delivered it.

As for the insufficiency of them admitted in commission, that error could not be prevented by the electors, there being no other choice and all strangers to each other's education, qualities, or disposition. And if any deem it a shame to our nation to have any mention made of those enormities, let them peruse the histories of the Spaniards' discoveries and plantations, where they may see how many mutinies, disorders, and dissensions have accompanied them and crossed their attempts; which, being known to be particular men's offences, doth take away the general scorn and contempt which malice, presumption, covetousness, or ignorance might produce, to the scandal and reproach of those whose actions and valiant resolutions deserve a more worthy respect.

Now whether it had been better for Captain Smith to have concluded with any of those several projects: to have abandoned the country with some ten or twelve of them who were called the better sort and have left Master Hunt our preacher, Master Anthony Gosnold, a most honest, worthy, and industrious gentleman, Master Thomas Wotton, and some twenty-seven others of his countrymen, to the fury of the savages, famine, and all manner of mischiefs and inconveniences (for they were but forty in all to keep possession of this large country); or starve himself with them for company, for want of lodging; or but adventuring abroad to make them provision; or by his opposition to preserve the action and save all their lives; I leave to the censure of all honest men to consider. But

> We men imagine in our jollity
> That 'tis all one or good or bad to be.
> But then anon we alter this again,
> If happily we feel the sense of pain;
> For then we're turn'd into a mourning vein.

Written by Thomas Studley, the first cape-merchant[23] in Virginia, Robert Fenton, Edward Harrington, and J. S.

## 23

# Captain Newport Reports Gold and Copper in Virginia (1607)

Captain Christopher Newport commanded the expedition of three ships that brought the first settlers to Jamestown. He was a veteran explorer and sea-captain, and, like many of his contemporaries, he was convinced that the English would find sources of gold to equal the rich hoards that the Spaniards had found. Below is a 'Copy of a Letter to the Earl of Salisbury from Captain

Newport, the 29th of July, 1607', from a manuscript at Alnwick Castle, printed by Alexander Brown, *The Genesis of the United States* (Boston, 1890), I, 105–6.

Right Honourable:

My very good lord, my duty in most humble wise remembered, it may please Your good Lordship, I arrived here in the sound of Plymouth this day from the discovery of that part of Virginia imposed upon me and the rest of the colony for the south part, in which we have performed our duties to the uttermost of our powers and have discovered into the country near 250 miles. The country is excellent and very rich in gold and copper. Of the gold we have brought a say[1] and hope to be with Your Lordship shortly to show it His Majesty and the rest of the Lords.

I will not deliver the expectance and assurance we have of great wealth but will leave it to Your Lordship's censure when you see the probabilities. I wish I might have come in person to have brought these glad tidings, but my inability of body and the not having any man to put in trust the ship and that in her makes me to defer my coming till wind and weather be favourable.

And so I most humbly take my leave.

From Plymouth this twenty-ninth of July, 1607,

Your Lordship's most humbly bounden,

Christopher Newport.

24

# Captain Newport, with Some Difficulty, Crowns Powhatan (1608)

From John Smith, *A Map of Virginia . . . Whereunto Is Annexed the Proceedings of Those Colonies* (1612). Reprinted by Edward Arber, *The Travels and Works of Captain John Smith*, I, 121–5. In September 1608, Captain John Smith was chosen 'President' of the infant colony at Jamestown. Captain Christopher Newport returned to Virginia with instructions to bring back a lump of gold, a certainty of having discovered the South Sea, or one of the members of Raleigh's 'Lost Colony'. The narrative, written by some of the participants, revised by William Symonds, and published by T. Abbay, continues.

How or why Captain Newport obtained such a private commission as not to return without a lump of gold, a certainty of the South Sea, or one of the lost company of Sir Walter Raleigh, I know not; nor why he brought such a five-pieced barge[1] not to bear us to that South Sea till we had borne her over the mountains (which how far they extend is yet unknown). As for the coronation of Powhatan and his presents of basin, ewer, bed, clothes, and such costly novelties, they had been much better well spared than so ill spent; for we had his favour much better only for a poor piece of copper till this stately kind of soliciting made him so much overvalue himself that he respected us as much as nothing at all.

As for the hiring of the Poles and Dutch to make pitch and tar, glass, mills, and soap-ashes, [that] was most necessary and well. But to send them and seventy more without victual to work was not so well considered; yet this could not have hurt us had they been two hundred, though then we were 130 that wanted for ourselves. For we had the savages in that decorum (their harvest being newly gathered) that we feared not to get victual sufficient had we been five hundred.

Now was there no way to make us miserable but to neglect that time to make our provision whilst it was to be had; the which was done to perform this strange discovery, but more strange coronation. To lose that time, spend that victual we had, tire and starve our men, having no means to carry victual, munition, the hurt or sick, but their own backs: how or by whom they were invented I know not.

But Captain Newport we only accounted the author, who to effect these projects had so gilded all our hopes with great promises that both company and Council concluded his resolution. I confess, we little understood then our estates, to conclude his conclusion[2] against all the inconveniences the foreseeing President alleged. There was added to the Council one Captain Waldo and Captain Wynne, two ancient soldiers and valiant gentlemen but ignorant of the business, being newly arrived. Ratcliffe was also permitted to have his voice; and Master Scrivener [was] desirous to see strange countries. So that although Smith was President, yet the Council had the authority and ruled it as they listed.

As for clearing Smith's objections how pitch and tar, wainscot, clapboard, glass, and soap-ashes could be provided to re-lade the ship, or provision got to live withal when none was in the country and that which we had spent before the ships departed, the answer was Captain Newport undertook to fraught the pinnace with corn in going and returning in his discovery, and to re-fraught her again from Werowocomoco, also promising a great proportion of victual from his ship, inferring that Smith's propositions were only devices to hinder his journey, to effect it himself, and that the cruelty Smith had used to the savages in his absence might occasion them to hinder his designs. For which all works were left and 120 chosen men were appointed for his guard.

And Smith, to make clear these seeming suspicions that the savages were not so desperate as was pretended by Captain Newport and how willing he was to further them to effect their projects, because the coronation would consume much time, undertook their message to Powhatan (to entreat him to come to Jamestown to receive his presents) accompanied only with Captain Waldo, Master Andrew Buckler, Edward Brinton, and Samuel Collier.

With these four he went overland against Werowocomoco, there passed the river of Pamunkey in the savages' canoes, Powhatan being thirty miles off, who presently was sent for. In the mean time, his women entertained Smith in this manner.

In a fair, plain field they made a fire, before which, he sitting on a mat, suddenly amongst the woods was heard such a hideous noise and shrieking that they betook them to their arms, supposing Powhatan with all his power came to surprise them; but the beholders, which were many, men, women, and children, satisfied the Captain there was no such matter, being presently presented with this antic.

Thirty young women came naked out of the woods (only covered behind and before with a few green leaves), their bodies all painted, some white, some red, some black, some parti-colour, but every one different. Their leader had a fair pair of stags' horns on her head and an otter skin at her girdle, another at her arm, a quiver of arrows at her back, and bow and arrows in her hand. The next, in her hand a sword; another a club; another a pot-stick: all horned alike. The rest every one with their several devices.

These fiends, with most hellish cries and shouts, rushing from amongst the trees, cast themselves in a ring about the fire, singing and dancing with excellent ill variety, oft falling into their infernal passions and then solemnly again to sing and dance. Having spent near an hour in this masquerade, as they entered [they] in manner departed.

Having re-accommodated themselves, they solemnly invited Smith to their lodging; but no sooner was he within the house but all these nymphs more tormented him than ever with crowding and pressing and hanging upon him, most tediously crying, 'Love you not me?'

This salutation ended, the feast was set, consisting of fruit in baskets, fish and flesh in wooden platters; beans and peas there wanted not (for twenty hogs) nor any savage dainty their invention could devise; some attending, others singing and dancing about them.

This mirth and banquet being ended, with firebrands (instead of torches) they conducted him to his lodging.

The next day came Powhatan. Smith delivered his message of the presents sent him and re-delivered him Namontack,[3] desiring him come to his Father Newport to accept those presents and conclude their revenge against the Monacans.

Whereunto the subtle savage thus replied:

If your king have sent me presents, I also am a king and this [is] my land. Eight days I will stay to receive them. Your father is to come to me, not I to him, nor yet to your fort; neither will I bite at such a bait. As for the Monacans, I can revenge my own injuries; and as for Atquanachuck, where you say your brother was slain, it is a contrary way from those parts you suppose it. But for any salt water beyond the mountains, the relations you have had from my people are false.

Whereupon he began to draw plots upon the ground, according to his discourse, of all those regions.

Many other discourses they had (yet both desirous to give each other content in complimental courtesies), and so Captain Smith returned with this answer.

Upon this, Captain Newport sent his presents by water, which is near a hundred miles; with fifty of the best shot himself went by land, which is but twelve miles; where he met with our three barges to transport him over.

All things being fit for the day of his coronation, the presents were brought, his basin, ewer, bed, and furniture set up, his scarlet cloak and apparel (with much ado) put on him (being persuaded by Namontack they would do him no hurt). But a foul trouble there was to make him kneel to receive his crown. He, neither knowing the majesty nor meaning of a crown, nor bending of the knee, endured so many persuasions, examples, and instructions as tired them all. At last, by leaning hard on his shoulders, he a little stooped, and Newport put the crown on his head, when, by the warning of a pistol, the boats were prepared with such a volley of shot that the king start up in a horrible fear, till he saw all was well; then, remembering himself to congratulate[4] their kindness, he gave his old shoes and his mantle[5] to Captain Newport.

But, perceiving his purpose was to discover the Monacans, he laboured to divert his resolution, refusing to lend him either men or guides more than Namontack. And so, after some complimental kindness on both sides, in requital of his presents, he presented Newport with a heap of wheat ears that might contain seven or eight bushels, and as much more we bought, ready dressed, in the town; wherewith we returned to the fort.

25

# Indians Sound Like Welshmen to Captain Wynne (1608)

A letter from Captain Peter Wynne to his patron, Sir John Egerton, in the Ellesmere Papers preserved in the Huntington Library.

To the Honourable Knight, Sir John Egerton, at York House, give these,

Most Noble Knight,

I was not so desirous to come into this country as I am now willing here to end my days, for I find it a far more pleasant and plentiful country than any report made mention of. Upon the river which we are seated I have gone six- or sevenscore miles, and so far is navigable; afterward I travelled between fifty or sixty miles by land into a country called Monacan, who owe no subjection to Powhatan. This land is very high ground and fertile, being very full of very delicate springs of sweet water, the air more healthful than the place where we are seated, by reason it is not subject to such fogs and mists as we continually have. The people of Monacan speak a far differing language from the subjects of Powhatan, their pronunciation being very like Welsh, so that the gentlemen in our company desired me to be their interpreter. The commodities as yet known in this country, whereof there will be great store, is pitch, tar, soap-ashes, and some dyes, whereof we have sent examples. As for things more precious, I omit till time (which I hope will be shortly) shall make manifest proof of it. As concerning your request of bloodhounds, I cannot learn that there is any such in this country; only the dogs which are here are a certain kind of curs like our warreners' hay-dogs[1] in England, and they keep them to hunt their land-fowls, as turkeys and such-like, for they keep nothing tame about them. Hereafter I doubt not but to give you at large a farther relation than as yet I am able to do, and do therefore desire you to take these few lines in good part and hold me excused for the rest until fitter opportunity. Thus commending my service to your good love with good love, with many thanks for all favours and kindnesses received from you, I do ever remain

Yours most devoted in
all service,
Peter Wynne

Jamestown in Virginia
this 21st of November [1608]

26

# King James Wants a Flying Squirrel from America (1610?)

A brief note from the Earl of Southampton to the Earl of Salisbury, dated December 15 [1610?], State Papers, Domestic, James I, Vol. 50, No. 65, has a curious footnote. Printed in Brown, *Genesis*, I, 356–7.

TALKING with the King, by chance I told him of the Virginia squirrels which they say will fly, whereof there are now divers brought into England. He presently and very earnestly asked me if none of them was provided for him and whether Your Lordship had none for him, saying that he was sure you would get him one of them. I would not have troubled you with this but that you know so well how he is affected to these toys, and with a little inquiry of any of your folks you may furnish yourself to present him at his coming to London, which will not be before Wednesday next, the Monday before to Theobalds, and the Saturday before that to Royston.

# 27

# Strachey's Description of the
# 'Still Vexed Bermoothes' (1610)

Excerpts from William Strachey, 'A True Reportory of the Wrack and Redemption of Sir Thomas Gates . . . upon and from the Islands of the Bermudas . . .' First printed by Purchas, *Pilgrims*, Bk. IV, Ch. 6, pp. 1734–58; reprinted by Louis B. Wright, *A Voyage to Virginia in 1609: Two Narratives* (Charlottesville, 1964).

It is presumed that Shakespeare read a manuscript version of the 'True Reportory' and in it found suggestions for *The Tempest*.

## I

*A most dreadful tempest (the manifold deaths whereof are here to the life described), their wrack on Bermuda, and the description of those islands.*

Excellent Lady,

Know that upon Friday late in the evening we brake ground out of the sound of Plymouth, our whole fleet then consisting of seven good ships and two pinnaces, all which from the said second of June unto the twenty-third of July kept in friendly consort together, not a whole watch at any time losing the sight each of other. Our course, when we came about the height of between 26 and 27 degrees, we declined to the northward and, according to our Governor's instructions, altered the trade and ordinary way used heretofore by Dominica and Nevis in the West Indies and found the wind to this course indeed as friendly as in the judgement of all seamen it is upon a more direct line. . . .

We had followed this course so long as now we were within seven or eight days at the most, by Captain Newport's reckoning, of making Cape Henry upon the coast of Virginia, when on St James his day, July 24, being Monday (preparing for no less all the black night before), the clouds gathering thick upon us and the winds singing and whistling most unusually (which made us to cast off our pinnace, towing the same until then astern), a dreadful storm and hideous began to blow from out the north-east, which swelling and roaring as it were by fits, some hours with more violence than others, at length did beat all light

188

from Heaven; which, like an hell of darkness, turned black upon us, so much the more fuller of horror as in such cases horror and fear use to overrun the troubled and overmastered senses of all, which taken up with amazement, the ears lay so sensible to the terrible cries and murmurs of the winds and distraction of our company as who was most armed and best prepared was not a little shaken.

For surely, noble lady, as death comes not so sudden nor apparent, so he comes not so elvish[1] and painful (to men, especially, even then in health and perfect habitudes of body) as at sea; who comes at no time so welcome but our frailty (so weak is the hold of hope in miserable demonstrations of danger) it makes guilty of many contrary changes and conflicts. For, indeed, death is accompanied at no time nor place with circumstances every way so uncapable of particularities of goodness and inward comforts as at sea. For it is most true, there ariseth commonly no such unmerciful tempest, compound of so many contrary and divers nations,* but that it worketh upon the whole frame of the body and most loathsomely affecteth all the powers thereof. And the manner of the sickness it lays upon the body, being so unsufferable, gives not the mind any free and quiet time to use her judgement and empire; which made the poet say:

> Hostium uxores, puerique caecos
> Sentiant motus orientis Haedi, et
> Aequoris nigri fremitum, et trementes
> Vere ripas.[2]

For four-and-twenty hours the storm in a restless tumult had blown so exceedingly as we could not apprehend in our imaginations any possibility of greater violence; yet did we still find it not only more terrible but more constant, fury added to fury, and one storm urging a second more outrageous than the former, whether it so wrought upon our fears or indeed met with new forces. Sometimes strikes* in our ship amongst women and passengers not used to such hurly and discomforts made us look one upon the other with troubled hearts and panting bosoms, our clamours drowned in the winds and the winds in thunder. Prayers might well be in the heart and lips but drowned in the outcries of the officers:[3] nothing heard that could give comfort, nothing seen that might encourage hope. It is impossible for me, had I the voice of Stentor and expression of as many tongues as his throat of voices, to express the outcries and miseries, not languishing but wasting his spirits, and art constant to his own principles but not prevailing.

Our sails wound up lay without their use, and if at any time we bore but a hullock,[4] or half fore-course, to guide her before the sea, six and sometimes eight men were not enough to hold the whipstaff[5] in the steerage and the tiller below in the gunner room: by which may be imagined the strength of the storm, in which the sea swelled above the clouds and gave battle unto Heaven. It could not be said to rain: the waters like whole rivers did flood in the air. And this I did still observe, that whereas upon the land, when a storm hath poured itself forth once in drifts of rain, the wind, as beaten down and vanquished therewith, not long after endureth, here the glut of water (as if throttling the wind erewhile) was no sooner a little emptied and qualified but instantly the winds (as having gotten their mouths now free and at liberty) spake more loud and grew more tumultuous and malignant. What shall I say? Winds and seas were as mad as fury and rage could make them. For mine own part, I had been in some storms before, as well upon the coast of Barbary and Algiers in the Levant, and once, more distressful, in the Adriatic gulf in a bottom of Candy,[6] so as I may well say: 'Ego quid sit ater Adriae novi sinus, et quid albus peccet Iapyx.'[7] Yet all that I had ever suffered gathered together might not hold comparison with this: there was not a moment in which the sudden splitting or instant oversetting of the ship was not expected.

Howbeit this was not all. It pleased God to bring a greater affliction yet upon us; for in the beginning of the storm we had received likewise a mighty leak. And the ship, in every joint almost having spewed out her oakum before we were aware (a casualty more desperate than any other that a voyage by sea draweth with it), was grown five foot suddenly deep with water above her ballast, and we almost drowned within whilst we sat looking when to perish from above. This, imparting no less terror than danger, ran through the whole ship with much fright and amazement, startled and turned the blood and took down the braves[8] of the most hardy mariner of them all, insomuch as he that before happily felt not the sorrow of others now began to sorrow for himself, when he saw such a pond of water so suddenly broken in and which he knew could not (without present avoiding)[9] but instantly sink him. So as, joining (only for his own sake, not yet worth the saving) in the public safety there might be seen master, master's mate, boatswain, quartermaster, coopers, carpenters, and who not, with candles in their hands, creeping along the ribs viewing the sides, searching every corner, and listening in every place if they could hear the water run. Many a weeping leak was this way found and hastily stopped, and at length one in the gunner room made up with I know not how many pieces of beef. But all was to no purpose; the leak (if it were but one) which drunk in our greatest seas and took in our destruction fastest could not then be found, nor ever was, by any labour, counsel, or search. The waters still increasing and the pumps going, which at length choked with bringing up whole and continual biscuit (and indeed all we had, ten thousandweight), it was conceived as most likely that the leak might be sprung in the bread room; whereupon the carpenters went down and ripped up all the room but could not find it so. . . .

Our Governor, upon the Tuesday morning (at what time, by such who had been below in the hold, the leak was first discovered) had caused the whole company, about 140, besides women, to be equally divided into three parts and, opening the ship in three places (under the forecastle, in the waist, and hard by the bittacle),[10] appointed each man where to attend; and thereunto each man came duly upon his watch, took the bucket or pump for one hour, and rested another. Then men might be seen to labour, I may well say, for life; and the better sort, even our Governor and admiral themselves, not refusing their turn and to spell each the other, to give example to other. The common sort, stripped naked as men in galleys, the easier both to hold out and to shrink from under the salt water, which continually leaped in among them, kept their eyes waking and their thoughts and hands working with tired bodies and wasted spirits three days and four nights, destitute of outward comfort and desperate of any deliverance, testifying how mutually willing they were yet by labour to keep each other from drowning, albeit each one drowned whilst he laboured.

Once so huge a sea brake upon the poop and quarter upon us as it covered our ship from stern to stem like a garment or a vast cloud; it filled her brim full for a while within, from the hatches up to the spardeck. The source or confluence of water was so violent as it rushed and carried the helm-man from the helm and wrested the whipstaff out of his hand, which so flew from side to side that when he would have seized* the same again it so tossed him from starboard to larboard as it was God's mercy it had not split him. It so beat him from his hold and so bruised him as a fresh man hazarding in by chance fair fell with it and, by main strength bearing somewhat up, made good[11] his place and with much clamour encouraged and called upon others, who gave her now up, rent in pieces and absolutely lost.

Our Governor was at this time below at the capstan, both by his speech and authority heartening every man unto his labour. It struck him from the place where he sat and grovelled him and all us about him on our faces, beating together with our breaths all thoughts from our bosoms else than that we were now sinking. For my part, I thought her already in the bottom of the sea; and I have heard him say, wading out of the flood thereof, all his ambition was but to climb up above hatches to die in *aperto coelo* and in the company of his old friends. It so stunned the ship in her full pace that she stirred no more than if she had been caught in a net, or than as if the fabulous remora[12] had stuck to her forecastle. Yet without bearing one inch of sail, even then she was making her way nine or ten leagues in a watch.

One thing it is not without his wonder (whether it were the fear of death in so great a storm, or that it pleased God to be gracious unto us), there was not a passenger, gentleman or other, after he began to stir and labour, but was able to relieve his fellow and make good his course. And it is most true, such as in all their lifetimes had never done hour's work before (their minds now helping their bodies) were able twice forty-eight hours together to toil with the best.

During all this time the heavens looked so black upon us that it was not possible the elevation of the Pole might be observed; nor a star by night nor sunbeam by day was to be seen. Only upon the Thursday night Sir George Somers, being upon the watch, had an apparition of a little, round light,[13] like a faint star, trembling and streaming along with a sparkling blaze, half the height upon the main mast and shooting sometimes from shroud to shroud, 'tempting to settle, as it were, upon any of the shrouds. And for three or four hours together, or rather more, half the night, it kept with us, running sometimes along the main-yard to the very end and then returning; at which Sir George Somers called divers about him and showed them the same, who observed it with much wonder and carefulness.[14] But upon a sudden, towards the morning watch, they lost the sight of it and knew not what way it made.

The superstitious seamen make many constructions of this sea-fire, which nevertheless is usual in storms; the same (it may be) which the Grecians were wont in the Mediterranean to call Castor and Pollux, of which if one only appeared without the other they took it for an evil sign of great tempest. The Italians and such who lie open to the Adriatic and Tyrrhenian Sea call it (a sacred body) *corpo sancto*; the Spaniards call it St Elmo and have an authentic and miraculous legend for it. Be it what it will, we laid other foundations of safety or ruin than in the rising or falling of it. Could it have served us now miraculously to have taken our height by, it might have strucken amazement and a reverence in our devotions according to the due of a miracle. But it did not light us any whit the more to our known way, who ran now (as do hoodwinked[15] men) at all adventures, sometimes north and north-east, then north and by west, and in an instant again varying two or three points, and sometimes half the compass. East and by south we steered away as much as we could to bear upright, which was no small carefulness nor pain to do, albeit we much unrigged our ship, threw overboard much luggage, many a trunk and chest (in which I suffered no mean loss), and staved many a butt of beer, hogsheads of oil, cider, wine, and vinegar, and heaved away all our ordnance on the starboard side, and had now purposed to have cut down the main mast the more to lighten her, for we were much spent and our men so weary as their strengths together failed them with their hearts, having travailed now from Tuesday till Friday morning, day and night, without either sleep or food: for, the leakage taking up all the hold, we could neither come by beer nor fresh water; fire we could keep none in the cookroom to dress any meat; and carefulness, grief, and our turn at the pump or bucket were sufficient to hold sleep from our eyes.

And surely, madam, it is most true, there was not any hour (a matter of admiration) all these days in which we freed not twelve hundred barricos[16] of water, the least whereof contained six gallons, and some eight; besides three deep pumps continually going, two beneath at the capstan and the other above in the half-deck, and at each pump four thousand strokes at the least in a watch. So as I may well say, every four hours we quitted one hundred tons of water. And from Tuesday noon till Friday noon we bailed and pumped two thousand ton; and yet, do what we could, when our ship held least in her (after Tuesday night second watch), she bore ten foot deep; at which stay our extreme working kept her one eight glasses,[17] forbearance whereof had instantly sunk us. And it being now Friday, the fourth morning, it wanted little but that there had been a general determination to have shut up hatches and, commending our sinful souls to God, committed the ship to the mercy of the sea. Surely, that night we must have done it, and that night had we then perished. But see the goodness and sweet introduction of better hope by our merciful God given unto us: Sir George Somers, when no man dreamed of such happiness, had discovered and cried land.

Indeed the morning, now three quarters spent, had won a little clearness from the days before, and it being better surveyed, the very trees were seen to move with the wind upon the shore side; whereupon our Governor commanded the helm-man to bear up. The boatswain, sounding at the first, found it thirteen fathom, and when we stood [in] a little, in seven fathom; and presently, heaving his lead the third time, had ground at four fathom; and by this, we had got her within a mile under the south-east point of the land, where we had somewhat smooth water. But having no hope to save her by coming to an anchor in the same, we were enforced to run her ashore as near the land as we could, which brought us within three quarters of a mile of shore; and by the mercy of God unto us, making out our boats, we had ere night brought all our men, women, and children, about the number of 150, safe into the island.

We found it to be the dangerous and dreaded island, or rather islands, of the Bermuda, whereof let me give Your Ladyship a brief description before I proceed to my narration. And that the rather because they be so terrible to all that ever touched on them, and such tempests, thunders, and other fearful objects are seen and heard about them, that they be called commonly the Devil's Islands and are feared and avoided of all sea travellers alive above any other place in the world. Yet it pleased our merciful God to make even this hideous and hated place both the place of our safety and means of our deliverance.

And hereby, also, I hope to deliver the world from a foul and general error, it being counted of most that they can be no habitation for men but rather given over to devils and wicked spirits; whereas indeed we find them now by experience to be as habitable and commodious as most countries of the same climate and situation, insomuch as, if the entrance into them were as easy as the place itself is contenting, it had long ere this been inhabited as well as other islands. Thus shall we make it appear that Truth is the daughter of Time, and that men ought not to deny everything which is not subject to their own sense. . . .

# 28

# Another Version of the Castaways
# on Bermuda (1610)

Shakespeare may have obtained further details and atmosphere for *The Tempest* from another vivid account of the wreck of the *Sea Venture* on an island in the Bermudas in 1609. The following account is taken from Silvester Jourdain, *A Discovery of the Bermudas, Otherwise Called the Isle of Devils* (1610). Reprinted by Wright in *A Voyage to Virginia in 1609*.

BEING in [a] ship called the *Sea Venture*, with Sir Thomas Gates our Governor, Sir George Somers, and Captain Newport, three most worthy, honoured gentlemen (whose valour and fortitude the world must needs take notice of, and that in most honourable designs) bound for Virginia, in the height of 30 degrees of northerly latitude or thereabouts we were taken with a most sharp and cruel storm upon the five-and-twentieth day of July, anno 1609, which did not only separate us from the residue of our fleet (which were eight in number), but with the violent working of the seas our ship became so shaken, torn, and leaked that she received so much water as covered two tier of hogsheads above the ballast; that our men stood up to the middles with buckets, barricos, and kettles to bail out the water and continually pumped for three days and three nights together without any intermission; and yet the water seemed rather to increase than to diminish. Insomuch that all our men, being utterly spent, tired, and disabled for longer labour, were even resolved, without any hope of their lives, to shut up the hatches and to have committed themselves to the mercy of the sea (which is said to be merciless), or rather to the mercy of their mighty God and redeemer (whose mercies exceed all His works), seeing no help nor hope in the apprehension of man's reason that any mother's child could escape that inevitable danger, which every man had proposed and digested to himself, of present sinking. So that some of them, having some good and comfortable waters in the ship, fetched them and drunk one to the other, taking their last leave one of the other until their more joyful and happy meeting in a more blessed world; when it pleased God out of His most gracious and merciful

195

providence so to direct and guide our ship (being left to the mercy of the sea) for her most advantage, that Sir George Somers (sitting upon the poop of the ship, where he sate three days and three nights together, without meal's meat and [with] little or no sleep), conning[1] the ship to keep her as upright as he could (for otherwise she must needs instantly have foundered), most wishedly-happily descried land. Whereupon he most comfortably encouraged the company to follow their pumping and by no means to cease bailing out of the water with their buckets, barricos, and kettles; whereby they were so overwearied, and their spirits so spent with long fasting and continuance of their labour, that for the most part they were fallen asleep in corners and wheresoever they chanced first to sit or lie; but, hearing news of land, wherewith they grew to be somewhat revived, being carried with will and desire beyond their strength, every man bustled up and gathered his strength and feeble spirits together, to perform as much as their weak force would permit him; through which weak means it pleased God to work so strongly as the water was stayed for that little time (which, as we all much feared, was the last period of our breathing) and the ship kept from present sinking, when it pleased God to send her within half an English mile of that land that Sir George Somers had not long before descried, which were the islands of the Bermudas.

And there neither did our ship sink but, more fortunately in so great a misfortune, fell in between two rocks, where she was fast lodged and locked for further budging; whereby we gained not only sufficient time, with the present help of our boat and skiff, safely to set and convey our men ashore (which were 150 in number) but afterwards had time and leisure to save some good part of our goods and provision, which the water had not spoiled, with all the tackling of the ship and much of the iron about her, which were necessaries not a little available[2] for the building and furnishing of a new ship and pinnace, which we made there for the transporting and carrying of us to Virginia. But our delivery was not more strange, in falling so opportunely and happily upon the land, as our feeding and preservation was beyond our hopes and all men's expectations most admirable.[3]

For the islands of the Bermudas, as every man knoweth that hath heard or read of them, were never inhabited by any Christian or heathen people but ever esteemed and reputed a most prodigious and enchanted place, affording nothing but gusts, storms, and foul weather; which made every navigator and mariner to avoid them as Scylla and Charybdis, or as they would shun the Devil himself; and no man was ever heard to make for the place but as, against their wills, they have by storms and dangerousness of the rocks, lying seven leagues unto the sea, suffered shipwreck. Yet did we find there the air so temperate and the country so abundantly fruitful of all fit necessaries for the sustentation and preservation of man's life that, most in a manner of all our provisions of bread, beer, and victual being quite spoiled in lying long drowned in salt water, notwithstanding we were there for the space of nine months (few days over or under) not only well received, comforted, and with good satiety contented, but out of the abundance thereof provided us some reasonable quantity and proportion of provision to carry us for Virginia and to maintain ourselves and that company we found there, to the great relief of them, as it fell out, in their so great extremities and, in respect of the shortness of time, until it pleased God that by My Lord's coming thither their store was better supplied. And greater and better provisions we might have made if we had had better means for the storing and transportation thereof. Wherefore my opinion sincerely of this island is that whereas it hath been and is still accounted the most dangerous, infortunate, and most forlorn place of the world, it is in truth the richest, healthfullest, and pleasing land (the quantity and bigness thereof considered) and merely natural, as ever man set foot upon. The particular profits and benefits whereof shall be more especially inserted and hereunto annexed, which every man to his own private knowledge, that was there, can avouch and justify for a truth.

Upon the eight-and-twentieth day of July 1609 (after the extremity of the storm was something qualified) we fell upon the shore at the Bermudas; where after our general, Sir Thomas Gates, Sir George Somers, and Captain Newport had by their provident carefulness landed all their men and so much of the goods and provisions out of the ship as was not utterly spoiled, every man disposed and applied himself to search for and to seek out such relief and sustentation as the country afforded. And Sir George Somers, a man inured to extremities (and knowing what thereunto belonged) was in this service neither idle nor backward but presently by his careful industry went and found out sufficient of many kind of fishes, and so plentiful thereof that in half an hour he took so many great fishes with hooks as did suffice the whole company one day. And fish is there so abundant that if a man step into the water they will come round about him; so that men were fain to get out for fear of biting. These fishes are very fat and sweet and of that proportion and bigness that three of them will conveniently lade two

o

men: those we called rock fish. Besides there are such abundance of mullets that with a seine might be taken at one draught one thousand at the least; and infinite store of pilchards; with divers kinds of great fishes, the names of them unknown to me; of crayfishes very great ones and so great store as that there hath been taken in one night with making lights even sufficient to feed the whole company a day. The country affordeth great abundance of hogs, as that there hath been taken by Sir George Somers, who was the first hunted for them, to the number of two-and-thirty at one time, which he brought to the company in a boat built by his own hands.

There is fowl in great num[ber] upon the islands where they breed, that there hath been taken in two or three hours a thousand at the least: the bird being of the bigness of a good pigeon and layeth eggs as big as hen eggs upon the sand, where they come and lay them daily although men sit down amongst them, that there hath been taken up in one morning by Sir Thomas Gates's men one thousand of eggs; and Sir George Somers's men, coming a little distance of time after them, have stayed there whilst they came and laid their eggs amongst them, that they brought away as many more with them, and many young birds very fat and sweet.

Another sea-fowl there is that lieth in little holes in the ground, like unto a cony-hole, and are in great numbers, exceeding good meat, very fat and sweet (those we had in the winter) and their eggs are white and of that bigness that they are not to be known from hen eggs. The other bird's eggs are speckled and of a different colour. There are also great store and plenty of herons, and those so familiar and tame that we beat them down from the trees with stones and staves—but such were young herons—besides many white herons without so much as a black or grey feather on them; with other small birds so tame and gentle that, a man walking in the woods with a stick and whistling to them, they will come and gaze on you, so near that you may strike and kill many of them with your stick; and with singing and holloing you may do the like.

There are also great store of tortoises (which some call turtles) and those so great that I have seen a bushel of eggs in one of their bellies, which are sweeter than any hen egg; and the tortoise itself is all very good meat and yieldeth great store of oil, which is as sweet as any butter; and one of them will suffice fifty men a meal, at the least; and of these hath been taken great store, with two boats, at the least forty in one day.

The country yieldeth divers fruits, as prickled pears, great abundance, which continue green upon the trees all the year; also great plenty of mulberries, white and red, and on the same are great store of silkworms, which yield cods of silk, both white and yellow, being some coarse and some fine.

And there is a tree called a palmetto tree, which hath a very sweet berry upon which the hogs do most feed; but our men, finding the sweetness of them, did willingly share with the hogs for them, they being very pleasant and wholesome, which made them careless almost of any bread with their meat; which occasioned us to carry in a manner all that store of flour and meal we did or could save for Virginia. The head of the palmetto tree is very good meat, either raw or sodden; it yieldeth a head which weigheth about twenty pound and is far better meat than any cabbage.

There are an infinite number of cedar trees (the fairest, I think, in the world) and those bring forth a very sweet berry and wholesome to eat.

The country (forasmuch as I could find myself or hear by others) affords no venomous creature, or so much as a rat or mouse or any other thing unwholesome.

There is great store of pearl, and some of them very fair, round, and oriental, and you shall find at least one hundred seed of pearl in one oyster. There hath been likewise found some good quantity of ambergris, and that of the best sort. There are also great plenty of whales, which I conceive are very easy to be killed, for they come so usually and ordinarily to the shore that we heard them oftentimes in the night abed, and have seen many of them near the shore in the day-time.

There was born upon the Bermudas, at the time of our being there, two children, the one a man-child, there baptized by the name of Bermudas, and a woman-child, baptized by the name of Bermuda;[4] as also there was a marriage between two English people upon the island. This island, I mean the main island, with all the broken islands adjacent, are made in the form of a half moon, but a little more rounder, and divided into many broken islands, and there are many good harbours in it; but we could find [only] one especial place to go in, or rather to go out from it, which was not altogether free from some danger, and that lieth on the south-east side, where there is three fathoms water at the entrance thereof, but within six, seven, or eight fathoms at the least, where you may safely be landlocked from the danger of all winds and weathers, and more to the trees. The coming into it is so narrow and strait between the rocks as that it will with small store of munition be fortified and easily defended with all advantage the place affords against the forces of the potentest king of Europe.

There are also plenty of hawks and very good tobacco, as I think, which through forgetfulness I had almost omitted.

Now, having finished and rigged our ship and pinnace, the one called the *Deliverance*, the pinnace the *Patience*, we prepared and made ourselves ready to ship for Virginia, having powdered[5] some store of hogs' flesh for provision thither and the company thereof for some reasonable time; but were compelled to make salt there for the same purpose, for all our salt was spent and spoiled before we recovered the shore. We carried with us also a good portion of tortoise oil, which either for frying or baking did us very great pleasure, it being very sweet, nourishing, and wholesome.

The greatest defects we found there was tar and pitch for our ship and pinnace, instead whereof we were forced to make lime there of a hard kind of stone and use it, which for the present occasion and necessity, with some wax we found cast up by the sea from some shipwreck, served the turn to pay[6] the seams of the pinnace Sir George Somers built, for which he had neither pitch nor tar.

So that God, in the supplying of all our wants beyond all measure, showed Himself still merciful unto us, that we might accomplish our intended voyage to Virginia, for which I confidently hope He doth yet reserve a blessing in store, and to the which I presume every honest and religious heart will readily give their Amen.

When all things were made ready and commodiously fitted, the wind coming fair, we set sail and put off from the Bermudas the tenth day of May in the year 1610, and arrived at Jamestown in Virginia the four-and-twentieth day of the same month, where we found some threescore persons living. And being then some three weeks or thereabouts past, and not hearing of any supply, it was thought fitting by a general consent to use the best means for the preservation of all those people that were living, being all in number two hundred persons. And so, upon the eighth of June 1610, we embarked at Jamestown, not having above fourteen days' victual, and so were determined to direct our course for Newfoundland, there to refresh us and supply ourselves with victual to bring us home.

But it pleased God to dispose otherwise of us and to give us better means. For being all of us shipped in four pinnaces and departed from the town, almost down half the river, we met My Lord De La Warr coming by with three ships well furnished with victual, which revived all the company and gave them great content. And after some few days My Lord, understanding of the great plenty of hogs and fish was at the Bermudas and the necessity of them in Virginia, was desirous to send thither to supply himself with those things for the better comforting of his men and the plantation of the country.

Whereupon Sir George Somers, being a man best acquainted with the place, and being willing to do service unto his prince and country without any respect of his own private gain, and being of threescore years of age at the least, out of his worthy and valiant mind offered himself to undertake to perform with God's help that dangerous voyage for the Bermudas, for the better relief and comfort of the people in Virginia and for the better plantation of it; which offer My Lord De La Warr very willingly and thankfully accepted. And so upon the nineteenth of June Sir George Somers embarked himself at Jamestown in a small barge of thirty ton or thereabout that he built at the Bermudas, wherein he laboured from morning until night, as duly as any work-man doth labour for wages, and built her all with cedar, with little or no ironwork at all, having in her but one bolt, which was in the kelson.[7] Notwithstanding, thanks be to God, she brought us in safety to Virginia, and so I trust He will protect him and send him well back again, to his heart's desire and the great comfort of all the company there.[8]

The Bermudas lieth in the height of $32\frac{1}{2}$ degrees of northerly latitude, Virginia bearing directly from it, west-northwest, 230 leagues.

29

# Bermuda Providentially Saved for the English Nation (1615)

Lewis Hughes, one of the first ministers sent to Bermuda when that colony was still under the control of the Virginia Company of London, evidently was under instruction to send back an account of the excellencies of the island paradise. Since the islands were known as a place of witches and devils, Hughes, who himself had gained some notoriety earlier for exorcizing witches, points out that the previous bad name of the islands is merely part of the divine plan. The excerpt printed below is taken from *A Letter Sent into England from the Summer Islands* [*Bermuda*]. *Written by Mr Lewis Hughes, Preacher of God's Word There* (1615).

BELOVED friends, the goodness of Almighty God, in keeping these islands secret from all people of the world (except some that have come hither against their wills, to their loss, by means of shipwreck) till now that it hath pleased His Holy Majesty to discover and bestow them upon His people of England, is so great as should stir them up with thankful hearts to praise His holy and great name and to send such to inhabit them as fear God and give themselves to serve Him in holiness and righteousness, that so God may love to dwell in those islands as He did in Sion when He said: 'This is my rest for ever; here will I dwell, for I have a delight therein' (Ps. 132: 14).

And whereas it is given out by some that we do wrong to the King of Spain, they that think so are in an error, for the King of Spain had never anything to do here, and I hope never shall. The King of Kings hath kept these islands from the King of Spain and all other kings in the world till now that it hath pleased His Holy Majesty to bestow them upon the King of England, and hath put us his subjects in quiet possession of them without doing any wrong to the King of Spain or any other; and our hope is that if the Spaniards shall come to invade us, that God will not suffer them to take that from us that He hath freely given us.

It may be that some are afraid to come hither because of the strange reports that have gone of these islands, as that they are the islands of devils and fearful thundering and lightning as though Heaven and earth did meet together: believe me, my beloved, here are no such things (thanks be to God). True it is, that as Almighty God set the cherubims and the blade of a sword shaking in fearful manner to keep Adam from coming into Paradise, so by fearful tempests and terrible lightning and thunder God hath terrified and kept all people of the world from coming into these islands to inhabit them, as appeareth by divers signs of shipwreck in divers places about the islands; and this, as I take it, is the cause that such reports have gone of these islands and that all navigators and mariners have been careful to avoid and shun them as they would shun the Devil himself; but now, since it hath pleased God to discover them unto and to bestow them upon His people of England, here have been no such tempests nor danger, His holy and great name be therefore praised. And the more to stir you up to praise His holy name, consider, I pray you, of the manner how He brought our men to the first sight and true knowledge of them.

He did not bring them to their loss and grief by shipwreck, as He did others, but to their great joy in saving them from shipwreck. . . .[1]

The eleventh of July, 1612, Master Richard Moore, now Deputy Governor, arrived safely and with him about fifty souls—men, women, and children—to inhabit these islands, and since that time (by the mercy of God) divers other ships out of England have arrived safely with good supplies; therefore, let not the report that hath gone of these islands discourage any of the people of England from coming hither.

Neither let the fear of foreign invasion discourage any. For, as I am persuaded and have heard mariners that have travelled far say, the like islands are not to be found in the world where men may dwell so safe from foreign invasion, because God hath so compassed them about with fearful rocks as ships are not able to come near but in two channels that lead into two goodly and large harbours: the one at a place called the Gurnards Head, the other at a place called Davies Point. The channels are so narrow and curious[2] as ships must come in very leisurely, one after another, so as the forts on both sides the channels may sink them with ease, by the help of God.

As it hath pleased God (for the safety of those islands) in their first creation to environ them about with fearful rocks, so now in their first plantation it hath pleased His Holy Majesty to put into the heart of Master Moore, now Deputy Governor, to fortify them within, so as in the judgement of man they are invincible. At the Gurnards Head he hath built three forts and planted them with great pieces and men to defend them; and at Davies Point he hath builded two forts and planted them with great pieces and men to defend them. He hath also built divers other forts to keep long-boats from landing and to clear the harbours, if ships should come in. If long-boats should venture to land any there, they will be but as men cast away, because ships cannot come near to rescue or help any way; therefore, let not fear of foreign invasion keep any from coming hither.

There is great hope that (by the blessing of God) men may in time live very comfortably here and grow rich, if they will provide seeds of indigo, etc., and plants of currants, figs, raisins, mulberry trees for the silkworms, and vines that they may have wine for their own drinking; I say for their own drinking, because wine, considering the leakage, trouble, and charge, will be one of the least commodities these islands will afford. For the present, tobacco is the best commodity. . . .

I wish that all they that hereafter shall come hither out of England would consider with themselves that these islands were never inhabited till now, and that therefore they must of necessity labour hard at first and be contented to endure hardness and some want of many necessaries.

In time (by the grace of God) the storehouse shall be furnished with all necessaries for such as have money, and they that have not, if they be honest and industrious, shall be trusted; but now, in regard that the greatest part of the people that be here came very rashly and carelessly, not considering whither they went nor what they might in time have need of, I think that all that can be brought into the store as yet will be taken up by them; and therefore I advise such as are to come to bring (every one that is able) a barrel or two of biscuits for his own eating till he have cleared his ground and have wheat of his own.

Also let them bring oil, vinegar, aqua-vitae, barrel butter, pots, kettles, frying-pans, trivets, bowls, trays, tankards or pots to drink in, pails to fetch water in, and little barrels or jars to keep it in for their drink. The water is very good and wholesome, such as many do delight in.

Also let them bring tongs, fire shovels, bellows, tinder boxes, brimstone, flintstones and steels, spits, dripping-pans, candlesticks, lamps, locks, spades, shovels, pickaxes, hatchets, whetstones, saws, hammers, piercers, pincers, and nails of all sorts, as many as will serve to build a house with, and leather to mend their shoes, and sparrow-bills or nails to drive into them, else the rocks will tear them out quickly.

Also let them bring bedding: flock-beds are better than feather-beds. And for apparel for the summer, let them bring canvas or stuffs: blue linen and good buckram the women do wish for. Also let them not forget to bring castile soap, pins, points, laces, needles, thread, thimbles, shears, and scissors. Also let them bring strong fishing lines of twelve or fourteen fathoms long, and some small of whipcords and strong hooks, the biggest and as divers as they can, and some small hooks for breams.

And above all things have a care to leave their sins behind them and come hither as it were into a new world to lead a new life; and for the comfort of their souls let them bring Bibles and other good books and pack up all their small stuff in barrels. The barrels will afterwards serve them for many good uses.

Idle persons and such as are given to filching do live here in great misery; so also do all whorish women in great disgrace, hated and loathed of all honest poeple, which makes them weep and sigh with tears to wish themselves in England again, and for their comfort, to cool them a little, they are now and then towed at a boat's tail up and down the harbour; so were a couple served together, a man and a woman that came in the ship that came in, and so have divers others. Also all such as are profaners of the Sabbath and come to the service of God but when they list, I see that God findeth them out and denieth them His blessing. . . .

From the Summer Islands this twenty-first of December, 1614.

Yours as his own,

Lewis Hughes.

30

# The Blessed Isles [The West Indies]

From *The Island Princess* (1619–21), a play by John Fletcher.

> We are arriv'd among the blessed islands,
> Where every wind that rises blows perfumes,
> And every breath of air is like an incense:
> The treasure of the sun dwells here; each tree,
> As if it envied the old Paradise,
> Strives to bring forth immortal fruit. . . .
> Nothing we see but breeds an admiration;
> The very rivers, as we float along,
> Throw up their pearls, and curl their heads to court us;
> The bowels of the earth swell with the births
> Of thousand unknown gems and thousand riches;
> Nothing that bears a life but brings a treasure.

# 31

# The Virginia Indians (1612)

William Strachey, companion of Sir Thomas Gates in the disastrous voyage of the *Sea Venture*, was named by Gates secretary of the colony soon after the Bermuda castaways reached Virginia in May 1610. Strachey served as secretary for almost two years and showed a keen interest in the Indians. Although much of the material that he included in his *History of Travel into Virginia Britannia* was taken from John Smith, the material on the Indians, part of which is included below, was written by Strachey himself. He intended his work to serve as propaganda for colonization, and he hoped for some further post in the colonial establishment—in which hope he was disappointed. His *History of Travel* was composed about 1612. One manuscript was presented to Henry Percy, ninth Earl of Southampton. It has been edited by Louis B. Wright and Virginia Freund, The Hakluyt Society, 2nd Ser., No. 103 (London, 1953).

## Chapter 3

. . . W E may well say how this tract or portion of land, which we call Virginia Britannia, by the inhabitants, as afore said, *Tsenacommacah*, is governed in chief by a great king, by them called by sundry names according to his divers places, qualities, or honours by himself obtained, either for his valour, his government, or some such-like goodness, which they use to admire and commend to succeeding times with memorable titles, and so commonly they of greatest merit amongst them aspire to many names.

The great emperor at this time amongst them we commonly call Powhatan, for by that name, true it is, he was made known unto us when we arrived in the country first; and so indeed he was generally called when he was a young man, as taking his denomination from the country Powhatan wherein he was born, which is above at the Falls, as before mentioned, right over against the islands at the head of our river, and which place or birthright of his he sold, anno 1609, about September, unto Captain Francis West. . . . The inhabitants themselves, especially his frontier neighbour princes, call him still Powhatan; his own people sometimes call him Ottaniack, sometimes Mamanatowick, which last signifies 'great king'; but his proper right name, which they salute him with (himself in presence), is Wahunsena-cawh. . . .

He is a goodly old man, not yet shrinking, though well beaten with many cold and stormy winters, in which he hath been patient of many necessities and attempts of his fortune to make his name and family great. He is supposed to be little less than eighty years old (I dare not say how much more others say he is). Of a tall stature and clean limbs, of a sad aspect, round, fat-visaged, with grey hairs, but plain and thin, hanging upon his broad shoulders, some few hairs upon his chin, and so on his upper lip. He hath been a strong and able savage, sinewy, active, and of a daring spirit, vigilant, ambitious, subtle to enlarge his dominions: for but the countries Powhatan, Arrohattock, Appomattox, Pamunkey, Youghtamond, and Mattapanient, which are said to come unto him by inheritance, all the rest of the territories before named and expressed in the map, and which are all adjoining to that river whereon we are seated, they report (as is likewise before mentioned) to have been either by force subdued unto him or through fear yielded. Cruel he hath been, and quarrellous, as well with his own werowances for trifles, and that to strike a terror and awe into them of his power and condition, as also with his neighbours in his younger days, though now delighted in security and pleasure, and therefore stands upon reasonable conditions of peace with all the great and absolute werowances about him and is likewise more quietly settled amongst his own.

Watchful he is over us and keeps good espial upon our proceedings, concerning which he hath his sentinels that, at what time soever any of our boats, pinnaces, or ships come in, fall down, or make up the river, give the alarm and take it quickly the one from the other until it reach and come even to the court or hunting house, wheresoever he and his *cronoccoes* [i.e.], counselors, and priests are; and then he calls to advise and gives out directions what is to be done, as more fearing than harmed at any time with the danger and mischief which he saith we intend unto him by taking away his land from him and conspiring to surprise him, which we never yet imagined nor attempted, and yet albeit the conceit[1] of as much as strongly possesseth him. He doth often send unto us to temporize with us, awaiting perhaps but a fit opportunity (inflamed by his bloody and furious priests) to offer us a taste of the same cup which he made our poor countrymen drink off at Roanoke; not yet seeming willing to hold any open quarrel or hostility with us, but in all advantages which he sometimes takes against our credulous and beguiled people he hath it always so carried as upon our complaint to him it is rather laid upon some of his worst and unruly people, of which he tells us even our King James (commanding so many divers men) must have some irregular and unruly people, or else upon some of his petty werowances, whom peradventure we have attempted (saith he) with offences of the like nature, than that it is any act of his or done by his command or according to his will; often flattering us that he will take order that it shall be no more so, but that the *tassantasses*, that is, the strangers, King James his people, and his people, shall be all one, brothers and friends. And thus he served us at what time he wrought the Chickahominies (a nation, as we have learned, before the coming in of us so far from being his subjects as they were ever his enemies) into a hatred of us (being, indeed, a mighty people and our neighbours, within some ten or twelve miles of Jamestown) and us into the suspicion of them, by telling us that they were naught[2] and not to be trusted by us, attending but opportunity to do us a mischief, and by urging them to betray such of our men as should come at any time to trade with them for corn. And true it is, upon an advantage at such a time they slew three of our men without cause or offence given, only put into this jealousy[3] of our fair dealing with them by Powhatan, and they had done as much for all the rest of ours at that time with them in the barge had not their own fear and cowardice more withheld them than the readiness of our people to stand upon their guard. And when this was complained of unto Powhatan he wholly laid the blame upon the unruliness and force of so mighty a people, excusing himself to us by their number and insolence; yea, so far he will herein go sometime that when some of his people have done us wrong (and by his provoking, too), he will not fail underhand, after the fact, to tell us the authors of our wrong, giving us leave and bidding us revenge us upon them, of such subtle understanding and politic carriage is he.

In all his ancient inheritances he hath houses built after their manner and at every house provision for his entertainment, according to the time. About his person ordinarily attendeth a guard of forty or fifty of the tallest men his country do afford. Every night upon the four quarters of his house are four sentinels drawn forth, each standing from other a flight shot, and at every half hour one from the *corps de garde* doth hollo, unto whom every sentinel returns answer round from his stand; if any fail, an officer is presently sent forth that beateth him extremely.

The word 'werowance', which we call and construe for a king, is a common word whereby they call all commanders, for they have but few words in their language and but few occasions to use any officers more than one commander, which commonly they call 'werowance'.

It is strange to see with what great fear and adoration all these people do obey this Powhatan, for at his feet they present whatsoever he commandeth, and at the least frown of his brow the greatest will tremble; it may be because he is very terrible and inexorable in punishing such as offend him. For example, he caused certain malefactors (at what time Captain Smith was prisoner with them, and to the sight whereof Captain Smith for some purpose was brought) to be bound hand and foot, when certain officers appointed thereunto, having from many fires gathered great store of burning coals, raked the coals round in form of a cockpit, and in the midst they cast the offenders to broil to death. Sometimes he causeth the heads of them that offend to be laid upon the altar or sacrificing stone, and one or two with clubs beat out their brains. When he would punish any notorious enemy or trespasser, he causeth him to be tied to a tree, and with mussel-shells or reeds the executioner cutteth off his joints one after another, ever casting what is cut off into the fire; then doth he proceeed with shells and reeds to case the skin from his head and face, after which they rip up his belly, tear out his bowels, and so burn him with the tree and all. Thus themselves reported that they executed an Englishman, one George Cawson, whom the women enticed up from the barge unto their houses at a place called Appocant. Howbeit, his ordinary correction is to have an offender whom he will only punish and not put to death to be beaten with cudgels as the Turks do. We have seen a man kneeling on his knees, and at Powhatan's command two men have beat him on the bare skin till the skin hath been all bollen[4] and blistered and all on a gore blood, and till he hath fallen senseless in a swound, and yet never cried, complained, nor seemed to ask pardon, for that they seldom do.

And, sure, it is to be wondered at how such a barbarous and uncivil prince should take into him (adorned and set forth with no greater outward ornament and munificence) a form and ostentation of such majesty as he expresseth, which oftentimes strikes awe and sufficient wonder into our people presenting themselves before him; but such is, I believe, the impression of the Divine Nature, and howsoever these (as other) heathens forsaken by the true light have not that portion of the knowing blessed Christian spirit, yet I am persuaded there is an infused kind of divineness and extraordinary (appointed that it shall be so by the King of Kings) to such who are His immediate instruments on earth. . . .

According to the order and custom of sensual heathenism in the allowance of polygamy, he may have as many women as he will, and hath (as is supposed) many more than one hundred; all which he doth not keep yet as the Turk in one seraglio or house but hath an appointed number which reside still in every their several places, amongst whom, when he lieth on his bed, one sitteth at his head and another at his feet, but when he sitteth at meat or in presenting himself to any strangers one sitteth on his right hand and another on his left. . . .

He was reported by the said Kemps, as also by the Indian Machumps, . . . I say, they often reported unto us that Powhatan had then living twenty sons and ten daughters, besides a young one by Winganuske, Machumps his sister and a great darling of the king's, and besides young Pocahontas, a daughter of his using sometime to our fort in times past, now married to a private captain called Kocoum some two years since.

As he is weary of his women he bestows them on those that best deserve them at his hands. When he dineth or suppeth, one of his women before and after meat bringeth him water in a wooden platter to wash his hands, another waiting with a bunch of feathers to wipe them instead of a towel, and the feathers, when he hath wiped, are washed and dried again.

A mile from Orapaks in a thicket of wood he hath a principal house in which he keepeth his kind of treasure, as skins, copper, pearl, and beads, which he storeth up against the time of his death and burial; here is also his store of red paint for ointment, and bows and arrows. This house is fifty or sixty yards in length, frequented only by priests. At the four quarters of this house stand four images, not as *atlantes* or *telamones*, supporters to bear up pillars, posts, or somewhat else in the stately building, nor as in the ancient times the images and pedigrees of the whole stock or family were wont to be set in porches or the first entrance into houses, with a porter of special trust, who had the charge of keeping and looking unto them, called *atrienses*; but these are merely set as careful sentinels, forsooth, to defend and protect the house (for so they believe of them). One is like a dragon, another like a bear, the third like a leopard, and the fourth a giant-like man, all made evil-favoured enough, according to their best workmanship.

## Chapter 4

The great king Powhatan hath divided his country into many provinces or shires, as it were, and over every one placed a several absolute commander or werowance, to him contributory, to govern the people there to inhabit; and his petty werowances in all may be in number about three- or four-and-thirty, all which have their precincts and bounds, proper and commodiously appointed out, that no one intrude upon the other, of several forces; and for the ground wherein each one soweth his corn, plants his apoke[5] and garden fruits, he tithes to the great king of all the commodities growing in the same, or of what else his shire brings forth appertaining to the land or river—corn, beasts, pearl, fowl, fish, hides, furs, copper, beads—by what means soever obtained, a peremptory rate set down, as shall be mentioned in the sixth chapter; nor have I thought it altogether amiss to remember here and offer to consideration for all after occasions a catalogue of the several werowances' names, with the denomination of the particular shire, as afore said, wherein they govern, together with what forces for the present day they are able to send unto the wars. . . .

Opossunoquonuske, sister to Coquonasum, a werowancqua or queen of a little *mussaran*, or small village, of Appomattox, not unlike an ancient *episcata villatica*, and she was of power to have spared upon command some twenty able fighting men, howbeit her town we burned and killed some of her people (herself miscarrying[6] with small shot, in pursuit in the woods in winter, 1610) for a treacherous massacre which she practised upon fourteen of our men, whom she caused her people to invite up into her town to feast and make merry, entreating our men beforehand to leave their arms in their boat because they said how their women would be afraid else of their pieces. . . .

Oholasc, queen of Quiyocahannock, which we commonly, though corruptly, call Tappahannock, and is the same which Captain Smith in his map calls Quiyoughcohanock, on the south or Salisbury side; whose son, being yet young, shall be by Powhatan's appointment werowance of the said Quiyocahannock: his name is Tatahcoop. The werowance Pepiscunimah, whom by construction[7] as well the Indians as we call Pipsco, was sometime possessed in right of this part, as by birth and possession descended the true and lawful werowance of the same, but upon a displeasure which Powhatan conceived against him (in that the said Pipsco, and that not many years since, had stolen away a chief woman from Opechancanough, one of Powhatan's brothers), he was deposed from that regiment and the aforesaid Tatahcoop (a supposed son of Powhatan's by this said Queen Oholasc) made werowance, who, being yet young, as is said, is for the most part in the government of Chopoke at Chawopo, one of Pipsco's brothers. Yet is Pipsco suffered to retain in this his country a little small *kaasun*, or village, upon the rivage[8] of the stream, with some few people about him, keeping the said woman still, whom he makes his best beloved, and she travels with him upon any remove in hunting-time or in his visitation of us, by which means twice or thrice in a summer she hath come unto our town. Nor is so handsome a savage woman as I have seen amongst them, yet with a kind of pride can take upon her a show of greatness; for we have seen her forbear to come out of her *quintan*, or boat, through the water, as the other both maids and married women usually do, unless she were carried forth between two of her servants. I was once early at her house (it being summer-time) when she was laid without-doors under the shadow of a broad-leaved tree, upon a pallet of osiers, spread over with four or five fine, grey mats, herself covered with a fair, white, dressed deerskin or two; and when she rose she had a maid who fetched her a frontal[9] of white coral and pendants of great but imperfect-coloured and worse-drilled pearls, which she put into her ears, and a chain with long links of copper, which they call *tapaantaminais*, and which came twice or thrice double about her neck, and they accompt a jolly ornament; and sure, thus attired, with some variety of feathers and flowers stuck in their hairs, they seem as debonair,[10] quaint,[11] and well-pleased[12] as, I wis, a daughter of the house of Austria behung with all her jewels. Likewise her maid fetched her a mantle, which they call *puttawus*, which is like a side cloak, made of blue feathers, so artificially and thick sewed together that it shows like a deep purple satin and is very smooth and sleek; and after she brought her water for her hands and then a bunch or two of fresh, green, ashen leaves, as for a towel to wipe them. I offend in this digression the willinger since these were ceremonies which I did little look for, carrying so much presentment of civility, and which are not ordinarily performed to any other amongst them; and the Quiyocahannocks may be able to make for the wars sixty fighting men.

Tackonekintaco, an old werowance of Warrasqueoc, whom Captain Newport brought prisoner with his son Tangoit about 1610 to our Lord General, lying then at Point Comfort, and whom again His Lordship released upon promises and a solemn contract made by the old man to exchange with His Lordship (after he should have gathered in his harvest in August following) five hundred bushels of wheat, beans, and peas, for copper, beads, and hatchets; and, for the better colour, carrying away his son, he left a nephew (as he said) of his with His Lordship as a pawn or hostage until the performance;

howbeit the imposture nephew, privy beforehand to the falsehood of the old man, watching his opportunity, leaped overboard one night (being kept in the *Delaware*, and to be more sure of him at that time fettered both legs together, with a sea-gown[13] upon him); yet, I say, he adventured to get from us by swimming, and sure either he recovered the south shore or sunk in the attempt; which of either was his fortune we know not, only if he miscarried we never found his body nor gown, and the Indians of Warrasqueoc would oftentimes afterwards mock us and call to us for him, and at length make a great laughter and tell us he was come home—how true or false is no great matter. But indeed the old king after that time refused to perform the former bargain, for which His Lordship, to give them to understand how he would not be so dealt with, sent forth two companies, the [blank] of [blank], His Lordship's own company, under the command of Captain Brewster, and some seamen under Captain Argall, who fell upon two towns of his and burned them to the ground, with all their goodly furniture of mats and dishes, wooden pots and platters, for of this sort is all their goodly *epitrapezia*, or vessels belonging to their use for the table or what else; and these Warrasqueocs may make sixty men. . . .

Wowinchopunck, werowance of Paspahegh, whom the ninth of February 1610, whilst he with a company of his people were attempting some practice upon our old blockhouse at Jamestown, and had been for the same skulking about there some two or three days and nights, Captain George Percy, governor of the town, sent forth Ensign Powell and Ensign Walker to make surprise of him, if they could possibly, and bring him alive into the town. But they, not finding him at any such advantages, yet loath to lose him or let him escape altogether, set upon him (he being one of the mightiest and strongest savages that Powhatan had under him and was therefore one of his champions and one who had killed treacherously many of our men, as he could beguile them or as he at any time found them by chance single in the woods, strayed beyond the command of the blockhouse), and Powell, running upon him, thrust him twice through the body with an arming-sword; howbeit his people came in so fast and shot their arrows so thick as our men, being unarmed, in their doublet and hose only and without pieces, were fain to retire whilst the Indians recovered the werowance's body and carried it away with a mighty quickness and speed of foot and with a horrible yell and howling; howbeit the lieutenant of the blockhouse, one Puttock, followed hard and overreached one of the *cronoccoes* or chief men and, closing with him, overthrew him and with his dagger

P

sent him to accompany his master in the other world. And the Paspaheghs may make in number for the wars forty.

Pochins, one of Powhatan's sons at Kecoughtan and was the young
werowance there at the same time when Sir Thomas Gates, Lieutenant
General, took possession of it. It is an ample and fair country indeed,
an admirable portion of land, comparatively high, wholesome, and
fruitful, the seat sometimes of a thousand Indians and three hundred
Indian houses, and those Indians, as it may well appear, better husbands
than in any part else that we have observed, which is the reason that
so much ground is there cleared and open, enough with little labour
already prepared to receive corn or make vineyards of two or three
thousand acres; and where besides we find many fruit trees, a kind of
gooseberry, cherries, and other plums, the mariock apple,[14] and many
pretty coppices or bosks, as it were, of mulberry trees; and is indeed
a delicate and necessary seat for a city or chief fortification, being so
near (within three miles by water) the mouth of our bay, and is well
appointed a fit seat for one of our chief commanders, since Point
Comfort being, out of all dispute, to be fortified, to secure our towns
above, to keep open the mouth of our river, by which our shipping
may be let in, it will require the faith and judgement of a worthy commander to be there always present. Besides, there will be good fishing,
and upon one of the capes may be placed a garrison to attend the
furnaces and boiling-pots for the making of salt, which without
question there (as in the Bermudas) may be made for all occasions, to
serve the colony and the fishing voyages for the same. Likewise, upon
Point Comfort a great quantity of one kind of silk-grass grows, there
as yet disorderly, which, having the ground prepared and fitted for it,
would retribute a commodity worthy the pains, if not going beyond
the expectation of the good which is hoped of it. Our Lord General
and Lieutenant General have erected here two forts, as is before
remembered, the one called Fort Henry, the other Charles Fort, as the
river which runs in and serves both His Lordship hath called Southampton River.[15]

Upon the death of an old werowance of this place some fifteen or
sixteen years since (being too powerful neighbours to side[16] the great
Powhatan), it is said Powhatan, taking the advantage, subtly stepped
in and conquered the people, killing the chief and most of them, and
the reserved he transported over the river, craftily changing their seat
and quartering them amongst his own people, until now at length
the remain of those living have with much suit obtained of him

Payankatank, which he not long since (as you have heard likewise) dispeopled. They might have made of able men for the wars thirty.

Upon the river of Chickahominy, some eight or twelve miles from Jamestown, which falls from the north side unto our King's River, are the Chickahominies, who, being a warlike and free people, albeit they pay certain duties to Powhatan and for copper will be waged to serve and help him in his wars, yet they will not admit of any werowance from him to govern over them but suffer themselves to be regulated and guided by their priests, with the assistance of their elders, whom they call *cawcawwassoughs*; and they make three hundred men. . . .

And thus it may appear how they are a people who have their several divisions, provinces, and princes, to live in and to command over, and do differ likewise (as amongst Christians) both in stature, language, and condition; some being great people, as the Susquehannas, some very little, as the Wicocomocos; some speaking likewise more articulate and plain, and some more inward and hollow, as is before remembered; some courteous and more civil, others cruel and bloody; Powhatan having large territories and many petty kings under him, as some have fewer.

## Chapter 5

*A true description of the people; of their colour, constitution, and disposition; their apparel*

They are generally of a colour brown, or rather tawny, which the mothers cast them into with a kind of arsenic-stone (like red patise[17] or orpiment),[18] or rather with red-tempered ointments of earth and the juice of certain scrused[19] roots, so soon as they are born; and this they do (keeping themselves still so smudged and besmeared) either for the custom of the country or the better to defend them (since they go most-what naked) from the stinging of mosquitoes (kinds of flies or biting gnats, such as the Greeks called *scynipes*, as yet in great swarms within the Arches[20] and which here breed abundantly amongst the marish whorts and fen-berries). And of the same hue are their women, howbeit it is supposed neither of them naturally born so discoloured, for Captain Smith (living sometime amongst them) affirmeth how they are from the womb indifferent white, but as the men so do the women dye and disguise themselves into this tawny colour, esteeming it the best beauty to be nearest such a kind of murrey as a sodden quince is of (to liken it to the nearest colour I can), for which they daily anoint both face and bodies all over with such a kind of fucus or unguent as can cast them into that stain. . . . Howbeit he or she that hath obtained the perfectest art in the tempering of this colour with any better kind of earth, herb, or root, preserves it not yet so secret and precious unto herself as do our great ladies their oil of talcum or other painting white and red, but they friendly communicate the secret and teach it one another. After their anointing, which is daily, they dry them in the sun and thereby make their skins, besides the colour more black and spotted, which the sun kissing oft and hard adds to their painting, the more rough and rugged.

Their heads and shoulders they paint oftenest, and those red, with the root puccoon brayed[21] to powder, mixed with oil of the walnut or bear's grease; this they hold in summer doth check the heat and in winter arms them in some measure against the cold. Many other forms of paintings they use; but he is the most gallant who is the most monstrous and ugly to behold.

Their hair is black, gross, long, and thick. The men have no beards; their noses are broad, flat, and full at the end; great big lips and wide mouths (yet nothing so unsightly as the Moors). They are generally tall of stature and straight, of comely proportions, and the women have handsome limbs, slender arms, and pretty hands; and when they sing they have a delightful and pleasant tang in their voices.

For their apparel, they are sometimes covered with the skins of wild beasts, which in winter are dressed with the hair but in the summer without. The better sort use large mantles of divers skins, not much differing from the Irish faldings, some embroidered with white beads, some with copper, other painting after their manner; but the common sort have scarce wherewithal to cover their nakedness but stick long blades [of] grass, the leaves of trees, or such-like under broad baldrics of leather, which covers them behind and before.

The better sort of women cover them (for the most part) all over with skin mantles, finely dressed, shagged and fringed at the skirt, carved and coloured, with some pretty works or the proportion of beasts, fowl, tortoises, or other such-like imagery as shall best please or express the fancy of the wearer. Their younger women go not shadowed amongst their own company until they be nigh eleven or twelve returns of the leaf old (for so they accompt and bring about the year, calling the fall of the leaf *taquitock*); nor are they much ashamed thereof; and therefore would the before-remembered Pocahontas, a well-featured but wanton young girl, Powhatan's daughter, sometimes resorting to our fort, of the age then of eleven or twelve years, get the boys forth with her into the market place and make them wheel, falling on their hands, turning their heels upwards, whom she would follow and so wheel herself, naked as she was, all the fort over. But being past once twelve years, they put on a kind of *semicinctum* leathern apron (as do our artificers or handicraftsmen) before their bellies and are very shamefaced to be seen bare. We have seen some use mantles made both of turkey feathers and other fowl, so prettily wrought and woven with threads that nothing could be discerned but the feathers, which were exceeding warm and very handsome. *Nuda mulier erat pulchra* (saith Plautus) *quam purpurata pulchrior?*[22] Indeed, the ornament of that sex, who receive an addition of delicacy by their garments. True it is, sometimes in cold weather, or when they go a-hunting, or seeking the fruits of the woods, or gathering bents[23] for their mats, both men and women, to defend them from the bushes, put on a kind of leather breeches and stockings, all fastened together, made of deerskins, which they tie and wrap about the loins after the fashion of the Turks or Irish trouses.

They adorn themselves most with copper beads and painting. Of the men there be some who will paint their bodies black, and some yellow, and being oiled all over they will stick therein the soft down of sundry coloured birds, of bluebirds, white heronshaws, and the feathers of the carnation bird, which they call *ahshowcutteis*, as if so many variety of laces were stitched to their skins, which makes a wondrous show. The men, being angry and prepared to fight, paint and cross their foreheads, cheeks, and the right side of their heads diversly, either with *terra sigillata* or with their root puccoon.

The women have their arms, breasts, thighs, shoulders, and faces cunningly embroidered with divers works; for, pouncing and searing their skins with a kind of instrument heated in the fire, they figure therein flowers and fruits of sundry lively kinds, as also snakes, serpents, efts, etc., and this they do by dropping upon the seared flesh sundry colours, which rubbed into the stamp will never be taken away again, because it will not only be dried into the flesh but grow therein.

The men shave their hair on the right side very close, keeping a ridge commonly on the top or crown like a cock's-comb; for their women with two shells will grate away the hair into any fashion they please. On the left side they wear their hair at full length, with a lock of an ell long, which they anoint often with walnut oil, whereby it is very sleek and shines like a raven's wing. Sometimes they tie up their lock with an artificial and well-laboured knot, in the same fashion as I have seen the *carazzaies*[24] of Scio and Pera, stuck with many coloured gewgaws, as the cast head or brow-antler of a deer, the hand of their enemy dried, croisetts of bright and shining copper, like the new moon. Many wear the whole skin of a hawk, stuffed, with the wings abroad, and buzzards' or other fowls' whole wings, and to the feathers they will fasten a little rattle about the bigness of the chape[25] of a rapier, which they take from the tail of a snake, and sometimes divers kinds of shells, hanging loose by small purflets or threads, that, being shaken as they move, they will make a certain murmuring or whistling noise by gathering wind, in which they seem to take great jollity and hold it a kind of bravery.[26]

Their ears they bore with wide holes, commonly two or three, and in the same they do hang chains of stained pearl, bracelets of white bone, or shreds of copper, beaten thin and bright and wound up hollow, and with a great pride certain fowls' legs—eagles, hawks, turkeys, etc.—with beasts' claws—bears, raccoons, squirrels, etc.— the claws thrust through, they let hang upon the cheek to the full view. And some of their men there be who will wear in these holes a small green-and-yellow-coloured live snake, near half a yard in length, which, crawling and lapping himself about his neck, oftentimes familiarly he suffers to kiss his lips; others wear a dead rat tied by the tail, and such-like conundrums.

The women are in themselves so modest as in the time of their sickness they have great care to be seen abroad, at what time they go apart and keep from the men in a several room which they have for themselves as a kind of *gynaceum*, nor will the men at such a time press into the nursery where they are.

The men are very strong, of able bodies and full of agility, accustoming themselves to endure hardness, to lie in the woods under a tree, by a small fire, in the worst of winter, in frost and snow, or in the reeds and grass, as in ambuscado, to accomplish their purposes in the summer.

They are inconstant in everything but what fear constraineth them to keep, crafty, timorous, quick of apprehension, ingenious enough in their own works: as may testify the weirs in which they take their fish, which are certain enclosures made of reeds and framed in the fashion of a labyrinth or maze, set a fathom deep in the water, with divers chambers or beds, out of which the entangled fish cannot return or get out, being once in (well may a great one by chance break the reeds and so escape, otherwise he remains a prey to the fisherman the next low water, which they fish with a net tied at the end of a pole); as like-wise may speak for them their nets, their artificial dressing of leather, their cordage, which they make of their natural hemp and flax, together with their cunning dressing of that and preserving the whole year great litches or bundles of the same to be used upon any occasion; and of their girdles, which they make of silk-grass, much like St Francis' cordon, their cloaks of feathers, their bows and bowstrings, their arrows, their crownets, which their werowances wear, and their queens' *fasciae crinales*, borders or frontals of white beads, coral, and copper; especially their boats, which they call *quintans* and are very shapeful, made of one piece of timber, like the ancient *monoxylum navigium*, their mats, and all their household implements and such-like. . . .

<br>

32

# Virginia's Natural Bounty (1613)

The Virginia Company of London, eager to disseminate favourable propaganda about its colony overseas, was instrumental in publishing an eye-witness account by a preacher in Jamestown, Alexander Whitaker, whose *Good News from Virginia* appeared in 1613 with a laudatory preface by William Crashaw as long as Whitaker's own essay. The excerpt from Whitaker, printed below, is a good example of the optimistic literature about colonization that the Virginia Company was publishing at this time.

. . . The whole continent of Virginia, situate within the degrees of 34 and 47, is a place beautified by God with all the ornaments of nature and enriched with His earthly treasures. That part of it which we already possess, beginning at the Bay of Chesapeake and stretching itself in northerly latitude to the degrees of 39 and 40, is interlined with seven most goodly rivers, the least whereof is equal to our river of Thames; and all these rivers are so nearly joined as that there is not very much distance[1] of dry ground between either of them, and those several mainlands are everywhere watered with many veins or creeks of water, which sundry ways do overthwart the land and make it almost navigable from one river to the other. The commodity[2] whereof to those that shall inhabit this land is infinite in respect of the speedy and easy transportance of goods from one river to the other. I cannot better manifest it unto you but in advising you to consider whether the water or land hath been more beneficial to the Low Countries; but here we shall have the commodity both of water and land more ready, with less charge and labour, than hath been bestowed by them in turning land into water.

The river which we inhabit (commonly called Powhatan's River)[3] ebbeth and floweth 140 miles from the main, at the mouth whereof are the two forts of Henrico and Charles. Forty-two miles upward is the first and mother Christian town seated, called Jamestown, and seventy miles beyond that upward is the new town of Henrico, built and so named in the memory of the noble Prince Henry of lasting and blessed memory. Ten miles beyond this town is a place called the Falls,[4] because the river hath there a great descent, falling down between many mineral rocks which be there; twelve miles farther beyond this place is there a crystal rock wherewith the Indians do head many of their arrows; three days' journey from thence is there a rock or stony hill found, which is in the top covered all over with a perfect and most rich silver ore. Our men that went to discover those parts had but two iron pickaxes with them, and those so ill tempered that the points of them turned again and bowed at every stroke, so that we could not search the entrails of that place; yet some trial was made of that ore with good success and argument of much hope.

Six days' journey beyond this mine a great ridge of high hills do run along the mainland, not far from whom the Indians report a great sea doth run, which we commonly call a South Sea, but in respect of our habitation is a West Sea, for there the sun setteth from us. The higher ground is much like unto the mould of France, clay and sand being proportionably mixed together at the top; but if we dig any depth (as we have done for our bricks) we find it to be red clay, full of glistering spangles. There be many rocky places in all quarters, and more than probable likelihoods of rich mines of all sorts: though I knew all, yet it were not convenient at this time that I should utter all, neither have we had means to search for anything as we ought, through present want of men and former wants of provision for the belly. As for iron, steel, antimonium, and *terra sigillata*, they have rather offered themselves to our eyes and hands than been sought for of us.

The air of the country (especially about Henrico and upward) is very temperate and agreeth well with our bodies. The extremity of summer is not so hot as Spain nor the cold of winter so sharp as the frosts of England. The spring and harvest are the two longest seasons and most pleasant; the summer and winter are both but short. The winter is for the most part dry and fair but the summer watered often with many great and sudden showers of rain, whereby the cold of winter is warmed and the heat of summer cooled. Many have died with us heretofore through their own filthiness and want of bodily comforts for sick men; but now very few are sick among us: not above three persons amongst all the inhabitants of Henrico. I would to God our souls were no sicker than our bodies and that other of God's blessings were as general and common as the bodily health. I have seen it by experience and dare boldly affirm it that sickness doth more rage in England quarterly than here yearly. I doubt that hereafter, when our hospital or guest house is built up, you hear of many more cut off by the sword of justice (unless the better people be sent over) than perished by the diseases of the country.

The natural people of the land are generally such as you heard of before: a people to be feared of those that come upon them without defensive armour, but otherwise faint-hearted (if they see their arrows cannot pierce) and easy to be subdued. Shirts of mail or quilted cotton are the best defence against them. There is but one or two of their petty kings that for fear of us have desired our friendship, and those keep good quarter with us, being very pleasant amongst us and (if occasion be) serviceable unto us. Our eldest friends be Pipsco and Chopoke, who are our overthwart neighbours at Jamestown and have been friendly to us in our great want. The other is the werowance of Chesapeake, who but lately traded with us peaceably. If we were once the masters of their country and they stood in fear of us (which might with few hands employed about nothing else be in short time brought to pass), it were an easy matter to make them willingly to forsake the Devil, to embrace the faith of Jesus Christ, and to be baptized. Besides, you cannot easily judge how much they would be available to us in our discoveries of the country, in our buildings and plantings and quiet provision for ourselves, when we may peaceably pass from place to place without need of arms or guard.

The means for our people to live and subsist here of themselves are many and most certain, both for beasts, birds, fish, and herbs. The beasts of the country are for the most part wild: as lions, bears, wolves, and deer; foxes, black and red; raccoons; beavers; possums; squirrels; wildcats, whose skins are of great price; and muskrats, which yield musk as the musk-cats do. There be two kinds of beasts among these most strange: one of them is the female possum, which will let forth her young out of her belly and take them up into her belly again at her pleasure without hurt to herself; neither think this to be a traveller's tale but the very truth, for Nature hath framed her fit for that service: my eyes have been witness unto it and we have sent of them and their young ones into England. The other strange-conditioned creature is the flying squirrel, which, through the help of certain broad flaps of skin growing on each side of her forelegs, will fly from tree to tree twenty or thirty paces at one flight and more, if she have the benefit of a small breath of wind. Besides these, since our coming hither we have brought both kine, goats, and hogs, which prosper well and would multiply exceedingly if they might be provided for.

This country besides is replenished with birds of all sorts, which have been the best sustenance of flesh which our men have had since they came; also eagles and hawks of all sorts, amongst whom are osprey, fishing hawk, and the cormorant. The woods be everywhere full of wild turkeys, which abound and will run as swift as a greyhound. In winter our fields be full of cranes, herons, pigeons, partridges, and blackbirds; the rivers and creeks be overspread everywhere with water-fowl of the greatest and least sort, as swans, flocks of geese and brants, duck and mallard, sheldrakes, divers, etc., besides many other kinds of rare and delectable birds whose names and natures I cannot yet recite; but we want the means to take them.

The rivers abound with fish both great and small. The sea-fish come into our rivers in March and continue until the end of September; great schools of herrings come in first; shads, of a great bigness, and rock fish, follow them. Trouts, bass, flounders, and other dainty fish come in before the other be gone; then come multitudes of great sturgeons, whereof we catch many and should do more but that we want good nets answerable to the breadth and depth of our rivers: besides our channels are so foul in the bottom with great logs and trees that we often break our nets upon them. I cannot reckon nor give proper names to the divers kinds of fresh fish in our rivers. I have caught with mine angle pike, carp, eel, perches of six several kinds, crayfish, and the torope[5] or little turtle, besides many smaller kinds.

Wherefore, since God hath filled the elements of earth, air, and waters with His creatures, good for our food and nourishment, let not the fear of starving hereafter, or of any great want, dishearten your valiant minds from coming to a place of so great plenty. If the country were ours and means for the taking of them (which shortly I hope shall be brought to pass), then all of these should be ours; we have them now but we are fain to fight for them; then should we have them without that trouble. Fear not, then, to want food, but only provide means to get it here. We have store of wild-fowl in England, but what are they better for them that cannot come by them, wanting means to catch them? Even such is and hath been our case heretofore.

But even these are not all the commodities which we may find here: for the earth will yield much more fruit to our industrious labours, as hath been proved by the corn and other things which we have planted this last year. I have made proof of it, with the help of three more, being a stranger to that business and having not a body inured to such labour, and set so much corn, *horis succisivus unius septimanae* (in the idle hours of one week), as will suffice me for bread one quarter of a year; and one commodity is besides in this corn, that from the time of setting unto the time of gathering five months will abundantly suffice: for we set corn from the beginning of March until the end of May, and reap or gather in July, August, and September. Our English seeds thrive very well here, as peas, onions, turnips, cabbages, coleflowers, carrots, thyme, parsley, hyssop, marjoram, and many other whereof I have tasted and eaten.

What should I name unto you the divers sorts of trees, sweet woods, and physical[6] plants; the divers kinds of oaks and walnut trees; the pines, pitch-trees, soap-ashes trees, sassafras, cedar, ash, maple, cypress, and many more which I daily see and admire at the beauty and riches which God hath bestowed upon this people that yet know not how to use them.

Wherefore, you (right wise and noble adventurers of Virginia) whose hearts God hath stirred up to build Him a temple, to make Him an house, to conquer a kingdom for Him here: be not discouraged with those many lamentable assaults that the Devil hath made against us: he now rageth most because he knoweth his kingdom is to have a short end. Go forward boldly and remember that you fight under the banner of Jesus Christ, that you plant His kingdom Who hath already broken the serpent's head. God may defer His temporal reward for a season, but be assured that in the end you shall find riches and honour in this world and blessed immortality in the world to come. And you, my brethren, my fellow labourers, send up your earnest prayers to God for His church in Virginia, that, since His harvest here is great but the labourers few, He would thrust forth labourers into His harvest. And pray also for me that the ministration of His Gospel may be powerful and effectual by me, to the salvation of many and advancement

of the kingdom of Jesus Christ, to whom, with the Father and the
Holy Spirit, be all honour and glory forevermore.

Amen.

## 33

# A Gossip Reports on Virginia, Including Pocahontas (1612–16)

John Chamberlain, a London gentleman of leisure, was the friend of many
eminent men of his day, but he himself appears to have had no ambition to
do more than observe and enjoy the little world around him. Like Horace
Walpole in a later age, he was an inveterate letter writer, and his letters to
Sir Dudley Carleton, at this time English ambassador to Venice, provide
fascinating sidelights on matters interesting Londoners. Chamberlain's
letters have had various printings. The most complete edition is that edited
by Norman McClure, *The Letters of John Chamberlain* (2 vols., Philadelphia,
1939).

London, July 9, 1612 [State Papers Domestic, James I, LXX, 4]:

It is generally looked for that he [the Spanish Ambassador, Don
Pedro de Zuñiga] will expostulate about our planting in Virginia,
wherein there will need no great contestation, seeing it is to be feared
that action will fall to the ground of itself by the extreme beastly idleness of our nation, which (notwithstanding any cost or diligence used
to support them) will rather die and starve than be brought to any
labour or industry to maintain themselves. Two or three of the last
ships that came thence bring nothing but discomfort and that Sir
Thomas Gates and Sir Thomas Dale are quite out of heart; and to mend
the matter, not past five days since here arrived a ship with ten men,
who (being sent forth to fish for their relief and having taken great
store) have given them the slip and run away, and fill the town with ill
reports, which will hinder that business more than the lottery[1] or any
other art they can use for the present will further it: and yet they have
taken good order to have these runaways apprehended and punished,
or at least sent back again.

London, August 1, 1613 [State Papers Domestic, James I, LXXIV, 49]:

There is a ship come from Virginia with news of their well-doing, which puts some life in that action that before was almost at the last cast. They have taken a daughter of a king that was their greatest enemy, as she was going a-feasting upon a river to visit certain friends; for whose ransom the father offers whatsoever is in his power and to become their friend, and to bring them where they shall meet with gold mines. They propound unto him three conditions: to deliver all the English fugitives, to render all manner of arms or weapons of theirs that are come to his hands, and to give them three hundred quarters of corn. The first two he performed readily and promiseth the other at their harvest, if his daughter may be well used in the mean time. But this ship brought no commodities from thence but only these fair tales and hopes. Marry, touching at the Bermudas, she hath brought thence some quantity of pearl and between twenty and thirty pound weight of ambergris, worth £900 at least, and by the next that is to come thence they are promised to have a return of four times as much. When the business of Virginia was at the highest, in that heat, many gentlemen and others were drawn by persuasion and importunity of friends to underwrite their names for Adventurers, but when it came to the payment (specially the second or third time), their hands were not so ready to go to their purses as they were to the paper, and in the end flatly refused, whereupon they are sued by the Company in the Chancery, where this action finds such favour that they have ready dispatch and the underwriters are forced to make payment, which amounts to a round sum between three and four thousand pound.

London, June 22, 1616 [State Papers Domestic, James I, LXXXVII, 67]:

Sir Thomas Dale is arrived from Virginia and brought with him some ten or twelve old and young of that country, among whom the most remarkable person is Pocahontas (daughter of Powhatan, a king or *cacique* of that country) married to one Rolfe, an Englishman. I hear not of any other riches or matter of worth but only some quantity of sassafras, tobacco, pitch, and clapboard, things of no great value unless there were more plenty and nearer hand. All I can learn of it is that the country is good to live in, if it were stored with people, and might in time become commodious, but there is no present profit to be expected.

# 34

# Pocahontas, Lured to Jamestown by a Stratagem, Marries John Rolfe (1614)

Excerpts from Ralph Hamor, *A True Discourse of the Present Estate of Virginia and the Success of the Affairs There until the Eighteenth of June 1614* ... (1615).

... N o w, after five years' intestine war with the revengeful, implacable Indians, a firm peace (not again easily to be broken) hath been lately concluded, not only with the neighbour and bordering Indians, as on Potomac, Tappahannock, and other rivers, but even with that subtle, old, revengeful Powhatan and all the people under his subjection, for all whom Powhatan himself stands firmly engaged. By which means we shall not only be furnished with what commodities their country yieldeth and have all the helps they may afford us in our endeavours, ... but also, which will be most for our benefit, our own men may, without hazard, I might say with security (by self-experience) follow their several labours, whereby twenty shall now be able to perform more than heretofore hath been forty. ...

It chanced Powhatan's delight and darling, his daughter Pocahontas (whose fame hath even been spread in England by the title of Nonpareil of Virginia),[1] in her princely progress, if I may so term it, took some pleasure, in the absence of Captain Argall, to be among her friends at Potomac (as it seemeth by the relation I had), employed thither as shopkeepers to a fair, to exchange some of her father's commodities for theirs. Where, residing some three months or longer, it fortuned, upon occasion either of promise or profit, Captain Argall to arrive there, whom Pocahontas, desirous to renew her familiarity with the English and delighting to see them as unknown, fearful perhaps to be surprised, would gladly visit. As she did, of whom no sooner had Captain Argall intelligence but he dealt with an old friend and adopted brother of his, Japazaws, how and by what means he might procure her captive, assuring him that now or never was the time to pleasure him if he intended indeed that love which he had made profession of, that in ransom of her he might redeem some of our Englishmen and arms now in the possession of her father, promising to use her with all fair and gentle entreaty.

Japazaws, well assured that his brother, as he promised, would use her courteously, promised his best endeavours and secrecy to accomplish his desire and thus wrought it, making his wife an instrument (which sex hath ever been most powerful in beguiling enticements) to effect his plot, which he had thus laid: he agreed that himself, his wife, and Pocahontas would accompany his brother to the waterside, whither come, his wife should feign a great and longing desire to go aboard and see the ship, which, being there three or four times before, she had never seen, and should be earnest with her husband to permit her. He seemed angry with her, making, as he pretended, so unnecessary a request, especially being without the company of women, which denial she, taking unkindly, must feign to weep (as who knows not that women can command tears), whereupon her husband, seeming to pity those counterfeit tears, gave her leave to go aboard, so that it would please Pocahontas to accompany her.

Now was the greatest labour to win her, guilty (perhaps) of her father's wrongs (though not known, as she supposed), to go with her; yet by her earnest persuasions she assented. So forthwith aboard they went. The best cheer that could be made was seasonably provided; to supper they went, merry on all hands, especially Japazaws and his wife, who, to express their joy, would e'er be treading upon Captain Argall's foot, as who should say, ' 'Tis done; she is your own.' Supper ended, Pocahontas was lodged in the gunner's room, but Japazaws and his wife desired to have some conference with their brother, which was only to acquaint him by what stratagem they had betrayed his prisoner, as I have already related. After which discourse, to sleep they went, Pocahontas nothing mistrusting this policy, who, nevertheless, being most possessed with fear and desire of return, was first up and hastened Japazaws to be gone.

Captain Argall, having secretly well rewarded him with a small copper kettle and some other less valuable toys, so highly by him esteemed that doubtless he would have betrayed his own father for them, permitted both him and his wife to return but told him that for divers considerations, as for that his father had then eight of our Englishmen, many swords, pieces, and other tools, which he had at several times by treacherous murdering our men taken from them, which, though of no use to him, he would not re-deliver, he would reserve Pocahontas, whereat she began to be exceeding pensive and discontented, yet ignorant of the dealing of Japazaws, who in outward appearance was no less discontented that he should be the means of her captivity. Much ado there was to persuade her to be patient, which with extraordinary courteous usage by little and little was wrought in her.

And so to Jamestown she was brought, a messenger to her father forthwith dispatched to advertise him that his only daughter was in the hands and possession of the English, there to be kept till such time as he would ransom her with our men, swords, pieces, and other tools treacherously taken from us. The news was unwelcome and troublesome unto him, partly for the love he bare to his daughter and partly for the love he bare to our men, his prisoners, of whom (though with us they were unapt for any employment) he made great use, and those swords and pieces of ours, which (though of no use to him) it delighted him to view and look upon.

He could not without long advice and deliberation with his council resolve upon anything, and it is true, we heard nothing of him till, three months after, by persuasions of others he returned us seven of our men, with each of them a musket unserviceable, and by them sent us word that whensoever we pleased to deliver his daughter he would give us, in satisfaction of his injuries done to us and for the rest of our pieces broken and stolen from him, five hundred bushels of corn and be forever friends with us. The men and pieces (in part of payment) we received and returned him answer that his daughter was very well and kindly entreated and so should be howsoever he dealt with us; but we could not believe that the rest of our arms were either lost or stolen from him, and therefore till he returned them all we would not by any means deliver his daughter, and then it should be at his choice whether he would establish peace or continue enemies with us. . . .

[Negotiations and threats alternated, until two of Powhatan's sons, anxious for Pocahontas's welfare, intervened.]

Long before this time, a gentleman of approved behaviour and honest carriage, Master John Rolfe, had been in love with Pocahontas and she with him, which thing, at the instant that we were in parley with them, myself made known to Sir Thomas Dale by a letter[2] from him, whereby he entreated his advice and furtherance in his love, if so it seemed fit to him for the good of the plantation, and Pocahontas herself acquainted her brethren therewith. Which resolution, Sir Thomas Dale well approving, was the only cause he was so mild amongst them, who otherwise would not have departed their river without other conditions.

The bruit of this pretended marriage came soon to Powhatan's knowledge, a thing acceptable to him, as appeared by his sudden consent thereunto, whom some ten days after sent an old uncle of hers, named Opachisco, to give her as his deputy in the church and two of his sons to see the marriage solemnized, which was accordingly done about the fifth of April, and ever since we have had friendly commerce and trade, not only with Powhatan himself but also with his subjects round about us; so as now I see no reason why the colony should not thrive apace.

Besides this love by this means with Powhatan concluded, it will be worth my pains to run over our friendship with our next neighbours, the Chickahominies, lately confirmed, a lusty and daring people, who have long time lived free from Powhatan's subjection, having laws and governors within themselves. These people, hearing of our concluded peace with Powhatan (as the noise thereof was soon bruited abroad), sent two of their men unto us and two fat bucks for present to our king (for so Sir Thomas Dale is generally reputed and termed amongst them) and offered themselves and service unto him, alleging that albeit in former times they had been our enemies and we theirs, yet they would now, if we pleased, become not only our trusty friends but even King James his subjects and tributaries and relinquish their old name of Chickahominies and take upon them, as they call us, the name of *tassantasses*; and because they have no principal commander or werowance, they would entreat Sir Thomas Dale, as King James his deputy, to be their supreme head, king, and governor, and in all just causes and quarrels to defend them, as they would be ready at all times to aid him. . . .

When the appointed day came, Sir Thomas Dale himself and Captain Argall, with fifty men in a barge and frigate well appointed, lest any treachery might be intended, set forward to Chickahominy. . . .

After long discourse of their former proceedings, Captain Argall told them that now since they had entreated peace and promised their love and friendship, he was sent unto them from the great werowance to conclude the same, all former injuries on both sides set apart and forgotten, which he would do upon these conditions.

First, that they should take upon them, as they promised, the name of *tassantasses*, or Englishmen, and be King James his subjects and be forever honest, faithful, and trusty unto his deputy in their country.

Q

Secondly, that they should never kill any of our men or cattle, but if either our men or cattle should offend them or run to them they should bring them home again and should receive satisfaction for the trespass done them.

Thirdly, they should at all times be ready and willing to furnish us with three or four hundred bowmen to aid us against the Spaniards (whose name is odious amongst them, for Powhatan's father was driven by them from the West Indies into those parts),[3] or against any other Indians which should, contrary to the established peace, offer us any injury.

Fourthly, they shall not, upon any occasion whatsoever, break down any of our pales or come into any of our towns or forts by any other ways, issues, or ports than ordinary, but first call and say the *tassantasses* are there, and, so coming, they shall at all times be let in and kindly entertained.

Fifthly, so many fighting men as they have, which may be at the least five hundred, should yearly bring into our storehouse, at the beginning of their harvest, two bushels of corn a man, as tribute of their obedience to His Majesty and to his deputy there, for which they should receive so many iron tomahawks, or small hatchets.

Lastly, the eight chief men which govern as substitutes and councilors under Sir Thomas Dale shall at all times see these articles and conditions duly performed, for which they shall receive a red coat or livery from our king yearly and each of them the picture of His Majesty, engraven in copper, with a chain of copper to hang it about his neck, whereby they shall be known to be King James his noblemen; so as, if these conditions, or any of them be broken, the offenders themselves shall not only be punished but also those commanders, because they stand engaged for them.

After these articles were thus proposed, the whole assembly, assenting thereunto, answered with a great shout and noise that they would readily and willingly perform them all. . . .

So soon as there was an end of speaking and the peace firmly concluded and assented unto, Captain Argall, by the gift of eight great pieces of copper and eight great tomahawks, bound the eight great men or councilors to the exact performance and keeping of the same, according to the conditions proclaimed, which they very gladly and thankfully accepted, and returned him, as testimonies of their loves, venison, turkeys, fresh fish, baskets, mats, and such-like things as they were then furnished with; and so the counsel broke up, and then every man brought to sell to our men skins, bowls, mats, baskets, tobacco, etc., and became as familiar amongst us as if they had been Englishmen indeed. . . .

The greatest and main enemies and disturbers of our proceedings, and that which hath hitherto deterred our people to address themselves into those parts have been only two: enmity with the naturals and the bruit of famine. One of these two (and that, indeed, which was some cause of the other) I have already removed and shall as easily take away the other; howbeit it were too great folly (I might say, impudency) in me to aver that there hath reigned no such infection in the colony, occasioned merely by misgovernment, idleness, and faction. . . . Yet now I dare and will boldly affirm to the greatest adversary of the plantation that shall aver the contrary that there is that plenty of food, which every man by his own industry may easily and doth procure, that the poorest there and most in want hath not been so much pinched with hunger this four years that if he would take any pains he knew not where to fetch a good meal's meat. . . .

Sir Thomas Dale hath taken a new course throughout the whole colony, by which means the general store (apparel only excepted) shall not be charged with anything; and this it is: he hath allotted to every man in the colony three English acres of clear corn-ground, which every man is to mature and tend, being in the nature of farmers (the Bermuda undertakers only excepted), and they are not called unto any service or labour belonging to the colony more than one month in the year, which shall neither be in seed-time or in harvest, for which, doing no other duty to the colony, they are yearly to pay into the store two barrels and a half of corn, there to be reserved to keep new men, which shall be sent over, the first year after their arrival. . . .

To proceed, therefore, in my encouragement to painful[4] people, such as either through crosses in this world, or racked rents, or else great charge of children and family, live here, and that not without much care and sweat, into extreme poverty, for those this country hath present remedy. Every such person so well disposed to adventure thither shall soon find the difference between their own and that country, the affairs in the colony being so well ordered and the hardest tasks already overpassed that whosoever (now or hereafter) shall happily arrive there shall find a handsome house of some four rooms, or more, if he have a family, to repose himself in, rent-free, and twelve English acres of ground adjoining thereunto, very strongly impaled, which ground is only allotted unto him for roots, garden herbs, and corn; neither shall he need to provide himself (as were wont the first planters) of a year's provision of victuals, for that the store there will be able to afford him, and upon these conditions he shall be entertained. He shall have for himself and family a competent twelvemonth's provision delivered unto him, in which time it must be his care to provide for himself and family ever after as those already there. To this end he shall be furnished with necessary tools of all sorts, and for his better subsistence he shall have poultry and swine, and, if he deserve it, a goat or two, perhaps a cow given him, which once compassed, how happily he may live, as do many there who, I am sure, will never return, I submit to their own future well-experienced judgements. . . .

[Hamor proceeds to tell of Sir Thomas Dale's project of building another town at the falls of the James, called Henrico in honour of Prince Henry.]

I should be too tedious if I should give up the accompt of every day's labour, which therefore I purposely omit and will only describe the town in the very state and perfection which I left it, and, first, for the situation: it stands upon a neck of a very high land, three parts thereof environed with the main river and cut over between the two rivers with a strong pale, which maketh the neck of land an island. There is in this town three streets of well-framed houses, a handsome church, and the foundation of a more stately one laid of brick, in length an hundred foot and fifty foot wide, besides storehouses, watchhouses, and such-like. There are also, as ornaments belonging to this town, upon the verge of this river, five fair blockhouses or commanders, wherein live the honester sort of people, as in farms in England, and there keep continual sentinel for the town's security, and about two miles from the town into the main a pale of two miles in length, cut over from river to river, guarded likewise with several commanders, with a great quantity of corn-ground impaled, sufficient, if there were no more in the colony secured, to maintain with but easy manuring and husbandry more men than I suppose will be addressed thither (the more is the pity) these three years. . . .

[There follows a description of Bermuda Hundred, established the previous Christmas, and then Jamestown proper.]

About fifty miles from this seat [Rochdale Hundred] on the other side of the rivers is Jamestown situate upon a goodly and fertile island, which although formerly scandaled with[5] unhealthful air, we have since approved as healthful as any other place in the country. And this I can say by mine own experience, that that corn and garden ground, which with much labour (being when we first seated upon it a thick wood) we have cleared and impaled, is as fertile as any other we have had experience and trial of. The town itself . . . is reduced into a handsome form and hath in it two fair rows of houses, all of framed timber, two stories and an upper garret or cornloft high, besides three large and substantial storehouses joined together, in length some hundred and twenty foot and in breadth forty; and this town hath been lately newly and strongly impaled and a fair platform for ordnance in the west bulwark raised. There are also without this town in the island some very pleasant and beautiful houses, two blockhouses to observe and watch lest the Indians at any time should swim over the back river and come into the island, and certain other farm-houses. . . .

## 35

# Rolfe Marries Pocahontas to Convert Her —So He Claims (1614)

'The Copy of the Gentleman's Letter to Sir Thomas Dale that after married Powhatan's daughter, containing the reasons moving him thereunto.' Printed in Hamor's *A True Discourse* (1615).

Honourable Sir and most worthy Governor:

When your leisure shall best serve you to peruse these lines, I trust in God the beginning will not strike you into a greater admiration than the end will give you good content. It is a matter of no small moment concerning my own particular, which here I impart unto you, and which toucheth me so nearly as the tenderness of my salvation. Howbeit I freely subject myself to your grave and mature judgement, deliberation, approbation, and determination, assuring myself of your zealous admonitions and godly comforts, either persuading me to desist or encouraging me to persist therein with a religious fear and godly care, for which (from the very instant that this began to root itself within the secret bosom of my breast) my daily and earnest prayers have been, still are, and ever shall be poured forth with as sincere a godly zeal as I possibly may to be directed, aided, and governed in all my thoughts, words, and deeds to the glory of God and for my eternal consolation. To persevere wherein I never had more need nor (till now) could ever imagine to have been moved with the like occasion.

But my case standing as it doth, what better unworldly refuge can I here seek than to shelter myself under the safety of your favourable protection? And did not my ease proceed from an unspotted conscience, I should not dare to offer to your view and approved judgement these passions of my troubled soul, so full of fear and trembling is hypocrisy and dissimulation. But knowing my own innocency and godly fervour in the whole prosecution hereof, I doubt not of your benign acceptance and clement construction. As for malicious depravers and turbulent spirits, to whom nothing is tasteful but what pleaseth their unsavoury palate, I pass[1] not for them, being well assured in my persuasion (by the often trial and proving of myself in my holiest meditations and prayers) that I am called hereunto by the spirit of God, and it shall be sufficient for me to be protected by yourself in all virtuous and pious endeavours. And for my more happy proceeding herein, my daily oblations[2] shall ever be addressed to bring to pass so good effects that yourself and all the world may truly say, 'This is the work of God and it is marvellous in our eyes.'

But to avoid tedious preambles and to come nearer the matter: first suffer me with your patience to sweep and make clean the way wherein I walk from all suspicions and doubts which may be covered therein and faithfully to reveal unto you what should move me hereunto.

Let, therefore, this my well-advised[3] protestation, which here I make between God and my own conscience, be a sufficient witness at the dreadful Day of Judgement (when the secret of all men's hearts shall be opened) to condemn me herein if my chiefest intent and purpose be not to strive with all my power of body and mind in the undertaking of so mighty a matter, no way led (so far forth as man's weakness may permit) with the unbridled desire of carnal affection, but for the good of this plantation, for the honour of our country, for the glory of God, for my own salvation, and for the converting to the true knowledge of God and Jesus Christ an unbelieving creature, namely Pocahontas, to whom my hearty and best thoughts are and have a long time been so entangled and enthralled in so intricate a labyrinth that I was even awearied to unwind myself thereout. But Almighty God, who never faileth His that truly invocate His holy name, hath opened the gate and led me by the hand that I might plainly see and discern the safe paths wherein to tread.

To you, therefore, most noble sir, the patron and father of us in this country, do I utter the effects of this my settled and long-continued affection (which hath made a mighty war in my meditations), and here I do truly relate to what issue this dangerous combat is come unto, wherein I have not only examined but thoroughly tried and pared my thoughts even to the quick before I could find any fit wholesome and apt applications to cure so dangerous an ulcer. I never failed to offer my daily and faithful prayers to God for His sacred and holy assistance. I forgot not to set before mine eyes the frailty of mankind, his proneness to evil, his indulgency of wicked thoughts, with many other imperfections wherein man is daily ensnared and oftentimes overthrown, and them compared to my present estate. Nor was I ignorant of the heavy displeasure which Almighty God conceived against the sons of Levi and Israel for marrying strange wives, nor of the inconveniencies which may thereby arise, with other the like motions[4] which made me look about warily and with good circumspections into the grounds and principal agitations which thus should provoke me to be in love with one whose education hath been rude, her manners barbarous, her generation[5] accursed, and so discrepant in all nurture from myself that oftentimes with fear and trembling I have ended my private controversy with this: 'Surely these are wicked instigations, hatched by him who seeketh and delighteth in man's destructions'; and so, with fervent praises to be ever preserved from such diabolical assaults (as I took those to be), I have taken some rest.

Thus, when I had thought I had obtained my peace and quietness, behold another but more gracious temptation hath made breaches into my holiest and strongest meditations, with which I have been put to a new trial in a straiter manner than the former; for besides the many passions and sufferings which I have daily, hourly, yea, and in my sleep, endured, even awaking me to astonishment, taxing me with remissness and carelessness, refusing and neglecting to perform the duty of a good Christian, pulling me by the ear and crying, 'Why dost not thou endeavour to make her a Christian?'[6] And these have happened, to my greater wonder, even when she hath been furthest separated from me, which in common reason (were it not an undoubted work of God) might breed forgetfulness of a far more worthy creature. Besides, I say, the holy spirit of God hath often demanded of me why I was

created. If not for transitory pleasures and worldly vanities, but to
labour in the Lord's vineyard, there to sow and plant, to nourish and
increase the fruits thereof, daily adding, with the good husband in the
Gospel, somewhat to the talent,[7] that in the end the fruits may be reaped,
to the comfort of the labourer in this life and his salvation in the world
to come. And if this be, as undoubtedly this is, the service Jesus Christ
requireth of His best servant, woe unto him that hath these instruments
of piety put into his hands and wilfully despiseth to work with them.
Likewise adding hereunto her great appearance of love to me, her
desire to be taught and instructed in the knowledge of God, her
capableness of understanding, her aptness and willingness to receive
any good impression, and also the spiritual, besides her own, incite-
ments stirring me up hereunto.

What should I do? Shall I be of so untoward a disposition as to refuse to lead the blind into the right way? Shall I be so unnatural as not
to give bread to the hungry? or uncharitable as not to cover the
naked? Shall I despise to actuate these pious duties of a Christian?
Shall the base fear of displeasing the world overpower and withhold
me from revealing unto man these spiritual works of the Lord, which
in my meditations and prayers I have daily made known unto him?
God forbid! I assuredly trust He hath thus dealt with me for my eternal
felicity and for His glory; and I hope so to be guided by His heavenly
grace that in the end, by my faithful pains and Christian-like labour, I
shall attain to that blessed promise, pronounced by that holy prophet
Daniel unto the righteous that bring many unto the knowledge of
God: namely, that they shall shine like the stars for ever and ever. A
sweeter comfort cannot be to a true Christian, nor a greater encouragement for him to labour all the days of his life in the performance
thereof, nor a greater game of consolation to be desired at the hour of
death and in the Day of Judgement.

Again, by my reading and conference with honest and religious persons have I received no small encouragement, besides *serena mea
conscientia*, the clearness of my conscience, clean from the filth of
impurity, *quae est instar muri ahenei*, which is unto me as a brazen wall.
If I should set down at large the perturbations and godly motions which
have striven within me, I should but make a tedious and unnecessary
volume. But I doubt not these shall be sufficient both to certify you of
my true intents in discharging of my duty to God and to yourself, to
whose gracious providence I humbly submit myself, for His glory,
your honour, our country's good, the benefit of this plantation, and

for the converting of one unregenerate to regeneration; which I beseech God to grant for His dear son Christ Jesus his sake.

Now if the vulgar sort, who square[8] all men's actions by the base rule of their own filthiness, shall tax or taunt me in this my godly labour, let them know it is not any hungry appetite to gorge myself with incontinency; sure, if I would and were so sensually inclined, I might satisfy such desire, though not without a seared conscience, yet with Christians more pleasing to the eye and less fearful in the offence unlawfully committed. Nor am I in so desperate an estate that I regard not what becometh of me; nor am I out of hope but one day to see my country, nor so void of friends nor mean in birth but there to obtain a match to my great content; nor have I ignorantly passed over my hopes there or regardlessly seek to lose the love of my friends by taking this course. I know them all and have not rashly overslipped any.

But shall it please God thus to dispose of me (which I earnestly desire, to fulfill my ends before set down) I will heartily accept of it as a godly tax appointed me, and I will never cease (God assisting me) until I have accomplished and brought to perfection so holy a work, in which I will daily pray God to bless me, to mine and her eternal happiness.

And thus, desiring no longer to live to enjoy the blessings of God than this my resolution doth tend to such godly ends as are by me before declared, not doubting of your favourable acceptance, I take my leave, beseeching Almighty God to rain down upon you such plentitude of His heavenly graces as your heart can wish and desire, and so I rest,

At your command most willing to be disposed of,

John Rolfe

## 36

# English Democratic Procedures
# Established in America (1619)

On July 30, 1619, a date important in the history of American popular government, Governor George Yeardley, his council, and twenty-two burgesses, two elected from each of the eleven settlements in Virginia, met to make laws for the colony. The assembly repealed martial laws decreed by Sir Thomas Dale and enacted statutes based on English common law. From this time onward American colonials jealously guarded their civil rights as Englishmen. The following account is taken from John Pory, 'A Report of the Manner of Proceeding in the General Assembly Convented at James City ... July 30–August 4, 1619', State Papers Domestic, James I, Vol. I, No. 45. It is reprinted by Susan M. Kingsbury, *The Records of the Virginia Company of London* (Washington, 1906–35), III, 153–77.

FIRST. Sir George Yeardley, Knight, Governor and Captain General of Virginia, having sent his summons all over the country, as well to invite those of the Council of Estate that were absent as also for the election of Burgesses, there were chosen and appeared: . . .

[Names of the Burgesses are omitted.]

The most convenient place we could find to sit in was the choir of the church, where Sir George Yeardley, the Governor, being set down in his accustomed place, those of the Council of Estate sate next him on both hands except only the Secretary, then appointed Speaker, who sat right before him, John Twine, Clerk of the General Assembly, being placed next the Speaker, and Thomas Peirce, the Sergeant, standing at the bar to be ready for any service the Assembly should command him. But forasmuch as men's affairs do little prosper where God's service is neglected, all the Burgesses took their places in the choir till a prayer was said by Mr Bucke, the minister, that it would please God to guide and sanctify all our proceedings to His own glory and the good of this plantation. Prayer being ended, to the intent that, as we had begun at God Almighty, so we might proceed with awful and due respect towards the lieutenant, our most gracious and dread sovereign, all the Burgesses were entreated to retire themselves into the body of the church; which being done, before they were fully admitted they were called in order and by name, and so every man (none staggering at it) took the Oath of Supremacy and entered the Assembly. At Captain Ward, the Speaker took exception as at one that without any commission or authority had seated himself, either upon the Company's, and then his plantation would not be lawful, or on Captain Martin's land, and so he was but a limb or member of him and there could be but two Burgesses for all. So Captain Ward was commanded to absent himself till such time as the Assembly had agreed what was fit for him to do. After much debate, they resolved on this order following. . . .

[A long passage concerning a controversy between Captain Ward and Captain Martin about representation is omitted.]

These obstacles removed, the Speaker, who for a long time has been extreme sickly and therefore not able to pass through long harangues, delivered in brief to the whole Assembly the occasions of their meeting. Which done, he read unto them the commission for establishing the Council of Estate and the General Assembly, wherein their duties were described to the life.

Having thus prepared them, he read over unto them the Great Charter or commission of privileges, orders, and laws sent by Sir George Yeardley out of England. Which, for the more ease of the committees, having divided into four books, he read the former two the same forenoon for expedition's sake a second time over; and so they were referred to the perusal of two committees, which did reciprocally consider of either and accordingly brought in their opinions. But some may here object to what end we should presume to refer that to the examination of committees which the Council and Company in England had already resolved to be perfect and did expect nothing but our assent thereunto. To this we answer that we did it not to the end to correct or control anything therein contained, but only in case we should find aught not perfectly squaring with the state of this colony, or any law which did press or bind too hard, that we might by way of humble petition seek to have it redressed, especially because this Great Charter is to bind us and our heirs for ever. . . .

After dinner, the Governor and those that were not of the committees sat a second time, while the said committees were employed in the perusal of those two books. And whereas the Speaker had propounded four several objects for the Assembly to consider on, namely: first, the Great Charter of orders, laws, and privileges; secondly, which of the instructions given by the Council in England to My Lord La Warr, Captain Argall, or Sir George Yeardley might conveniently put on the habit of laws; thirdly, what laws might issue out of the private conceit of any of the Burgesses or any other of the colony; and lastly, what petitions were fit to be sent home for England: it pleased the Governor for expedition sake to have the second object of the four to be examined and prepared by himself and the non-committees. Wherein, after having spent some three hours' conference, the two committees brought in their opinions concerning the two former books (the second of which beginneth at these words of the Charter: 'And forasmuch as our intent is to establish one equal and uniform kind of government over all Virginia', etc.), which the whole Assembly, because it was late, deferred to treat of till the next morning.

*Saturday, July 31*

The next day, therefore, out of the opinions of the said committees, it was agreed these petitions ensuing should be framed, to be presented to the Treasurer, Council, and Company in England. Upon the committee's perusal of the first book, the General Assembly do become most humble suitors to Their Lordships and to the rest of that honourable Council and renowned Company that albeit they have been pleased to allot unto the Governor, to themselves, together with the Council of Estate here, and to the officers of incorporations, certain land portions of land to be laid out within the limits of the same, yet that they would vouchsafe also that grounds as heretofore had been granted by patent to the ancient planters by former Governors that had from the Company received commission so to do might not now after so much labour and cost and so many years' habitation be taken from them. And, to the end that no man might do or suffer any wrong in this kind, that they would favour us so much (if they mean to grant this our petition) as to send us notice what commission or authority for granting of lands they have given to each particular Governor in times past.

The second petition of the General Assembly framed by the committee out of the second book is that the Treasurer and Company in England would be pleased with as much convenient speed as may be to send men hither to occupy their lands belonging to the four incorporations, as well for their own behoof and profit as for the maintenance of the Council of Estate, who are now to their extreme hindrance often drawn far from their private businesses; and likewise that they will have a care to send tenants to the ministers of the four incorporations to manure[1] their glebe. . . .

A third petition humbly presented by this General Assembly to the Treasurer, Council, and Company is that it may plainly be expressed in the Great Commission (as indeed it is not) that the ancient planters of both sorts, *viz.*, such as before Sir Thomas Dale's depart were come hither upon their own charges, and such also as were brought hither upon the Company's cost, may have their second, third, and more divisions successively in as large and free manner as any other planters. Also that they will be pleased to allow to the male children of them and of all others begotten in Virginia, being the only hope of a posterity, a single share apiece and shares for their issues or for themselves, because that in a new plantation it is not known whether man or woman be more necessary.

Their fourth petition is to beseech the Treasurer, Council, and Company that they would be pleased to appoint a Sub-Treasurer here to collect their rents, to the end that the inhabitants of this colony be not tied to an impossibility of paying the same yearly to the Treasurer in England, and that they would enjoin the said Sub-Treasurer not precisely according to the letter of the Charter to exact money of us (whereof we have none at all, as we have no mint) but the true value of the rent in commodity.

The fifth petition is to beseech the Treasurer, Council, and Company that, towards the erecting of the University and College, they will send, when they shall think it most convenient, workmen of all sorts fit for that purpose.

The sixth and last is they will be pleased to change the savage name of Kecoughtan[2] and to give that incorporation a new name.

These are the general petitions drawn by the committees out of the two former books, which the whole General Assembly, in manner and form above set down, do most humbly offer up and present to the honourable construction of the Treasurer, Council, and Company in England. . . .

This being dispatched, we fell once more debating of such instructions, given by the Council in England to several Governors, as might be converted into laws, the last whereof was the establishment of the price of tobacco, namely, of the best at 3*s*. and the second at 18*d*. the pound. At the reading of this the Assembly thought good to send for Mr Abraham Persey, the cape-merchant, to publish this instruction to him and to demand of him if he knew of any impediment why it might not be admitted of. His answer was that he had not as yet received any such order from the Adventurers of the [Company] in England. And notwithstanding he saw the authority was good, yet was he unwilling to yield till such time as the Governor and Assembly had laid their commandment upon him, out of the authority of the foresaid instructions. . . .

*Here begin the laws drawn out of the instructions given by His Majesty's Council of Virginia in England to My Lord La Warr, Captain Argall, and Sir George Yeardley, Knight*

By this present General Assembly be it enacted that no injury or oppression be wrought by the English against the Indians whereby the present peace might be disturbed and ancient quarrels might be revived.

And farther be it ordained that the Chickahominy are not to be excepted out of this law until either that such order come out of England or that they do provoke us by some new injury.

Against idleness, gaming, drunkenness, and excess in apparel the Assembly hath enacted as followeth:

First, in detestation of idleness be it enacted that if any man be found to live as an idler or runagate, though a freedman, it shall be lawful for that incorporation of plantation to which he belongeth to appoint him a master to serve for wages, till he show apparent signs of amendment.

Against gaming at dice and cards be it ordained by this present Assembly that the winner or winners shall lose all his or their winnings and both winners and losers shall forfeit 10s. a man, one 10s. whereof to go to the discoverer and the rest to charitable and pious uses in the incorporation where the fault is committed.

Against drunkenness be it also decreed that if any private person be found culpable thereof, for the first time he is to be reproved privately by the minister, the second time publicly, the third time to lie in bolts twelve hours in the house of the Provost-marshal and to pay his fee; and if he still continue in that vice, to undergo such severe punishment as the Governor and Council of Estate shall think fit to be inflicted on him. But if any officer offend in this crime, the first time he shall receive reproof from the Governor, the second time he shall openly be reproved in the church by the minister, and the third time he shall be committed and then degraded, provided it be understood that the Governor hath always power to restore him when he shall in his discretion think fit.

Against excess in apparel, that every man be assessed in the church for all public contributions: if he be unmarried, according to his own apparel; if he be married, according to his own and his wife's or either of their apparel.

As touching the instruction of drawing some of the better disposed of the Indians to converse with our people and to live and labour amongst them, the Assembly, who know well their dispositions, think it fit to enjoin [or at] least to counsel those of the colony neither utterly to reject them nor yet to draw them to come in. But in case they will of themselves come voluntarily to places well peopled, there to do service in killing of deer, fishing, beating of corn, and other works, that then five or six may be admitted into every such place and no more, and that with the consent of the Governor: provided that good guard in the night be kept upon them, for generally (though some amongst many may prove good) they are a most treacherous people and quickly gone when they have done a villainy. And it were fit a house were built for them to lodge in apart by themselves and lone inhabitants by no means to entertain them.

Be it enacted by this present Assembly that, for laying a surer foundation of the conversion of the Indians to Christian religion, each town, city, borough, and particular plantation do obtain unto themselves by just means a certain number of the natives' children to be educated by them in true religion and civil course of life, of which children the most towardly boys in wit and graces of nature to be brought up by them in the first elements of literature, so to be fitted by the college intended for them that from thence they may be sent to that work of conversion.

As touching the business of planting corn, this present Assembly doth ordain that year by year all and every householder and householders have in store for every servant he or they shall keep, and also for his or their own persons, whether they have any servants or no, one spare barrel of corn to be delivered out yearly, either upon sale or exchange as need shall require. For the neglect of which duty he shall be subject to the censure of the Governor and Council of Estate: provided always that the first year of every new man this law shall not be of force.

About the plantation of mulberry trees, be it enacted that every man, as he is seated upon his division, do for seven years together, every year, plant and maintain in growth six mulberry trees at the least, and as many more as he shall think convenient and as his virtue and industry shall move him to plant, and that all such persons as shall neglect the yearly planting and maintaining of that small proportion shall be subject to the censure of the Governor and the Council of Estate.

Be it farther enacted as concerning silk-flax that those men that are upon their division of settled habitation do this next year plant and dress a hundred plants, which, being found a commodity, may farther be increased. And whosoever do fail in the performance of this shall be subject to the punishment of the Governor and Council of Estate.

For hemp, also, both English and Indian, and for English flax and aniseeds, we do require and enjoin all householders of this colony that have any of those seeds to make trial thereof the next season.

Moreover, be it enacted by this present Assembly that every householder do yearly plant and maintain ten vines until they have attained to the art and experience of dressing a vineyard either by their own industry or by the instruction of some *vigneron*, and that upon what penalty soever the Governor and Council of Estate shall think fit to impose upon the neglecters of this act.

Be it also enacted that all necessary tradesmen, or so many as need shall require, such as are come over since the departure of Sir Thomas Dale or that shall hereafter come, shall work at their trades for any other man, each one being paid according to the quality of his trade and work, to be estimated, if he shall not be contented, by the Governor and officers of the place where he worketh.

Be it further ordained by this General Assembly, and we do by these presents enact, that all contracts made in England between the owners of the land and their tenants and servants which they shall send hither may be caused to be duly performed, and that the offenders be punished as the Governor and Council of Estate shall think just and convenient.

Be it established also by this present Assembly that no crafty or advantageous means be suffered to be put in practice for the enticing away the tenants or servants of any particular plantation from the place where they are seated. And that it shall be the duty of the Governor and Council of Estate most severely to punish both the seducers and the seduced and to return these latter into their former places.

Be it further enacted that the orders for the magazine lately made be exactly kept and that the magazine be preserved from wrong and sinister practices, and that according to all the orders of court in England all tobacco and sassafras be brought by the planters to the cape-merchant till such time as all the goods now or heretofore sent for the magazine be taken off their hands at the prices agreed on; that by this means, the same going for England with one hand, the price thereof may be upheld the better; and to that end that all the whole colony may take notice of the last order of court made in England and all those whom it concerneth may know how to observe it, we hold it fit to publish it here for a law among the rest of our laws. . . .

*Tuesday, August 3, 1619*

This morning a third sort of laws (such as might proceed out of every man's private conceit) were read and referred by halves to the same committees which were from the beginning. . . .

*Wednesday, August 4th*

*A third sort of laws, such as may issue out of every man's private conceit*

It shall be free for every man to trade with the Indians, servants only excepted, upon pain of whipping, unless the master will redeem it off with the payment of an angel, one-fourth part whereof to go to the Provost-marshal, one-fourth part to the discoverer, and the other moiety to the public uses of the incorporation.

That no man do sell or give any of the greater howes[3] to the Indians, or any English dog of quality, as a mastiff, greyhound, blood-hound, land- or water-spaniel, or any other dog or bitch whatsoever, of the English race, upon pain of forfeiting 5s. sterling to the public uses of the incorporation where he dwelleth.

That no man do sell or give any Indians any piece, shot, or powder, or any other arms, offensive or defensive, upon pain of being held a traitor to the colony and of being hanged as soon as the fact is proved, without all redemption.

That no man may go above twenty miles from his dwelling-place, nor upon any voyage whatsoever shall be absent from thence for the space of seven days together without first having made the Governor or commander of the same place acquainted therewith, upon pain of paying 20s. to the public uses of the same incorporation where the party delinquent dwelleth.

That no man shall purposely go to any Indian towns, habitations, or places, or resorts without leave from the Governor or commander of that place where he liveth, upon pain of paying 40s. to public uses as afore said.

That no man living in this colony but shall between this and the first of January next ensuing come or send to the Secretary of Estate to enter his own and all his servants' names, and for what term or upon what conditions they are to serve, upon penalty of paying 40s. to the said Secretary of Estate. Also, whatsoever masters or people do come over to this plantation that within one month of their arrival (notice being first given them of this very law) they shall likewise resort to the Secretary of Estate and shall certify him upon what terms or conditions they be come hither, to the end that he may record their grants and commissions and for how long time and upon what conditions their servants (in case they have any) are to serve them, and that upon pain of the penalty next above mentioned.

All ministers in the colony shall once a year, namely, in the month of March, bring to the Secretary of Estate a true account of all christen-ings, burials, and marriages, upon pain, if they fail, to be censured for their negligence by the Governor and Council of Estate; likewise,

R

where there be no ministers, that the commanders of the place do supply the same duty.

No man without leave of the Governor shall kill any neat cattle whatsoever, young or old, especially kine, heifers, or cow-calves, and shall be careful to preserve their steers and oxen and to bring them to the plough and such profitable uses; and without he have obtained leave as afore said shall not kill them, upon penalty of forfeiting the value of the beast so killed.

Whosoever shall take any of his neighbours' boats, oars, or canoes without leave from the owner shall be held and esteemed a felon and so proceeded against; though he that shall take away by violence or stealth any canoes or other things from the Indians shall make valuable restitution to the said Indians and shall forfeit, if he be a freeholder, £5; if a servant 40s., or endure a whipping; and anything under the value of 13d. shall be accounted petty larceny.

All ministers shall duly read divine service and exercise their ministerial function according to the ecclesiastical laws and orders of the Church of England and every Sunday in the afternoon shall catechize such as are not yet ripe to come to the Com[munion]. And whosoever of them shall be found negligent or faulty in this kind shall be subject to the censure of the Governor and Council of Estate.

The ministers and churchwardens shall seek to present all ungodly disorders, the committers whereof, if upon good admonitions and mild reproof they will not forbear the said scandalous offences, as, suspicions of whoredoms, dishonest company-keeping with women, and suchlike, they are to be presented and punished accordingly.

If any person after two warnings do not amend his or her life in point of evident suspicion of incontinency or of the commission of any other enormous sins, that then he or she be presented by the churchwardens and suspended for a time from the church by the minister. In which interim if the same person do not amend and humbly submit him or herself to the church he is then fully to be excommunicate and soon after a writ or warrant to be sent from the Governor for the apprehending of his person and seizing on all his goods. Provided always that all the ministers do meet once a quarter, namely, at the feast of St Michael the Archangel, of the Nativity of our Saviour, of the Annunciation of the Blessed Virgin, and about midsummer, at James City or any other place where the Governor shall reside, to determine whom it is fit to excommunicate; and that they first present their opinion to the Governor ere they proceed to the act of excommunication.

For the reformation of swearing, every freeman and master of a family after thrice admonition shall give 5*s.*, or the value upon present demand, to the use of the church where he dwelleth; and every servant after the like admonition, except his master discharge the fine, shall be subject to whipping. Provided that, the payment of the fine notwithstanding, the said servant shall acknowledge his fault publicly in the church.

No man whatsoever, coming by water from above, as from Henrico, Charles City, or any place from the westward of James City, and being bound for Kecoughtan or any other part on this side, the same shall presume to pass either by day or by night without touching first here at James City to know whether the Governor will command him any service. And the like shall they perform that come from Kecoughtanward, or from any place between this and that, to go upward; upon pain of forfeiting £10 sterling a time to the Governor. Provided that if a servant, having had instructions from his master to observe this law, do notwithstanding transgress the same, that then the said servant shall be punished at the Governor's discretion; otherwise that the master himself shall undergo the foresaid penalty.

No man shall trade into the bay, either in shallop, pinnace, or ship, without the Governor's licence and without putting in security that neither himself nor his company shall force or wrong the Indians, upon pain that, doing otherwise, they shall be censured at their return by the Governor and Council of Estate.

All persons whatsoever upon the Sabbath Day shall frequent divine service and sermons both forenoons and afternoon, and all such as bear arms shall bring their pieces, swords, powder, and shot. And every one that shall transgress this law shall forfeit 3*s.* a time to the use of the church, all lawful and necessary impediments excepted. But if a servant in this case shall wilfully neglect his master's command, he shall suffer bodily punishment.

No maid- or woman-servant, either now resident in the colony or hereafter to come, shall contract herself in marriage without either the consent of her parents, or of her master or mistress, or of the magistrate and minister of the place both together. And whatsoever minister shall marry or contract any such persons without some of the foresaid consents shall be subject to the severe censure of the Governor and Council of Estate.

Be it enacted by this present Assembly that whatsoever servant hath heretofore or shall hereafter contract himself in England, either by way of indenture or otherwise, to serve any master here in Virginia, and shall afterward against his said former contract depart from his master without leave, or, being once embarked, shall abandon the ship he is appointed to come in and so, being left behind, shall put himself into the service of any other man that will bring him hither, that then at the same servant's arrival here he shall first serve out his time with that master that brought him hither, and afterward also shall serve out his time with his former master according to his covenant.

Here end the laws.

All these laws being thus concluded and consented to as afore said, Captain Henry Spelman[4] was called to the bar to answer to certain misdemeanours laid to his charge by Robert Poole, interpreter, upon his oath (whose examination the Governor sent into England in the *Prosperous*), of which accusations of Poole, some he acknowledged for true but the greatest part he denied. Whereupon the General Assembly, having thoroughly heard and considered his speeches, did constitute this order following against him:

*August 4, 1619*

This day Captain Henry Spelman was convented before the General Assembly and was examined by a relation upon oath of one Robert Poole, interpreter, what conference had passed between the said Spelman and Opechancanough at Poole's meeting with him in Opechancanough's court. Poole chargeth him he spake very unreverently and maliciously against the present Governor, whereby the honour and dignity of his place and person, and so of the whole colony, might be brought into contempt, by which means what mischiefs might ensue from the Indians, by disturbance of the peace or otherwise, may easily be conjectured. Some things of this relation Spelman confessed, but the most part he denied; except only one matter of importance, and that was that he had informed Opechancanough that within a year there would come a Governor greater than this that now is in place. By which and by other reports it seemeth he hath alienated the mind of Opechancanough from this present Governor and brought him in much disesteem, both with Opechancanough and the Indians, and the whole colony in danger of their slippery designs.

The General Assembly, upon Poole's testimony only not willing to put Spelman to the rigour and extremity of the law, which might, perhaps, both speedily and deservedly have taken his life from him (upon the witness of one whom he much excepted against), were pleased for the present to censure him rather out of that his confession above written than out of any other proof. Several and sharp punishments were pronounced against him by divers of the Assembly, but in fine the whole court by voices united did incline to the most favourable, which was that for this misdemeanour he should first be degraded of his title of captain, at the head of the troop, and should be condemned to perform seven years' service to the colony in the nature of interpreter to the Governor.

This sentence being read to Spelman, he, as one that had in him more of the savage than of the Christian, muttered certain words to himself, neither showing any remorse for his offences nor yet any thankfulness to the Assembly for their so favourable censure, which he at one time or another (God's grace not wholly abandoning him) might with some one service have been able to have redeemed. . . .

The last act of the General Assembly was a contribution to gratify their officers, as followeth:

*August 4, 1619*

It is fully agreed at this General Assembly that in regard of the great pains and labour of the Speaker of this Assembly (who not only first formed the same Assembly and to their great ease and expedition reduced all matters to be treated of into a ready method, but also, his indisposition notwithstanding, wrote or dictated all orders and other expedients, and is yet to write several books for all the general incorporations and plantations, both of the Great Charter and of all the laws), and likewise in respect of the diligence of the Clerk and Sergeant, officers thereto belonging; that every man and man-servant of above sixteen years of age shall pay into the hands and custody of the Burgesses of every incorporation and plantation one pound of the best tobacco, to be distributed to the Speaker and likewise to the Clerk and Sergeant of the Assembly, according to their degrees and ranks, the whole bulk whereof to be delivered into the Speaker's hands, to be divided accordingly. And in regard the Provost-marshal of James City hath also given some attendance upon the said General Assembly, he is also to have a share out of the same. And this is to begin to be gathered the twenty-fourth of February next.

In conclusion, the whole Assembly commanded the Speaker (as now he doth) to present their humble excuse to the Treasurer, Council, and Company in England for being constrained by the intemperature of the weather and the falling sick of divers of the Burgesses to break up so abruptly before they had so much as put their laws to the engrossing. This they wholly committed to the fidelity of their Speaker, who therein (his conscience tells him) hath done the part of an honest man, otherwise he would be easily found out by the Burgesses themselves, who with all expedition are to have so many books of the same laws as there be both incorporations and plantations in the colony.

In the second place, the Assembly doth most humbly crave pardon that in so short a space they could bring their matter to no more perfection, being for the present enforced to send home titles rather than laws, propositions rather than resolutions, attempts than achievements, hoping their courtesy will accept our poor endeavour and their wisdom will be ready to support the weakness of this little flock.

Thirdly, the General Assembly doth humbly beseech the said Treasurer, Council, and Company that albeit it belongeth to them only to allow or to abrogate any laws which we shall here make, and that it is their right so to do, yet that it would please them not to take it in ill part if these laws which we have now brought to light do pass current and be of force till such time as we may know their farther pleasure out of England: for otherwise this people (who now at length have gotten the reins of former servitude into their own swinge)[5] would in short time grow so insolent as they would shake off all government and there would be no living among them.

Their last humble suit is that the said Council and Company would be pleased, so soon as they shall find it convenient, to make good their promise set down at the conclusion of their commission for establishing the Council of Estate and the General Assembly; namely, that they will give us power to allow or disallow of their orders of court, as His Majesty hath given them power to allow or to reject our laws.

In sum, Sir George Yeardley, the Governor, prorogued the said General Assembly till the first of March, which is to fall out this present year of 1619, and in the mean season dissolved the same.

# 37

# Promise of Prosperity in Virginia (1619)

A letter from John Pory, probably to Sir Dudley Carleton, dated September 30, 1619, in the Barlow Collection in the New York Public Library; printed by Kingsbury, *Records of the Virginia Company*, III, 219–22.

Right Honourable and my singular good lord,

Having met with so fit a messenger as this man-of-war of Flushing, I could not but impart with Your Lordship (to whom I am so everlastingly bound) these poor fruits of our labours here; wherein though Your Lordship will espy many errors and imperfections and matters of low esteem, yet withal you will be content to observe the very principle and rudiments of our infant commonwealth, which, though now contemptible, Your Lordship may live to see a flourishing estate, maugre both Spaniards and Indians. The occasion of this ship's coming hither was an accidental consortship in the West Indies with the *Treasurer*, an English man-of-war also, licensed by a commission from the Duke of Savoy to take Spaniards as lawful prize. This ship, the *Treasurer*, went out of England in April was twelvemonth, about a month, I think, before any peace was concluded between the King of Spain and that prince. Hither she came to Captain Argall, then Governor of this colony, being part-owner of her. He more for love of gain, the root of all evil, than for any true love he bore to this plantation, victualled and manned her anew and sent her with the same commission to range the Indies. The event whereof (we may misdoubt) will prove some attempt of the Spaniard upon us, either by way of revenge, or by way of prevention, lest we might in time make this place *sedem belli* against the West Indies. But our Governor, being a soldier truly bred in that university of war, the Low Countries, purposeth, at a place or two upon the river fortifiable, to provide for them, animating in the mean while this warlike people (than whom for their small number no prince can be served with better) by his example to prepare their courages.

Both those of our nation and the Indians also have this torrid summer been visited with great sickness and mortality; which our good God (His name be blessed for it) hath recompensed with a marvellous plenty, such as hath not been seen since our first coming into the land.

For myself, I was, partly at land and partly at sea, vexed with a calenture[1] of some four or five months. But (praised be God) I am now as healthful as ever I was in my life. Here (as Your Lordship cannot be ignorant) I am, for fault of a better, Secretary of Estate, the first that ever was chosen and appointed by commission from the Council and Company in England, under their hands and common seal. By my fees I must maintain myself; which, the Governor tells me, may this year amount to a matter of £300 sterling, whereof fifty I do owe to himself, and I pray God the remainder may amount to a hundred more. As yet I have gotten nothing, save only (if I may speak it without boasting) a general reputation of integrity, for having spoken freely to all matters according to my conscience and, as near as I could discern, done every man right.

As touching the quality of this country, three things there be which in few years may bring this colony to perfection: the English plough, vineyards, and cattle. For the first, there be many grounds here cleared by the Indians to our hands which, being much worn out, will bear no more of their corn, which requireth an extraordinary deal of sap and substance to nourish it; but of our grain of all sorts it will bear great abundance. We have had this year a plentiful crop of English wheat, though the last harvest 1618 was only shed upon the stubble and so self-sown, without any other manure.[2] In July last, so soon as we had reaped this self-sown wheat, we set Indian corn upon the same ground, which is come up in great abundance; and so by this means we are to enjoy two crops in one year from off one and the same field. The greatest labour we have yet bestowed upon English wheat hath been upon new broken-up grounds, one ploughing only and one harrowing, far short of the tilth used in Christendom, which when we shall have ability enough to perform, we shall produce miracles out of this earth.

Vines here are in such abundance as wheresoever a man treads they are ready to embrace his foot. I have tasted here of a great black grape as big as a damascene that hath a true muscatel taste; the vine whereof, now spending itself even to the tops of high trees, if it were reduced into a vineyard and there domesticated, would yield incomparable fruit. The like or a better taste have I found in a lesser sort of black grapes. White grapes, also, of great excellency I have heard to be in the country; but they are very rare, nor did I ever see or taste of them.

For cattle, they do mightily increase here, both kine, hogs, and goats, and are much greater in stature than the race of them first brought out of England. No less are our horses and mares likely to multiply, which prove of a delicate shape and of as good spirit and mettle.

All our riches for the present do consist in tobacco, wherein one man by his own labour hath in one year raised to himself to the value of £200 sterling; and another by the means of six servants hath cleared at one crop £1,000 English. These be true, yet indeed rare, examples, yet possible to be done by others. Our principal wealth (I should have said) consisteth in servants; but they are chargeable to be furnished with arms, apparel, and bedding, and for their transportation and casual,[3] both at sea and for their first year commonly at land also; but if they escape they prove very hardy and sound, able men.

Now that Your Lordship may know we are not the veriest beggars in the world, our cow-keeper here of James City on Sundays goes accoutered all in fresh, flaming silks, and a wife of one that in England had professed the black art, not of a scholar but of a collier of Croydon, wears her rough beaver hat, with a fair pearl hatband and a silken suit thereto correspondent. But to leave the populace and to come higher, the Governor here, who at his first coming, besides a great deal of worth in his person, brought only his sword with him, was at his late being in London together with his lady able to disburse very near £3,000 to furnish himself for his voyage. And once within seven years I am persuaded (*absit invidia verbo*)[4] that the Governor's place here may be as profitable as the Lord Deputy's of Ireland.

All this notwithstanding, I may say of myself that when I was the last year with Your Lordship at Middelburg, *si mens non laeva fuisset,*[5] I might have gone to The Hague[6] with you and found myself there now in far better company, which indeed is the soul of this life, and might have been deeply engrafted into Your Lordship's service, which since I have a thousand times affected in vain. And therefore, seeing I have missed that singular happiness, I must for what remains depend upon God's providence, Who, my hope is, will be so merciful towards me as once more before I die to vouchsafe me the sight of your countenance, wherein, I speak unfeignedly, I shall enjoy as much happiness as in any other thing I can imagine in this world.

At my first coming hither, the solitary uncouthness of this place, compared with those parts of Christendom or Turkey where I had been, and likewise my being sequestered from all occurrents[7] and passages which are so rife there, did not a little vex me. And yet, in these five months of my continuance here there have come at one time or another eleven sail of ships into this river, but freighted more with ignorance than with any other merchandise. At length, being hardened to this custom of abstinence from curiosity, I am resolved wholly to mind my business here and, next after my pen, to have some good book always in store, being in solitude the best and choicest company.

Besides, among these crystal rivers and odoriferous woods I do escape much expense, envy, contempt, vanity, and vexation of mind. Yet, good my lord, have a little compassion upon me and be pleased to send me what pamphlets and relations of the interim since I was with you as Your Lordship shall think good, directing the same (if you please) in a box to Mr Ralph Yeardley, apothecary (brother to Sir George Yeardley, our Governor) dwelling at the Sign of the Artichoke in Great Wood Street, to be sent to me by the first, together with his brother's things. This packet I delivered to one Marmaduke Rayner, an Englishman who goes entertained as pilot in this Flemish man-of-war. If he come to Your Lordship, as he hath promised, he will be the fittest messenger. All possible happiness I wish to Your Lordship and to my most honoured Lady; and though remote in place, yet near in affection do rest

Your Lordship's, ever most humbly at your command,

John Pory

James City in Virginia    September 30, 1619

38

# King James Tells How to Ensure Prosperity in America (1622)

That all the Virginians needed to make them producers of silk and wine, two commodities that English authorities particularly desired from their colonists, were orders from the King and a book of instructions is evident in a book published in 1622 with the title, *His Majesty's Gracious Letter to the Earl of Southampton . . . Commanding the Present Setting-Up of Silkworks and Planting of Vines in Virginia*. The King's letter, and a further letter from Southampton ordering that silk culture be taken in hand immediately, together with a treatise by a Frenchman, John Bonoeil, compose the book. The King's and Southampton's letters were reprinted by Purchas, *Pilgrims*, and may be found in the Maclehose edition (Glasgow, 1906), XIX, 154–7.

JAMES R.

RIGHT trusty and well-beloved, we greet you well. Whereas we understand that the soil in Virginia naturally yieldeth store of excellent mulberry trees, we have taken into our princely consideration the great benefit that may grow to the adventurers and planters by the breed of silkworms and setting up of silkworks in those parts. And therefore of our gracious inclination to a design of so much honour and advantage to the public, we have thought good, as at sundry other times, so now more particularly, to recommend it to your special care, hereby charging and requiring you to take speedy order that our people there use all possible diligence in breeding silkworms and erecting silkworks, and that they rather bestow their travail in compassing this rich and solid commodity than in tobacco, which besides much unnecessary expense brings with it many disorders and inconveniences. And forasmuch as our servant, John Bonoeil, hath taken pains in setting down the true use of the silkworm, together with the art of silkmaking and of planting vines, and that his experience and abilities may much conduce to the advancement of this business; we do hereby likewise require you to cause his directions both for the said silkworks and vineyards to be carefully put in practice throughout our plantations there, that so the work may go on cheerfully and receive no more interruptions nor delays.

Given under our signet, at our palace of Westminster, the ninth day of July, in the twentieth year of our reign of England, France, and Ireland; and of Scotland the five-and-fiftieth.

To our right trusty and right well-beloved cousin and Councilor, Henry, Earl of Southampton, Treasurer of our plantation in Virginia, and to our trusty and well-beloved, the Deputy and others of our said plantation.

[Letter from the Earl of Southampton to the Treasurer,
Council, and Company of Virginia]

The Treasurer, Council, and Company of Virginia, to the
Governor and Council of State in Virginia residing

After our very hearty commendations, His Sacred Majesty, out of his high wisdom and care of the noble plantation of Virginia, hath been graciously pleased to direct his letters to us here in England, thereby commanding us to advance the setting up of silkworks and planting of vineyards, as by the copy herewith sent you may perceive.

The intimation of His Majesty's pleasure we conceive to be a motive sufficient to induce you to employ all your endeavours to the setting forward those two staple commodities of silk and wine, which, brought to their perfection, will infinitely redound to the honour, benefit, and comfort of the colony and of this whole kingdom; yet we in discharge of our duties do again renew our often and iterated instructions and invite you cheerfully to fall upon these two so rich and necessary commodities. And if you shall find any person, either through negligence or wilfulness, to omit the planting of vines and mulberry trees in orderly and husbandly manner as by the book is prescribed, or the providing of convenient rooms for the breeding of worms, we desire they may by severe censures and punishment be compelled thereunto. And on the contrary, that all favour and possible assistance be given to such as yield willing obedience to His Highness' commands therein. The breach or performance whereof, as we are bound to give a strict account, so will it also be required of you, the Governor and Council, especially. Herein there can be no plea, either of difficulty or impossibility; but all the contrary appears by the natural abundance of those two excellent plants afore named everywhere in Virginia. Neither will such excuses be admitted, nor any other pretences serve, whereby the business be at all delayed. And as we formerly sent at our great charge the French *vignerons* to you, to teach you their art, so for the same purpose we now commend this book unto you, to serve as an instructor to everyone, and send you store of them to be dispersed over the whole colony, to every master of a family one. Silk-feed you shall receive also by this ship, sufficient to store every man. So that there wants nothing but industry in the planter suddenly to bring the making of silk to its perfection; which either for their own benefit (we hope) they will willingly endeavour, or by a wholesome and necessary severity they must be enforced.

This particular advice we thought necessary to give you, lest that if it should have come to you mingled with others you would have interpreted it as a common instruction or a business that was not taken so to heart as this is by us and we hope will be by you in humble obedience to His Sacred Majesty's royal instructions. The pains and industry of the author for the benefit of the plantations (being a member of our Company) are sufficient arguments of his good affection to the action, and they both deserve your best acceptance and ours, that others may thereby be invited to impart their knowledge in business of this and the like nature; whereby the colony may not only be supported for the present but brought to that perfection that may redound to the glory of God, the honour of His Majesty, and the inestimable benefit of his noble kingdoms; which, as they are the true aim and end the adventurers and planters have proposed unto themselves, so ought they to be still the honourable seeds to put others also forward in this action. We commend this business again to your special care. And so we commit you all, and your weighty affairs, to the protection of the Almighty.

[Preface to John Bonoeil's treatise]

To the right noble Company of Virginia, health

My Lords and others,

I have been induced to present this small tract unto you from the superabundant desire I have to further and advance the good success of that noble plantation. This discourse is therefore touching the feeding and entertainment of your silkworms. It shows how mulberry trees must be planted and their leaves gathered; how to sow the seeds of mulberry trees for him that will set up a seminary or orchard of the best trees of that nature; also how to erect, set up, and build houses for the silkworms. Withal, this gives direction how to plant and set the vine, how to dress and till it, of sundry sorts and fashions. Likewise it shows when the grapes are fit to be gathered, and how they are to make wine. Furthermore, how to plant and set peach trees and fig trees, which in hot countries are commonly set amongst vines, in vineyards in the open fields. Also, how to set the stones of divers kinds of fruits, and how to dry both raisins, figs, and peaches, to keep and preserve long.

I have a servant of mine, who hath dwelt in Virginia these six years, besides others of my friends and acquaintance of the country of Languedoc in France (which now dwell in Virginia also, being sent thither at the great charge of the Company to make silk and dress vines), all which have certified me by their letters, which I have received from thence, that the woods in Virginia are full of mulberry trees, of the tallest and broadest that ever they saw in any country, and great numbers there are of sundry sizes and bigness; and namely, that they have seen there some special trees, of which one alone is able to bring forth as many leaves as will feed so many silkworms as shall yield five pound of silk *per annum*. Also, they inform me that there is great abundance of vines in Virginia, and many of them well loaden with grapes. But because that young growing wood, bushes, and weeds so much choke and cover them, they cannot come to their full ripeness; and the vermin, by reason the grapes grow in the woods, eat many of them up before they come to maturity. Moreover, they avouch that Virginia is a better country than Languedoc, which is one of the fruitfullest provinces in all France, by reason of the heat thereof and the richness of the soil; which, notwithstanding, if so be Virginia be once well inhabited and peopled, it must needs exceed it: namely, for this reason, because the mulberry trees and the vines do both grow naturally in Virginia, with many other good things, which come only by force and labour in the best parts of France. And none may doubt hereof, to wit, that the vine being chosen of the best plants there and well dressed, but that it will assuredly bring forth very good fruit. Also other vine plants may be sent thither from other countries to try which of them will prove best.

And of that which we have formerly said, that the mulberry trees grow in abundance naturally in Virginia, it must needs thence follow that the worms will feed much better and with less labour of man than those in other countries do, where mulberry trees grow only with main labour and toil; and the silk also of them will be far better; and such quantity of silk may easily be made in Virginia (if there were store of hands) as in a very short time it would serve all Christendom. What an honour and wealth it would be to this kingdom of England all men may judge.

39

# Fish, Furs, and Timber Better than Gold (1616)

Captain John Smith, whose vigorous control of the unruly colonists at Jamestown in 1608–9 had helped save the settlement from disaster, returned to England in the autumn of 1609, but his interest in colonial ventures did not diminish. During the spring and summer of 1614 he commanded two ships that explored the New England coast, and two years later he published

a tract praising the valuable commodities of the region. From that work,
*A Description of New England* (1616), the following excerpt is taken.

AND surely, by reason of those sandy cliffs and cliffs of rocks, both
which we saw so planted with gardens and corn-fields and so well inhabited with a goodly, strong, and well-proportioned people, besides
the greatness of the timber growing on them, the greatness of the fish,
and the moderate temper of the air (for of twenty-five,[1] not any was
sick but two that were many years diseased before they went, notwithstanding our bad lodging and accidental diet), who can but approve
this a most excellent place, both for health and fertility? And of all the
four parts of the world that I have yet seen not inhabited, could I have
but means to transport a colony, I would rather live here than anywhere; and if it did not maintain itself, were we but once indifferently
well fitted, let us starve.

The main staple, from hence to be extracted for the present to produce the rest, is fish, which, however it may seem a mean and a base
commodity, yet who will but truly take the pains and consider the
sequel, I think will allow it well worth the labour. It is strange to see
what great adventures[2] the hopes of setting forth men of war to rob the
industrious innocent would procure, or such massy promises in gross,
though more are choked then well fed with such hasty hopes. But who
doth not know that the poor Hollanders, chiefly by fishing at a great
charge and labour in all weathers in the open sea, are made a people so
hardy and industrious? And by the venting this poor commodity to the
Easterlings[3] for as mean, which is wood, flax, pitch, tar, rosin, cordage,
and such-like (which they exchange again to the French, Spaniards,
Portugals, and English, etc., for what they want), are made so mighty,
strong, and rich as no state but Venice, of twice their magnitude, is so
well furnished with so many fair cities, goodly towns, strong fortresses,
and that abundance of shipping and all sorts of merchandise, as well of
gold, silver, pearls, diamonds, precious stones, silks, velvets, and cloth
of gold, as fish, pitch, wood, or such gross commodities? What voyages
and discoveries east and west, north and south, yea, about the world,
make they? What an army by sea and land have they long maintained
in despite of one of the greatest princes of the world? And never could
the Spaniard, with all his mines of gold and silver, pay his debts, his
friends and army, half so truly as the Hollanders still have done by this
contemptible trade of fish. Divers (I know) may allege many other
assistances, but this is their mine and the sea the source of those silvered

streams of all their virtue, which hath made them now the very miracle of industry, the pattern of perfection for these affairs; and the benefit of fishing is that *primum mobile* that turns all their spheres to this height of plenty, strength, honour, and admiration.

Herring, cod, and ling is that triplicity that makes their wealth and shippings multiplicities, such as it is, and from which (few would think it) they yearly draw at least one million and a half of pounds sterling, yet it is most certain (if records be true); and in this faculty they are so naturalized, and of their vents so certainly acquainted, as there is no likelihood they will ever be paralleled, having two or three thousand busses, flat-bottoms, sword-pinks,[4] todes,[5] and such-like, that breeds them sailors, mariners, soldiers, and merchants, never to be wrought out of that trade and fit for any other. I will not deny but others may gain as well as they; they will use it, though not so certainly, nor so much in quantity, for want of experience. And this herring they take upon the coast of Scotland and England, their cod and ling upon the coast of Ireland and in the North Seas.

Hamburg and the East Countries for sturgeon and caviar gets many thousands of pounds from England and the Straits; Portugal, the Biscayans, and the Spaniards make forty or fifty sail yearly to Cape Blanc,[6] to hook for porgos, mullet, and make puttargo;[7] and Newfoundland doth yearly fraught[8] near eight hundred sail of ships with a silly,[9] lean, skinny Poor John and cor-fish, which at least yearly amounts to 3 or 400,000 pound. If from all those parts such pains is taken for this poor gains of fish, and by them hath neither meat, drink, nor clothes, wood, iron, nor steel, pitch, tar, nets, leads, salt, hooks, nor lines for shipping, fishing, nor provision but at the second, third, fourth, or fifth hand, drawn from so many several parts of the world ere they come together to be used in this voyage; if these, I say, can gain, and the sailors live going for shares less than the third part of their labours, and yet spend as much time in going and coming as in staying there, so short is the season of fishing, why should we more doubt than Holland, Portugal, Spaniard, French, or other but to do much better than they where there is victual to feed us, wood of all sorts to build boats, ships, or barks, the fish at our doors, pitch, tar, masts, yards, and most of other necessaries only for making?

And here are no hard landlords to rack us with high rents or extorted fines to consume us, no tedious pleas in law to consume us with their many years' disputations for justice, no multitudes to occasion such impediments to good orders as in popular[10] states. So freely hath God and

His Majesty bestowed those blessings on them that will attempt to obtain them as here every man may be master and owner of his own labour and land, or the greatest part, in a small time. If he have nothing but his hands, he may set up this trade and by industry quickly grow rich, spending but half that time well which in England we abuse in idleness, worse, or as ill. Here is ground also as good as any lieth in the height of 41, 42, 43, etc., which is as temperate and as fruitful as any other parallel in the world. . . .

First, the ground is so fertile that, questionless, it is capable of producing any grain, fruits, or seeds you will sow or plant, growing in the regions afore named; but it may be not every kind to that perfection of delicacy, or some tender plants may miscarry because the summer is not so hot and the winter is more cold in those parts we have yet tried near the sea-side than we find in the same height in Europe or Asia. Yet I made a garden upon the top of a rocky isle in 43½, four leagues from the main, in May, that grew so well as it served us for sallets[11] in June and July. All sorts of cattle may here be bred and fed in the isles or peninsulas securely for nothing. In the interim till they increase, if need be (observing the seasons), I durst undertake to have corn enough from the savages for three hundred men for a few trifles; and if they should be untoward[12] (as it is most certain they are), thirty or forty good men will be sufficient to bring them all in subjection and make this provision, if they understand what they do; two hundred whereof may nine months in the year be employed in making merchantable fish, till the rest provide other necessaries fit to furnish us with other commodities.

In March, April, May, and half June here is cod in abundance; in May, June, July, and August mullet and sturgeon, whose roes do make caviar and puttargo. Herring, if any desire them, I have taken many out of the bellies of cods, some in nets; but the savages compare their store in the sea to the hairs of their heads, and surely there are an incredible abundance upon this coast. In the end of August, September, October, and November you have cod again to make cor-fish or Poor John, and each hundred is as good as two or three hundred in Newfoundland. So that half the labour in hooking, splitting, and turning is saved, and you may have your fish at what market you will before they can have any in Newfoundland, where their fishing is chiefly but in June and July, whereas it is here in March, April, May, September, October, and November, as is said. So that by reason of this plantation, the merchants may have fraught both out and home, which yields an advantage worth consideration.

s

Your cor-fish you may in like manner transport as you see cause to serve the ports in Portugal (as Lisbon, Aveiro, Portaport,[13] and divers others, or what market you please) before your islanders return. They being tied to the season in the open sea, you, having a double season and fishing before your doors, may every night sleep quietly ashore with good cheer and what fires you will, or when you please with your wives and family; they only their ships in the main ocean.

The mullets here are in that abundance you may take them with nets, sometimes by hundreds, where at Cape Blanc they hook them; yet those but one foot and a half in length, these two, three, or four, as oft I have measured. Much salmon some have found up the rivers, as they have passed; and here the air is so temperate as all these at any time may well be preserved.

Now, young boys and girls, savages or any other, be they never such idlers, may turn, carry, and return fish without either shame or any great pain; he is very idle that is past twelve years of age and cannot do so much, and she is very old that cannot spin a thread to make engines[14] to catch them. . . .

Of the muskrat may be well raised gains, well worth their labour that will endeavour to make trial of their goodness.

Of beavers, otters, martens, black foxes and furs of price may yearly be had six or seven thousand and, if the trade of the French were prevented, many more: 25,000 this year were brought from those northern parts into France, of which trade we may have as good part as the French, if we take good courses.

Of mines of gold and silver, copper, and probabilities of lead, crystal, and alum, I could say much if relations were good assurances. It is true, indeed, I made many trials according to those instructions I had, which do persuade me I need not despair but there are metals in the country; but I am no alchemist nor will promise more than I know, which is: who will undertake the rectifying of an iron forge, if those that buy meat, drink, coals, ore, and all necessaries at a dear rate gain, where all these things are to be had for the taking up, in my opinion cannot lose.

Of woods, seeing there is such plenty of all sorts, if those that build ships and boats buy wood at so great a price as it is in England, Spain, France, Italy, and Holland, and all other provision for the nourishing of man's life, live well by their trade when labour is all required to take those necessaries without any other tax, what hazard will be here but do much better? And what commodity in Europe doth more decay than wood? For the goodness of the ground, let us take it fertile or barren or as it is, seeing it is certain it bears fruits to nourish and feed man and beast as well as England, and the sea those several sorts of fish I have related.

Thus, seeing all good provisions for man's sustenance may with this facility be had by a little extraordinary labour till that transported be increased, and all necessaries for shipping only for labour, to which may be added the assistance of the savages (which may easily be had if they be discreetly handled in their kinds, towards fishing, planting, and destroying woods), what gains might be raised if this were followed (when there is but once men to fill your storehouses dwelling there, you may serve all Europe better and far cheaper than can the Iceland fishers or the Hollanders, Cape Blanc, or Newfoundland, who must be at much more charge than you), may easily be conjectured by this example.

Who can desire more content, that hath small means or but only his merit to advance his fortune, than to tread and plant that ground he hath purchased by the hazard of his life? If he have but the taste of virtue and magnanimity, what to such a mind can be more pleasant than planting and building a foundation for his posterity, got from the rude earth by God's blessing and his own industry without prejudice to any? If he have any grain of faith or zeal in religion, what can he do less hurtful to any, or more agreeable to God, than to seek to convert those poor savages to know Christ and humanity, whose labours with discretion will triple requite the charge and pain?

40

# The Pilgrims Seek a Refuge in America— and Find a Villain at Merrymount (1620–28)

From William Bradford, *Of Plymouth Plantation*, written between 1620 and 1647; first published in 1856. A scholarly edition was published by the Massachusetts Historical Society (2 vols., 1912); a well-printed recent edition is that by Samuel E. Morison (New York, 1952). Bradford begins his narrative with an account of the background of the Separatist movement, the sojourn in the Netherlands, and the departure from England on September 6, 1620. After a rough and stormy passage of the Atlantic, they finally reached Cape Cod in November of the same year.

... BUT to omit other things (that I may be brief), after long beating at sea they fell with that land which is called Cape Cod; the which being made and certainly known to be it, they were not a little joyful. After some deliberation had amongst themselves and with the master of the ship, they tacked about and resolved to stand for the southward (the wind and weather being fair) to find some place about Hudson's River for their habitation. But after they had sailed that course about half the day, they fell amongst dangerous shoals and roaring breakers, and they were so far entangled therewith as they conceived themselves in great danger; and the wind shrinking upon them withal, they resolved to bear up again for the Cape and thought themselves happy to get out of those dangers before night overtook them, as by God's good providence they did. And the next day they got into the Cape harbour, where they rid in safety.

A word or two by the way of this cape. It was thus first named by Captain Gosnold and his company, anno 1602, and after by Captain Smith was called Cape James; but it retains the former name amongst seamen. Also, that point which first showed those dangerous shoals unto them they called Point Care and Tucker's Terror; but the French and Dutch to this day call it Malabar by reason of those perilous shoals and the losses they have suffered there.

Being thus arrived in a good harbour and brought safe to land, they fell upon their knees and blessed the God of Heaven who had brought them over the vast and furious ocean and delivered them from all the perils and miseries thereof, again to set their feet on the firm and stable earth, their proper element. And no marvel if they were thus joyful, seeing wise Seneca was so affected with sailing a few miles on the coast of his own Italy as he affirmed that he had rather remain twenty years on his way by land than pass by sea to any place in a short time, so tedious and dreadful was the same to him.

But here I cannot but stay and make a pause and stand half amazed at this poor people's present condition; and so I think will the reader too when he well considers the same. Being thus past the vast ocean and a sea of troubles before in their preparation (as may be remembered by that which went before), they had now no friends to welcome them nor inns to entertain or refresh their weather-beaten bodies, no houses or much less towns to repair to, to seek for succour. It is recorded in Scripture as a mercy to the Apostle and his shipwrecked company that the barbarians showed them no small kindness in refreshing them; but these savage barbarians, when they met with them (as after will appear), were readier to fill their sides full of arrows than otherwise. And for the season, it was winter, and they that know the winters of that country know them to be sharp and violent and subject to cruel and fierce storms, dangerous to travel to known places, much more to search an unknown coast. Besides, what could they see but a hideous and desolate wilderness, full of wild beasts and wild men—and what multitudes there might be of them they knew not. Neither could they, as it were, go up to the top of Pisgah to view from this wilderness a more goodly country to feed their hopes; for which way soever they turned their eyes (save upwards to the heavens) they could have little solace or content in respect of any outward objects. For, summer being done, all things stand upon them with a weather-beaten face, and the whole country, full of woods and thickets, represented a wild and savage hue. If they looked behind them, there was the mighty ocean which they had passed and was now as a main bar and gulf to separate them from all the civil parts of the world. If it be said they had a ship to succour them, it is true; but what heard they daily from the master and company but that with speed they should look out a place (with their shallop) where they would be, at some near distance? For the season was such as he would not stir from thence till a safe harbour was discovered by them, where they would be and he might go without danger, and that victuals [were] consumed apace but he must and would keep sufficient for themselves and their return. Yea, it was muttered by some that if they got not a place in time they would turn them and their goods ashore and leave them. Let it also be considered what weak hopes of supply and succour they left behind them that might bear up their minds in this sad condition and trials they were under, and they could not but be very small. . . .

Being thus arrived at Cape Cod the eleventh of November, and necessity calling them to look out a place for habitation (as well as the master's and mariners' importunity), they having brought a large shallop with them out of England, stowed in quarters in the ship, they now got her out and set their carpenters to work to trim her up; but, being much bruised and shattered in the ship with foul weather, they saw she would be long in mending. Whereupon a few of them tendered themselves to go by land and discover those nearest places whilst the shallop was in mending; and the rather because as they went into that harbour there seemed to be an opening some two or three leagues off, which the master judged to be a river. It was conceived there might be some danger in the attempt yet, seeing them resolute, they were permitted to go, being sixteen of them well armed under the conduct of Captain Standish, having such instructions given them as was thought meet.

They set forth the fifteenth of November, and when they had marched about the space of a mile by the sea-side they espied five or six persons with a dog coming towards them, who were savages; but they fled from them and ran up into the woods, and the English followed them, partly to see if they could speak with them and partly to discover if there might not be more of them lying in ambush. But the Indians, seeing themselves thus followed, they again forsook the woods and ran away on the sands as hard as they could, so as they could not come near them but followed them by the track of their feet sundry miles and saw that they had come the same way. So, night coming on, they made their rendezvous and set out their sentinels and rested in quiet that night; and the next morning followed their track till they had headed a great creek and so left the sands and turned another way into the woods. But they still followed them by guess, hoping to find their dwellings; but they soon lost both them and themselves, falling into such thickets as were ready to tear their clothes and armour in pieces, but were most distressed for want of drink. But at length they found water and refreshed themselves, being the first New England water they drunk of and was now, in great thirst, as pleasant unto them as wine or beer had been in foretimes.

Afterwards they directed their course to come to the other shore, for they knew it was a neck of land they were to cross over, and so at length got to the sea-side and marched to this supposed river, and by the way found a pond of clear, fresh water and, shortly after, a good quantity of clear ground, where the Indians had formerly set corn, and some of their graves. And proceeding further they saw new stubble where corn had been set the same year; also they found where lately a house had been, where some planks and a great kettle was remaining, and heaps of sand newly paddled with hands. Which, they digging up, found in them divers fair Indian baskets filled with corn and some in ears, fair and good, of divers colours, which seemed to them a very goodly sight (having never seen any such before). This was near the place of that supposed river they came to seek, unto which they went and found it to open itself into two arms with a high cliff of sand in the entrance, but more like to be creeks of salt water than any fresh, for aught they saw, and that there was good harbourage for their shallop, leaving it further to be discovered by their shallop when she was ready. So, their time limited them being expired, they returned to the ship, lest they should be in fear of their safety, and took with them part of the corn and buried up the rest. And so, like the men from Eshcol,[1] carried with them of the fruits of the land and showed their brethren; of which, and their return, they were marvellously glad and their hearts encouraged.

After this, the shallop being got ready, they set out again for the better discovery of this place, and the master of the ship desired to go himself. So there went some thirty men but found it to be no harbour for ships but only for boats. There was also found two of their houses covered with mats and sundry of their implements in them, but the people were run away and could not be seen. Also there was found more of their corn and of their beans of various colours; the corn and beans they brought away, purposing to give them full satisfaction when they should meet with any of them, as, about some six months afterward, they did, to their good content. . . .

The month of November being spent in these affairs, and much foul weather falling in, the sixth of December they sent out their shallop again with ten of their principal men and some seamen upon further discovery, intending to circulate that deep bay of Cape Cod. The weather was very cold and it froze so hard as, the spray of the sea lighting on their coats, they were as if they had been glazed. Yet that night betimes they got down into the bottom of the bay, and as they drew near the shore they saw some ten or twelve Indians very busy about something. They landed about a league or two from them and had much ado to put ashore anywhere, it lay so full of flats. Being landed, it grew late, and they made themselves a barricado with logs and boughs as well as they could in the time, and set out their sentinel and betook them to rest, and saw the smoke of the fire the savages made that night. When morning was come they divided their company, some to coast along the shore in the boat, and the rest marched through the woods to see the land, if any fit place might be for their dwelling. They came also to the place where they saw the Indians the night before and found they had been cutting up a great fish like a grampus, being some two inches thick of fat like a hog, some pieces whereof they had left by the way. And the shallop found two more of these fishes dead on the sands, a thing usual after storms in that place, by reason of the great flats of sand that lie off.

So they ranged up and down all that day, but found no people nor any place they liked. When the sun grew low, they hasted out of the woods to meet with their shallop, to whom they made signs to come to them into a creek hard by, the which they did at high water; of which they were very glad, for they had not seen each other all that day since the morning. So they made them a barricado as usually they did every night, with logs, stakes, and thick pine boughs, the height of a man, leaving it open to leeward, partly to shelter them from the cold and wind (making their fire in the middle and lying round about it) and partly to defend them from any sudden assaults of the savages, if they should surround them; so, being very weary, they betook them to rest. But about midnight they heard a hideous and great cry, and their sentinel called 'Arm! arm!' So they bestirred them and stood to their arms and shot off a couple of muskets, and then the noise ceased. They concluded it was a company of wolves or such-like wild beasts, for one of the seamen told them he had often heard such a noise in Newfoundland.

So they rested till about five of the clock in the morning, for the tide and their purpose to go from thence made them be stirring betimes. So after prayer they prepared for breakfast, and it being day dawning, it was thought best to be carrying things down to the boat. But some said it was not best to carry the arms down, others said they would be the readier, for they had lapped them up in their coats from the dew; but some three or four would not carry theirs till they went themselves. Yet as it fell out, the water being not high enough, they laid them down on the bank-side and came up to breakfast.

But presently, all on the sudden, they heard a great and strange cry, which they knew to be the same voices they heard in the night, though they varied their notes; and one of their company, being abroad, came running in and cried, 'Men, Indians! Indians!' And withal, their arrows came flying amongst them. Their men ran with all speed to recover their arms, as by the good providence of God they did. In the mean time, of those that were there ready, two muskets were discharged at them and two more stood ready in the entrance of their rendezvous but were commanded not to shoot till they could take full aim at them. And the other two charged again with all speed, for there were only four had arms there and defended the barricado, which was first assaulted. The cry of the Indians was dreadful, especially when they saw their men run out of the rendezvous toward the shallop to recover their arms, the Indians wheeling about upon them. But some running out with coats of mail on and cutlasses in their hands, they soon got their arms and let fly amongst them and quickly stopped their violence. Yet there was a lusty man, and no less valiant, stood behind a tree within half a musket shot and let his arrows fly at them; he was seen [to] shoot three arrows, which were all avoided. He stood three shots of a musket, till one taking full aim at him and made the bark or splinters of the tree fly about his ears, after which he gave an extraordinary shriek and away they went, all of them. They left some to keep the shallop, and followed them about a quarter of a mile, and shouted once or twice, and shot off two or three pieces, and so returned. This they did that they might conceive that they were not afraid of them or any way discouraged. . . .

On Monday they sounded the harbour and found it fit for shipping, and marched into the land and found divers corn-fields and little running brooks, a place (as they supposed) fit for situation. At least it was the best they could find, and the season and their present necessity made them glad to accept of it. So they returned to their ship again with this news to the rest of their people, which did much comfort their hearts.

On the fifteenth of December they weighed anchor to go to the place they had discovered and came within two leagues of it, but were fain to bear up again; but the sixteenth day the wind came fair and they arrived safe in this harbour. And afterwards took better view of the place and resolved where to pitch their dwelling; and the twenty-fifth day began to erect the first house for common use to receive them and their goods. . . .

I shall a little return back and begin with a combination made by them before they came ashore, being the first foundation of their government in this place, occasioned partly by the discontented and mutinous speeches that some of the strangers amongst them had let fall from them in the ship: that when they came ashore they would use their own liberty, for none had power to command them, the patent they had being for Virginia and not for New England, which belonged to another government with which the Virginia Company had nothing to do; and partly that such an act by them done, this their condition considered, might be as firm as any patent, and in some respects more sure.

The form was as followeth:

### IN THE NAME OF GOD, AMEN.

We whose names are underwritten, the loyal subjects of our dread sovereign lord King James, by the Grace of God of Great Britain, France, and Ireland King, Defender of the Faith, etc.,

Having undertaken, for the glory of God and advancement of the Christian faith and honour of our king and country, a voyage to plant the first colony in the northern parts of Virginia, do by these presents solemnly and mutually in the presence of God and one of another, covenant and combine ourselves together into a civil body politic for our better ordering and preservation and furtherance of the ends afore said; and by virtue hereof to enact, constitute, and frame such just and equal laws, ordinances, acts, constitutions, and offices, from time to time, as shall be thought most meet and convenient for the general good of the colony, unto which we promise all due submission and obedience. In witness whereof we have hereunder subscribed our names at Cape Cod, the eleventh of November, in the year of the reign of our sovereign lord King James, of England, France, and Ireland the eighteenth, and of Scotland the fifty-fourth. Anno Domini 1620.

After this they chose, or rather confirmed, Mr John Carver (a man godly and well approved amongst them) their Governor for that year. And after they had provided a place for their goods or common store (which were long in unlading for want of boats, foulness of the winter weather, and sickness of divers) and began some small cottages for their habitation, as time would admit they met and consulted of laws and orders, both for their civil and military government as the necessity of their condition did require, still adding thereunto as urgent occasion in several times and as cases did require.

In these hard and difficult beginnings they found some discontents and murmurings arise amongst some, and mutinous speeches and carriages in other; but they were soon quelled and overcome by the wisdom, patience, and just and equal carriage of things by the Governor and better part, which clave faithfully together in the main.

But that which was most sad and lamentable was that in two or three months' time half of their company died, especially in January and February, being the depth of winter, and wanting houses and other comforts, being infected with the scurvy and other diseases which this long voyage and their inaccommodate condition had brought upon them. So as there died some times two or three of a day in the fore said time, that of a hundred and odd persons scarce fifty remained. And of these, in the time of most distress, there was but six or seven sound persons who, to their great commendations be it spoken, spared no pains night nor day, but with abundance of toil and hazard of their own health fetched them wood, made them fires, dressed them meat, made their beds, washed their loathsome clothes, clothed and unclothed them. In a word, did all the homely and necessary offices for them which dainty and queasy stomachs cannot endure to hear named; and all this willingly and cheerfully, without any grudging in the least, showing herein their true love unto their friends and brethren, a rare example and worthy to be remembered. Two of these seven were Mr William Brewster, their reverend elder, and Miles Standish, their captain and military commander, unto whom myself and many others were much beholden in our low and sick condition. And yet the Lord so upheld these persons as in this general calamity they were not at all infected either with sickness or lameness. And what I have said of these I may say of many others who died in this general visitation, and others yet living: that whilst they had health, yea, or any strength continuing, they were not wanting to any that had need of them. And I doubt not but their recompense is with the Lord.

But I may not here pass by another remarkable passage not to be forgotten. As this calamity fell among the passengers that were to be left here to plant, and were hasted ashore and made to drink water that the seamen might have the more beer, and one in his sickness desiring but a small can of beer, it was answered that if he were their own father he should have none, the disease began to fall amongst them also, so as almost half of their company died before they went away and many of their officers and lustiest men, as the boatswain, gunner, three quartermasters, the cook, and others. At which the master was something strucken and sent to the sick ashore and told the Governor he should send for beer for them that had need of it, though he drunk water homeward bound.

But now amongst his company there was far another kind of carriage in this misery than amongst the passengers. For they that before had been boon companions in drinking and jollity in the time of their health and welfare began now to desert one another in this calamity, saying they would not hazard their lives for them, they should be infected by coming to help them in their cabins, and so, after they came to lie by it, would do little or nothing for them but, 'if they died, let them die'. But such of the passengers as were yet aboard showed them what mercy they could, which made some of their hearts relent, as the boatswain (and some others), who was a proud young man and would often curse and scoff at the passengers. But when he grew weak, they had compassion on him and helped him; then he confessed he did not deserve it at their hands, he had abused them in word and deed. 'Oh!' (saith he) 'you, I now see, show your love like Christians indeed one to another, but we let one another lie and die like dogs.' Another lay cursing his wife, saying if it had not been for her he had never come this unlucky voyage, and anon cursing his fellows, saying he had done this and that for some of them, he had spent so much and so much amongst them, and they were now weary of him and did not help him, having need. Another gave his companion all he had, if he died, to help him in his weakness; he went and got a little spice and made him a mess of meat once or twice. And because he died not so soon as he expected he went amongst his fellows and swore the rogue would cozen[2] him, he would see him choked before he made him any more meat; and yet the poor fellow died before morning.

All this while the Indians came skulking about them and would sometimes show themselves aloof off, but when any approached near them, they would run away; and once they stole away their tools where they had been at work and were gone to dinner. But about the sixteenth of March a certain Indian came boldly amongst them and spoke to them in broken English, which they could well understand but marvelled at it. At length they understood by discourse with him that he was not of these parts but belonged to the eastern parts where some English ships came to fish, with whom he was acquainted and could name sundry of them by their names, amongst whom he had got his language. He became profitable to them in acquainting them with many things concerning the state of the country in the east parts where he lived, which was afterwards profitable unto them; as also of the people here, of their names, number, and strength, of their situation and distance from this place, and who was chief amongst them. His name was Samoset. He told them also of another Indian whose name was Squanto, a native of this place, who had been in England and could speak better English than himself. . . .

### [*The First Thanksgiving*]

They began now to gather in the small harvest they had and to fit up their houses and dwellings against winter, being all well recovered in health and strength and had all things in good plenty. For as some were thus employed in affairs abroad, others were exercised in fishing, about cod and bass and other fish, of which they took good store, of which every family had their portion. All the summer there was no want, and now began to come in store of fowl as winter approached, of which this place did abound when they came first (but afterward decreased by degrees). And besides water-fowl there was a great store of wild turkeys, of which they took many, besides venison, etc. Besides they had about a peck of meal a week to a person or, now since harvest, Indian corn to that proportion. Which made many afterwards write so largely of their plenty here to their friends in England, which were not feigned but true reports. . . .

[Thomas Morton, a companion of Captain Wollaston, who had come to Massachusetts in 1625, set up a Maypole at Mount Wollaston, which he re-christened Mare Mount or Merrymount, and scandalized the pious Pilgrims of Plymouth. They sent Captain Miles Standish to arrest him and in 1628 shipped him off to England, charged, among other villainies, with selling arms to the Indians.]

About some three or four years before this time there came over one Captain Wollaston (a man of pretty parts) and with him three or four more of some eminency, who brought with them a great many servants, with provisions and other implements for to begin a plantation, and pitched themselves in a place within the Massachusetts which they called, after their Captain's name, Mount Wollaston. Amongst whom was one Mr Morton, who it should seem had some small adventure[3] of his own or other men's amongst them but had little respect amongst them and was slighted by the meanest servants. Having continued there some time and not finding things to answer their expectations, nor profit to arise as they looked for, Captain Wollaston takes a great part of the servants and transports them to Virginia, where he puts them off at good rates, selling their time to other men, and writes back to one Mr Rasdall (one of his chief partners and accounted their merchant) to bring another part of them to Virginia likewise, intending to put them off there as he had done the rest. And he, with the consent of the said Rasdall, appointed one Fitcher to be his lieutenant and govern the remains of the plantation till he or Rasdall returned to take further order thereabout. But this Morton above said, having more craft than honesty (who had been a kind of pettifogger of Furnival's Inn) in the others' absence watches an opportunity (commons being but hard[4] amongst them) and got some strong drink and other junkets and made them a feast; and after they were merry he began to tell them he would give them good counsel. 'You see,' saith he, 'that many of your fellows are carried to Virginia, and if you stay till this Rasdall return you will also be carried away and sold for slaves with the rest. Therefore I would advise you to thrust out this Lieutenant Fitcher, and I, having a part in the plantation, will receive you as my partners and consociates; so may you be free from service and we will converse, plant, trade, and live together as equals and support and protect one another,' or to like effect. This counsel was easily received, so they took opportunity and thrust Lieutenant Fitcher out o' doors and would suffer him to come no more amongst them, but forced him to seek bread to eat and other relief from his neighbours till he could get passage for England.

After this they fell to great licentiousness and led a dissolute life, pouring out themselves into all profaneness. And Morton became Lord of Misrule and maintained (as it were) a school of atheism. And after they had got some goods into their hands and got much by trading with the Indians, they spent it as vainly in quaffing and drinking both wine and strong waters in great excess and (as some reported) £10 worth in a morning. They also set up a Maypole, drinking and dancing about it many days together, inviting the Indian women for their consorts, dancing and frisking together like so many fairies, or furies, rather, and worse practices, as if they had anew revived and celebrated the feasts of the Roman goddess Flora or the beastly practices of the mad Bacchanalians. Morton likewise, to show his poetry, composed sundry rhymes and verses, some tending to lasciviousness and others to the detraction and scandal of some persons, which he affixed to this idle, or idol, Maypole. They changed also the name of their place, and instead of calling it Mount Wollaston they call it Merrymount, as if this jollity would have lasted ever. But this continued not long, for after Morton was sent for England (as follows to be declared) shortly after came over that worthy gentleman Mr John Endicott, who brought over a patent under the broad seal for the government of the Massachusetts, who, visiting those parts, caused that Maypole to be cut down and rebuked them for their profaneness and admonished them to look there should be better walking. So they or others now changed the name of their place again and called it Mount Dagon.

Now to maintain this riotous prodigality and profuse excess, Morton, thinking himself lawless and hearing what gain the French and fishermen made by trading of pieces, powder, and shot to the Indians, he as the head of this consortship began the practice of the same in these parts. And first he taught them how to use them, to charge and discharge, and what proportion of powder to give the piece, according to the size or bigness of the same, and what shot to use for fowl and what for deer. And having thus instructed them, he employed some of them to hunt and fowl for him, so as they became far more active in that employment than any of the English, by reason of their swiftness of foot and nimbleness of body, being also quick-sighted and by continual exercise well knowing the haunts of all sorts of game. So as when they saw the execution that a piece would do and the benefit that might come by the same, they became mad (as it were) after them and would not stick to give any price they could attain to for them, accounting their bows and arrows but baubles in comparison of them.

And here I may take occasion to bewail the mischief that this wicked man began in these parts, and which since, base covetousness prevailing in men that should know better, has now at length got the upper hand and made this thing common, notwithstanding any laws to the contrary. So as the Indians are full of pieces all over, both fowling-pieces, muskets, pistols, etc.; they have also their moulds to make shot of all sorts, as musket bullets, pistol bullets, swan and goose shot, and of smaller sorts. Yea, some have seen them have their screw-plates to make screw-pins themselves when they want them, with sundry other implements wherewith they are ordinarily better fitted and furnished than the English themselves. Yea, it is well known that they will have powder and shot when the English want it nor cannot get it; and that in a time of war or danger, as experience hath manifested, that when lead hath been scarce and men for their own defence would gladly have given a groat a pound, which is dear enough, yet hath it been bought up and sent to other places and sold to such as trade it with the Indians at 12*d.* the pound. And it is like they give 3*s.* or 4*s.* the pound, for they will have it at any rate. And these things have been done in the same times when some of their neighbours and friends are daily killed by the Indians, or are in danger thereof and live but at the Indians' mercy. Yea, some, as they have acquainted them with all other things, have told them how gunpowder is made and all the materials in it, and that they are to be had in their own land; and I am confident, could they attain to make saltpetre, they would teach them to make powder.

O, the horribleness of this villainy! How many both Dutch and English have been lately slain by those Indians thus furnished, and no remedy provided; nay, the evil more increased and the blood of their brethren sold for gain (as is to be feared); and in what danger all these colonies are in is too well known. O that princes and parliaments would take some timely order to prevent this mischief and at length to suppress it by some exemplary punishment upon some of these gain-thirsty murderers, for they deserve no better title, before their colonies in these parts be overthrown by these barbarous savages, thus armed with

their own weapons by these evil instruments and traitors to their neighbours and country! But I have forgot myself and have been too long in
this digression; but now to return.

This Morton having thus taught them the use of pieces, he sold them
all he could spare, and he and his consorts determined to send for many
out of England and had by some of the ships sent for above a score. The
which being known, and his neighbours meeting the Indians in the
woods armed with guns in this sort, it was a terror unto them who lived
stragglingly and were of no strength in any place. And other places
(though more remote) saw this mischief would quickly spread over all
if not prevented. Besides, they saw they should keep no servants, for
Morton would entertain any, how vile soever, and all the scum of the
country or any discontents would flock to him from all places if this
nest was not broken. And they should stand in more fear of their lives
and goods in short time from this wicked and debased crew than from
the savages themselves.

So sundry of the chief of the straggling plantations, meeting together,
agreed by mutual consent to solicit those of Plymouth (who were then
of more strength than them all) to join with them to prevent the further
growth of this mischief and suppress Morton and his consorts before
they grew to further head and strength. Those that joined in this action
and after contributed to the charge of sending him for England, were
from Piscataqua, Naumkeag,[5] Winnisimmet,[6] Wessagusset,[7] Nan-
tasket,[8] and other places where any English were seated. Those of Plymouth being thus sought to by their messengers and letters, and weighing both their reasons and the common danger, were willing to afford
them their help though themselves had least cause of fear or hurt. So,
to be short, they first resolved jointly to write to him and in a friendly
and neighbourly way to admonish him to forbear those courses, and
sent a messenger with their letters to bring his answer.

But he was so high[9] as he scorned all advice and asked who had to do
with him,[10] he had and would trade pieces with the Indians, in despite
of all, with many other scurrilous terms full of disdain. They sent to
him a second time and bade him be better advised and more temperate
in his terms, for the country could not bear the injury he did. It was
against their common safety and against the King's proclamation. He
answered in high terms as before, and that the King's proclamation was
no law, demanding what penalty was upon it. It was answered, more
than he could bear—His Majesty's displeasure. But insolently he persisted and said the King was dead and his displeasure with him, and

many the like things, and threatened withal that if any came to molest him let them look to themselves, for he would prepare for them.

Upon which they saw there was no way but to take him by force, and having so far proceeded, now to give over would make him far more haughty and insolent. So they mutually resolved to proceed and obtained of the Governor of Plymouth to send Captain Standish and some other aid with him to take Morton by force. The which accordingly was done. But they found him to stand stiffly in his defence, having made fast his doors, armed his consorts, set divers dishes of powder and bullets ready on the table; and if they had not been over-armed with drink, more hurt might have been done. They summoned him to yield, but he kept his house and they could get nothing but scoffs and scorns from him. But at length, fearing they would do some violence to the house, he and some of his crew came out, but not to yield but to shoot; but they were so steeled with drink as their pieces were too heavy for them. Himself with a carbine, overcharged and almost half filled with powder and shot, as was after found, had thought to have shot Captain Standish, but he stepped to him and put by his piece and took him. Neither was there any hurt done to any of either side, save that one was so drunk that he ran his own nose upon the point of a sword that one held before him as he entered the house; but he lost but a little of his hot blood.

Morton they brought away to Plymouth, where he was kept till a ship went from the Isle of Shoals for England, with which he was sent to the Council of New England and letters written to give them information of his course and carriage. And also one was sent at their common charge to inform Their Honours more particularly and to prosecute against him. But he fooled of the messenger after he was gone from hence, and though he went for England, yet nothing was done to him, not so much as rebuked, for aught was heard, but returned the next year. Some of the worst of the company were dispersed and some of the more modest kept the house till he should be heard from. But I have been too long about so unworthy a person and bad a cause. . . .

T

# Profits in Virginia for Shoemakers (*c.* 1624)

The following letter from Captain John Smith, addressed to the Society of Cordwainers, is found on the flyleaf of a copy in the Huntington Library of Smith's *General History of Virginia* (1624) which the author presented to that guild of shoemakers.

To the Worshipful the Master Wardens and Society of the Cordwainers of the city of London

Worthy gentlemen:

Not only in regard of your courtesy and love, but also of the continual use I have had of your labours and the hope you may make some use of mine, I salute you with this chronological discourse, whereof you may understand with what infinite difficulties and dangers these plantations first began, with their yearly proceedings and the plain description and condition of those countries. How many of your company have been adventurers whose names are omitted or not nominated in the alphabet, I know not; therefore I entreat you better to inform me, that I may hereafter imprint you among the rest. But of this I am sure, for want of shoes among the oyster banks we tore our hats and clothes, and, those being worn, we tied barks of trees about our feet to keep them from being cut by the shells among which we must go or starve. Yet how many thousand of shoes have been transported to these plantations, how many soldiers, mariners, and sailors have been and are likely to be increased thereby, what vent your commodities have had and still have, and how many ships and men of all faculties have been and are yearly employed, I leave to your own judgements; and yet by reason of ill managing the returns have neither answered the general expectation nor my desire. The causes thereof you may read at large in this book for your better satisfaction; and I pray you take it not in ill part that I present the same to you in this manuscript epistle so late, for both it and myself have been so overtired by attendances that this work of mine does seem to be superannuated before its birth; notwithstanding let me entreat you to give it lodging in your hall freely to be perused for ever, in memory of your nobleness towards me and my love to God, my country, your society, and those plantations, ever resting

Yours to use,
John Smith.

# The Health-Preserving Climate of New England (1630)

Francis Higginson landed at Naumkeag, later Salem, in the Massachusetts Bay colony in April 1629 with his wife and seven children. Like Alexander Whitaker and other clergymen who were writing propaganda for colonization, Higginson, also a minister of the gospel, was an enthusiastic advocate of emigration to the new country. Soon after his arrival he sent back to London a vivid account of the land that he regarded as little short of paradise. His tract was published as *New England's Plantation, Or A Short and True Description of the Commodities and Discommodities of That Country* (1630). Despite Higginson's faith in the wholesome tonic of his new environment, he died of tuberculosis in August 1630—not long after his praise of New England was printed.

### Of the Air of New England with the Temper and Creatures in It

THE temper of the air of New England is one special thing that commends this place. Experience doth manifest that there is hardly a more healthful place to be found in the world that agrees better with our English bodies. Many that have been weak and sickly in old England by coming hither have been thoroughly healed and grown healthful and strong. For here is an extraordinary clear and dry air that is of a most healing nature to all such as are of a cold, melancholy, phlegmatic, rheumatic temper of body. None can more truly speak hereof by their own experience than myself. My friends that knew me can well tell how very sickly I have been and continually in physic, being much troubled with a tormenting pain, through an extraordinary weakness of my stomach and abundance of melancholic humours; but since I came hither on this voyage I thank God I have had perfect health and freed from pain and vomitings, having a stomach to digest the hardest and coarsest fare who before could not eat finest meat; and whereas my stomach could only digest and did require such drink as was both strong and stale, now I can and do oftentimes drink New England water very well; and I that have not gone without a cap for many years together, neither durst leave off the same, have now cast away my cap and do wear none at all in the day-time; and whereas before-time I clothed myself with double clothes and thick waistcoats to keep me warm, even in the summer-time, I do now go as thin clad as any, only wearing a light stuff cassock upon my shirt and stuff breeches of one thickness without linings. Besides, I have one of my children that was formerly most lamentably handled with sore breaking-out of both his hands and feet of the king's evil, but since he came hither he is very well over[1] he was, and there is hope of perfect recovery shortly, even by the very wholesomeness of the air, altering, digesting, and drying up the cold and crude humours[2] of the body. And therefore I think it is a wise course for all cold complexions[3] to come to take physic in New England; for a sup of New England's air is better than a whole draught of old England's ale.

In the summer-time, in the midst of July and August, it is a good deal hotter than in old England; and in winter, January and February are much colder, as they say; but the spring and autumn are of a middle temper.

Fowls of the air are plentiful here and of all sorts as we have in England, as far as I can learn, and a great many of strange fowls which we know not. Whilst I was writing these things, one of our men brought home an eagle which he had killed in the wood; they say they are good meat. Also here are many kinds of excellent hawks, both sea-hawks and land-hawks; and myself, walking in the woods with another in company, sprung a partridge so big that through the heaviness of his body could fly but a little way; they that have killed them say they are as big as our hens. Here are likewise abundance of turkeys often killed in the woods, far greater than our English turkeys and exceeding fat, sweet, and fleshy, for here they have abundance of feeding all the year long, as strawberries—in summer all places are full of them and all manner of berries and fruits. In the winter-time I have seen flocks of pigeons and have eaten of them. They do fly from tree to tree as other birds do, which our pigeons will not do in England; they are of all colours as ours are, but their wings and tails are far longer, and therefore it is likely they fly swifter to escape the terrible hawks in this country. In winter-time this country does abound with wild geese, wild ducks, and other sea-fowl, that a great part of winter the planters have eaten nothing but roast meat of divers fowls which they have killed.

Thus you have heard of the earth, water, and air of New England, now it may be you expect something to be said of the fire proportionable to the rest of the elements.

Indeed, I think New England may boast of this element more than of all the rest: for though it be here something cold in the winter, yet here we have plenty of fire to warm us, and that a great deal cheaper than they sell billets and faggots in London; nay, all Europe is not able to afford to make so great fires as New England. A poor servant here that is to possess but fifty acres of land may afford to give more wood for timber and fire as good as the world yields than many noblemen in England can afford to do. Here is good living for those that love good fires.

# Notes

*Introduction*

[1] The text for this long and important paper is found in E. G. R. Taylor, *The Original Writings and Correspondence of the Two Richard Hakluyts*, The Hakluyt Society, 2nd Ser., Nos. 76, 77 (London, 1935), II, 211–326.

[2] See Document No. 4, pp. 36–45.

[3] See Document No. 6, pp. 54–62.

[4] See Document No. 5, pp. 46–54.

[5] David B. Quinn (ed.), *The Voyages and Colonising Enterprises of Sir Humphrey Gilbert*, The Hakluyt Society, 2nd Ser., Nos. 83, 84 (London, 1938–9), I, 33–4.

[6] Quinn, *Voyages*, I, 35.

[7] *Ibid.*, I, 46.

[8] *Ibid.*, I, 36. The pamphlet was printed by Hakluyt in *Divers Voyages touching the Discovery of America* (1582) and reprinted by Taylor, *Original Writings and Correspondence of the Two Richard Hakluyts*, I, 116–22. See Document No. 1.

[9] Quinn, *Voyages*, I, 62.

[10] See Document No. 9, pp. 82–94.

[11] See Document No. 11, pp. 97–102.

[12] See Document No. 12, pp. 103–13.

[13] See Document No. 14, pp. 115–33.

[14] See Document No. 15, pp. 133–6.

[15] See Document No. 16, pp. 137–44.

[16] See Document No. 17, pp. 144–54.

[17] This theme is treated in some detail by Louis B. Wright, *The Dream of Prosperity in Colonial America* (New York, 1965).

[18] See Document No. 38, pp. 254–8.

[19] See Document No. 13, pp. 113–14.

[20] See Document No. 39, pp. 258–63.

[21] See Document No. 31, pp. 206–19.

[22] This subject is discussed by Louis B. Wright in *Religion and Empire: The Alliance between Piety and Commerce in English Expansion, 1558–1625* (Chapel Hill, N.C., 1943), 84–114.

[23] See Document No. 32, pp. 219–24.

[24] See Document No. 27, pp. 188–94.

[25] See Document No. 29, pp. 201–5.

[26] See Document No. 20, pp. 160–2.
[27] See Document No. 30, pp. p. 205.

## 1. *Purposes and Policies to Be Observed in Colonization*

[1] *very*] mere.
[2] *let*] hindrance.
[3] La Rochelle.
[4] Perhaps the Bay of Setúbal is meant.
[5] *stammels*] coarse woollens, usually dyed red.
[6] *suckets*] candied fruits; sweetmeats.
[7] The Baltic countries.
[8] *stapling place*] trade centre.
[9] *doubles of coarse linen*] the younger Hakluyt includes in a list of recommended provisions in his *Discourse of Western Planting* 'swift boats and barges ... covered with quilted canvas of defence against shot from the shore' and credits Roger Bodenham with their invention.
[10] *dryfats*] barrels.

## 2. *England's Time Approaches for Appropriating Part of the New World*

[1] *part stakes*] share in the profits.
[2] *forslown*] delayed.
[3] *pestered*] crowded.
[4] Don Antonio de Castilio, according to E. G. R. Taylor, *Original Writings*, I, 176.
[5] Michael Lok, secretary to the Muscovy Company.
[6] A river in Quebec province.
[7] A name applied to the unexplored northern region around Greenland and Labrador, apparently first used by Antonio and Niccolò Zeno, Venetian explorers. The account of their adventures was published in Italian in 1558 and Hakluyt included it in his *Principal Navigations* under the title, 'The Discovery of the Isles of Friesland, Iceland, Engroneland [Greenland], Estotiland, Drogeo, and Icaria'.
[8] *jealous*] zealous.
[9] His *Tractado de la sphera* was published in 1545.
[10] Although Hakluyt never succeeded in getting permanent lectureships established, Thomas Hood, a Cambridge Master of Arts, was commissioned in 1587 by Sir Thomas Smith and John Wolstenholme to lecture privately on the application of mathematics to navigation. Hakluyt in the mean time continued to press influential men for the sort of permanent public lectures he considered desirable. After 1598 lectures in navigation were given regularly at Gresham College. See D. W. Waters, *The Art of Navigation in England in Elizabethan and Early Stuart Times* (New Haven, 1958), pp. 185, 242, 243, and Appendices 16 and 19.

[11] The Gulf of St Lawrence.

[12] Jacques Cartier's name for the St Lawrence River.

### 3. *Reasons for Colonization*

[1] *woad*] a blue dye-stuff prepared from the leaves of *Isatis tinctoria* powdered and fermented.

[2] *factory*] trading centre.

[3] *hoys*] small boats.

[4] *busses*] fishing vessels, used principally by the Dutch herring industry.

[5] *manurance*] occupation.

[6] *ancient*] experienced.

[7] Presumably a garbled version of a Spanish place name. The English word 'shroff', from the Persian *saraf*, means 'banker'.

[8] *frails*] rush baskets.

[9] *poldavies*] coarse canvas used for sailcloth.

[10] *whittawers*] workers of leather into light, pliable skins.

### 4. *John Hawkins Investigates the Coast of Florida*

[textual note, p. 37] *\*are*] 1589 edition; the 1598–1600 edition changed to 'abode', reflecting the destruction of the French colony by the Spanish in 1565, after Hawkins's visit.

[1] The Saint Johns River in Florida.

[2] *mill*] millet.

[3] *antic*] grotesque.

[4] *sleighter*] more skilful.

[5] The island now comprising Haiti and the Dominican Republic.

[6] *pilled*] pillaged.

[7] *indurate*] harden.

[8] *galliass*] a warship somewhat larger than a galley, propelled by both sail and oars.

[9] *incontinent*] without delay.

[10] *sodden*] boiled.

[11] *at the Spaniards' finding*] victualled by the Spaniards.

[12] Tobacco, as Hawkins indicates in a marginal note.

[13] Probably *Liquidambar styraciflua*, which yields a balsam similar to that from *Liquidambar orientalis*. The balsam was used as an expectorant and sometimes in perfumes.

[14] *had estimation of*] valued.

[15] *graven*] engraved.

[16] *bring them out of estimation*] decrease their value (by bringing up too many at a haul).

[17] *ounces*] lynxes, or some other small felines.

[18] *whereas*] where.

[19] *admiration of us*] amazement on our part.
[20] *passeth*] surpasses.

### 5. Hawkins's and Drake's Slaving Expedition Comes to Grief at San Juan de Ulúa

[1] The Gold Coast.
[2] *concluded*] agreed.
[3] *meant nothing less*] had no such intention.
[4] Probably Cape Velas in Costa Rica.
[5] Riohacha, one of the oldest towns in Colombia.
[6] *circumstance*] advantage.
[7] *detract*] delay.
[8] *furicanos*] an early English form of the word 'hurricane', allied to the Old Spanish *furacán*.
[9] *jut*] shock.
[10] Don Martin Henriquez de Almansa.
[11] *bemean*] so behave as to.
[12] *meant nothing less*] as earlier, 'had no such intention'.
[13] *warded*] kept guard.
[14] *leesing*] loosing; casting off.
[15] *annoy*] damage.
[16] The early Spanish name for the Bahamas.
[17] *painful*] painstaking.

### 6. David Ingram Reports an Incredible Journey on Foot from Mexico to Nova Scotia

[1] The Sloane MS reads 'Camina'. This is possibly the Escambia River, which flows into Pensacola Bay in Florida. Hawkins's account of putting men ashore 'in the bottom of the same bay of Mexico in $23\frac{1}{2}$ degrees' need not be taken literally. For the most part, Ingram's details are too scanty for possible identification.
[2] Le Havre.
[3] *curiets*] breastplates. See also Hawkins's description of the gold and silver which the natives of Florida wore around their necks.
[4] An early name for the area north of Florida.

[textual note, p. 56] *\*Bariniah*] the Sloane MS reads 'Barimashe'.

[5] *bombax*] a tropical tree bearing a silky fibre.
[6] John Winter, nephew of Sir William Winter.
[7] *bastard*] a sweet Spanish wine.

[textual note, p. 58] *\*buyathos*] 'guiathos' in the Sloane MS.

[8] *grain*] maize.

[textual note, p. 59] *and very many unlike ours*] added from the Sloane MS.

⁹ The mouth of the St Mary's River (?).

¹⁰ *proper to the inhabitants*] individually owned.

¹¹ From Hakluyt's time to the late nineteenth century, reports persisted that certain white Indians spoke Welsh and were descendants of Welsh voyagers to America. For an example, see Document 25, pp. 186–7. Scientific investigation has revealed no Welsh word in any Indian dialect.

¹² Curaçao.

### 7. *Henry Hawks Reveals the Rich Commodities of New Spain*

¹ Crocodiles, identified by Hawks in the margin.

² Hakluyt's second edition changes to 'Acapulco', which was at this time the chief port for Spanish trade to the Philippines, the 'China, which they have newly found'. Manila had just been settled in 1571, although the Philippine Islands were discovered by Magellan in 1521.

³ Pine-trees.

⁴ Bison.

⁵ *Opuntia tuna*, the prickly pear.

⁶ *lions and tigers*] pumas and cougars.

⁷ *defended*] prohibited.

⁸ *oblations*] offerings.

⁹ *caddis*] cotton tape.

¹⁰ *rial of plate*] a coin worth six and a quarter pence.

¹¹ *cacique*] chief.

### 8. *Fish in Newfoundland Come at Command of Fisherman!*

¹ *For that*] because.

² *in proper person*] personally.

³ *train*] train oil, rendered whale fat, used for lamp fuel, lubricants, and in soap.

⁴ *lightly*] usually.

⁵ Pine-trees.

⁶ *meet*] suitable.

⁷ *find*] supply.

⁸ *doubteth*] fears.

⁹ Lynxes.

¹⁰ *beasts like to camels*] probably moose.

¹¹ *kerned*] granulated.

¹² Anticosti Island.

¹³ *tender*] have a tender care for.

### 9. *Sir Humphrey Gilbert's Tragic Adventure in Newfoundland*

¹ The Basque name for cod-fish. The island is now called Baccalieu.

[2] Now Cape Francis.

[3] *fights*] defensive screens.

[4] *sea-gate*] i.e., where there was no rolling swell to make handling of the ship difficult.

[5] *gratify*] reward.

[6] *advice*] consideration.

[7] *expedition*] speedy execution.

[8] *had been*] would have been.

[9] Possibly Hayes means the Strait of Belle Isle, at the northern end of the Gulf of St Lawrence.

[10] *bases*] small cannon.

[11] *hard success*] bad luck.

[12] *good conceit*] favourable opinion.

[13] *flaw*] storm.

[14] *happily*] perhaps.

## 10. *Poetical Mariners Praise a Colonial Propagandist*

[1] *prest*] ready.

[2] *purchase*] acquire.

[3] *white*] target.

[4] *frame*] succeed.

[5] *sequel*] result.

## 11. *Francis Drake on the California Coast*

[1] These were probably Indians of the now extinct Coast Miwok tribe.

[2] *artificially*] skilfully.

[3] *cognizance*] identification badge.

[4] Also spelled *tobáh* or *tobáh* elsewhere in the document. The word is not identifiable by comparison with any local Indian word. Probably the narrator confused the herb with tobacco, which was not grown in the area at this time.

[5] Anthropologists have suggested that the Indians regarded the white men with respectful dread as the spirits of the departed dead.

[6] *entreat*] treat.

[7] Possibly to be identified with a Coast Miwok word for chief—*hoipu, hoipa.*

## 12. *A New Land Like unto That of the Golden Age*

[1] *disbogging*] disemboguing, i.e., emptying into the open sea.

[2] Probably Port Ferdinando, on the coast of North Carolina. The identification of most sites mentioned is in dispute. For detailed discussion of the possibilities see the notes in Quinn's reprint.

[3] *Pistacia lentiscus*. Quinn suggests *Liquidambar styraciflua* as the nearest equivalent in this region.

<sup>4</sup> Simon Fernandez, a Portuguese pilot who took part in several of the Virginia voyages.

<sup>5</sup> *pointing*] appointing.

<sup>6</sup> The meaning of this word has never been satisfactorily determined; but it is clear that the English were mistaken in taking it for the name of the country.

[textual note, p. 106] * *called Wingina*] these words appear to be misplaced by the printer. Perhaps they should go after 'king' in the preceding sentence.

<sup>7</sup> *depart*] part.

<sup>8</sup> In his edition of 1598–1600, Hakluyt identifies them as Wanchese and Manteo.

<sup>9</sup> *set*] propel their craft.

<sup>10</sup> *for*] because of.

<sup>11</sup> *frumenty*] porridge made of Indian maize.

<sup>12</sup> *jealousy*] suspicion.

[textual notes, pp. 110–11] * *day's*] altered to 'hour's' in Hakluyt's 1598–1600 edition.

* *sunset*] altered to 'southwest' in 1598–1600 edition.

* *westernmost*] 'southermost' in 1598–1600 edition.

<sup>13</sup> This may be a misspelling of 'Bromwich', possibly the same man as the 'Master Bremige' who is mentioned in Grenville's expedition of 1585. See Quinn, *Roanoke Voyages*, I, p. 180.

### 13. *Glowing Prospects for Raleigh's Colony*

<sup>1</sup> *terra samia . . . terra sigillata*] two types of medicinal earth, valued for their astringent qualities, from the islands of Samos and Lemnos.

### 14. *Harriot Tells of the Goodness of Virginia*

<sup>1</sup> *skill*] knowledge.

<sup>2</sup> John Frampton's translation from the Spanish of Nicolás Monardes, *Joyful News out of the New-Found Land* (1577).

<sup>3</sup> *teston*] tester, sixpence.

<sup>4</sup> *orientness*] lustre.

<sup>5</sup> *seething*] boiling.

<sup>6</sup> *pompions*] pumpkins.

<sup>7</sup> The sunflower.

<sup>8</sup> Persimmons (*Diospyros virginiana*), which are too astringent to be palatable until fully ripened.

<sup>9</sup> The prickly pear.

<sup>10</sup> The Carolina parakeet, which was exceedingly numerous along the Atlantic coast from Florida to New York until exterminated by wholesale slaughter.

15. *Return to Roanoke Island; the Birth of Virginia Dare*

[1] Now Cape Lookout.
[2] *Menatonon his wife*] i.e., Menatonon's wife.

16. *A Promising Description of New England*

[1] On Cape Neddick, along the southern coast of Maine.
[2] Cape Cod.
[3] *proper*] fine; notable.
[4] Martha's Vineyard.
[5] Cuttyhunk.
[6] *light horseman*] light boat, later known as a gig.
[7] *artificial*] skilful in craftsmanship.
[8] *gratulations*] greetings; welcome.
[9] *grudging*] touch of illness.
[10] *saving voyage*] i.e., hope of profit.

17. *Captain Waymouth Explores the New England Coast*

[1] *a mean highland*] a land of moderate height. This was Monhegan Island, off the coast of Maine.
[2] Probably George's Islands.
[3] *waft*] wave.
[4] Now St George's Harbour.
[5] On Allen's Island.
[6] Benner's Island.
[7] *capacity*] intelligence.
[8] *flank his light horseman*] i.e., equip it with some sort of defensive screen.
[9] '*Baugh, waugh*'] this is possibly the source of the refrain of Ariel's song in *The Tempest*, I, ii.
[10] *tender*] offer.
[11] *consented*] accorded.
[12] What is presumably meant is that some acclaimed this river as surpassing the Rio Grande and other rivers mentioned.

18. *Seafarers' Tall Tales of Virginia*

[1] *intelligencers*] spies.
[2] *Gods me*] God save me.

19. *Prudent Advice to Guide Settlers in Establishing Themselves*

[1] *stour*] palisade.
[2] The ancient Greek name for the Don.
[3] Black.
[4] Perhaps a latinization for the Russian name for the White Sea (*Beloe More*), into which the Northern Dvina empties.
[5] *kedge*] a small anchor.

20. *Michael Drayton's Ode, 'To the Virginian Voyage'*

[1] *hinds*] cowards.

21. *George Percy Gives an Account of Jamestown and the Early Hardships*

[1] Marginal note: 'The next day Captain Smith was suspected for a supposed mutiny, though never no such matter.'

[2] An error for eight-and-twentieth.

[3] Modern Old Point Comfort, near Elizabeth City, Virginia.

[4] Modern Hampton, Virginia.

[5] *artificial*] skilfully fashioned.

[6] The Chickahominy.

[7] I.e., the king of Rappahannock's.

[8] *watchet*] light blue.

[9] *murrey*] purplish red.

[10] *Irish pace*] a narrow path through dense woods.

[11] *mainly*] with all speed.

[12] The James.

[13] *pounce and race*] scratch.

22. *Captain John Smith's Explorations and Troubles with the Indians*

[1] The Gunpowder River, which falls into the upper Chesapeake Bay.

[2] Conjectured by some to be the Iroquois.

[3] There is a Tuckahoe Creek, a tributary of the Choptank River, on the eastern shore of Maryland.

[4] *fear no colours*] feel confident of their self-sufficiency.

[5] *walkt a wayless way with uncouth pace*] travelled an uncharted course and unfamiliar paths.

[6] Persimmons.

[7] *Tuftaffeta humorists*] silken mollycoddles.

[8] *much failed not*] i.e., nearly succeeded in cutting off, etc.

[9] *buckler*] shield.

[10] *demeaned*] behaved.

[11] *quiyouckosucks*] priests.

[12] Usually described as Powhatan's brother, his successor as head of the Powhatan confederacy.

[13] One of Powhatan's chief residences; see Strachey's description (p. 210).

[14] *pieces*] guns.

[15] *performed the form of a besom*] i.e., spread out in a fan-like formation (?).

[16] *vambrace*] shield for the forearm.

[17] A plant from which they obtained red dye.

[18] Apparently an error for Werowocomoco, Powhatan's principal stronghold.

[19] *suspected*] doubtful of continuance.

[20] *demi-culverins*] cannons with bores of about 4½ inches.

[21] *saker*] a cannon smaller than a demi-culverin.

[22] *falcon*] another type of light cannon.

[23] *cape-merchant*] an officer who had charge of stores and trading transactions.

### 23. *Captain Newport Reports Gold and Copper in Virginia*

[1] *say*] the aphetic form of 'assay'.

### 24. *Captain Newport, with Some Difficulty, Crowns Powhatan*

[1] Newport had brought a barge made in five pieces that could be disassembled and carried above the fall-line of the river, there to be put together in order to traverse the upper reaches of the river to its source. It did not prove to be a success; Smith sardonically commented in a letter to the Treasurer and Council for Virginia that 'if he had burnt her to ashes, one might have carried her in a bag; but as she was, five hundred cannot'.

[2] *conclude his conclusion*] agree to his plan.

[3] An Indian boy whom Powhatan called his son and presented to Captain Newport in exchange for an English boy named Thomas Savage whom Newport (falsely) identified as his son. Namontack had just returned from a trip to England with Newport.

[4] *congratulate*] reciprocate.

[5] *mantle*] This is now preserved in a hall of the Ashmolean Museum (Bradford Smith, *Captain John Smith, His Life and Legend* [Philadelphia, 1953], p. 138).

### 25. *Indians Sound Like Welshmen to Captain Wynne*

[1] *hay-dogs*] since 'hays' are nets used to catch conies and other small game, a 'hay-dog' is presumably a dog used to retrieve the game.

### 27. *Strachey's Description of the 'Still Vexed Bermoothes'*

[1] *elvish*] spitefully.

[textual note p. 189] * *nations*] perhaps an error for 'motions'.

* *strikes*] probably an error for 'shrieks', as Frank Kermode suggests in his edition of *The Tempest* in the Arden series.

[2] 'May the wives and children of our foes be the ones to feel the blind onset of rising Auster and the roaring of the darkling sea and the shores quivering with the shock!' (Horace, *Odes*, iii. 27, 21–4). For 'Haedi' read 'Austri' (the south wind).

[3] Compare the Boatswain's complaint, 'A plague upon this howling! They are louder than the weather or our office' (*The Tempest*, I, i).

[4] *hullock*] a mere fragment of sail.

[5] *whipstaff*] the upper end of the lever by which the ship was steered above deck by the helmsman; the section below deck controlled the rudder.

[6] *bottom of Candy*] Cretan vessel.

[7] 'Full well I know what Hadria's [the Adriatic Sea's] black gulf can be and what the sins of clear Iapyx [the north-west wind]' (Horace, *Odes*, iii. 27, 18–19).

[8] *braves*] bravados.

[9] *avoiding*] bailing out.

[10] *bittacle*] compass box. The modern 'binnacle' is a corruption.

[textual note, p. 191] * *seized*] 'ceased' in Purchas' text.

[11] *made good*] supplied.

[12] Marginal note: 'Remora is fabled to be a small fish able to withstand a ship in her course.'

[13] See *The Tempest*, I, ii: 'Now on the beak, | Now in the waist, the deck, in every cabin, | I flamed amazement. Sometime I'ld divide | And burn in many places; on the topmast, | The yards, and bowsprit would I flame distinctly, | Then meet and join.'

[14] *carefulness*] anxiety.

[15] *hoodwinked*] blindfolded.

[16] *barricos*] kegs.

[17] *our extreme . . . eight glasses*] that is, continual pumping kept the water level at ten feet for four hours. The sailor's sand-glass ran for thirty minutes.

## 28. *Another Version of the Castaways on Bermuda*

[1] *conning*] keeping a watch and directing the steersman. The original is misprinted 'couning'.

[2] *available*] advantageous.

[3] *admirable*] wonderful.

[4] This was the child of John Rolfe by his first wife. The child died before the castaways left the island and the mother soon after their arrival in Virginia.

[5] *powdered*] salted.

[6] *pay*] cover with a waterproof substance.

[7] *kelson*] a line of timbers bolted to the keel to secure it to the floor timbers.

[8] Unfortunately, Somers died 'of a surfeit in eating a pig' while in the Bermudas. See the *D.N.B.* and Edmund Howes's continuation of the *Annals* of John Stow (1614), p. 942.

## 29. *Bermuda Providentially Saved for the English Nation*

[1] Hughes's brief account of the storm and the abundance of provisions the castaways found on Bermuda is omitted, since it seems to derive entirely from Jourdain's narrative, as indicated by numerous echoes of Jourdain's phraseology.

[2] *curious*] intricate.

31. *The Virginia Indians*

[1] *conceit*] imagination.

[2] *naught*] wicked.

[3] *jealousy*] suspicion.

[4] *bollen*] swollen.

[5] *apoke*] tobacco.

[6] *miscarrying*] dying.

[7] *construction*] i.e., contraction (?).

[8] *rivage*] bank.

[9] *frontal*] forehead band.

[10] *debonair*] fine.

[11] *quaint*] elegant.

[12] *well-pleased*] pleasing.

[13] *sea-gown*] a loose mantle, generally worn by seamen for warmth while on watch.

[14] *mariock apple*] the maracock or maypop, *Passiflora incarnata*, which bears an insipid, apple-like fruit.

[15] Strachey probably means the waters now known as Hampton Roads.

[16] *side*] live alongside.

[17] *patise*] red pigment.

[18] *orpiment*] arsenic trisulphide, used for a yellow pigment.

[19] *scrused*] crushed.

[20] *Arches*] Greek Archipelago.

[21] *brayed*] pounded.

[22] 'A pretty girl is prettier undressed than dressed in purple' (Plautus, *Mostellaria*, I, 3, 289, where it reads 'pulchra mulier nuda erit quam purpurata pulchrior'). Strachey seems to be inverting the meaning.

[23] *bents*] reeds or rushes.

[24] *caraʒʒaies*] apparently a word for 'girls' that Strachey learned in his travels in the Mediterranean area.

[25] *chape*] scabbard-tip.

[26] *bravery*] splendid ornament.

32. *Virginia's Natural Bounty*

[1] Marginal note: 'As 14 or 16 miles.'

[2] *commodity*] advantage.

[3] The James.

[4] The site of Richmond.

[5] *torope*] apparently the Algonkian 'turupe'.

[6] *physical*] medicinal.

33. *A Gossip Reports on Virginia, Including Pocahontas*

[1] *lottery*] the Treasurer and Colony of the Virginia Company were

granted a new charter on March 12, 1612, and with it permission to hold a lottery to further the plantation.

### 34. *Pocahontas, Lured to Jamestown by a Stratagem, Marries John Rolfe*

[1] Pocahontas was so described in Smith's *Map of Virginia* (1612)

[2] Printed following this document.

[3] The facts behind this statement have not been established. 'West Indies' probably means some Spanish settlement on the mainland of North America. A story long circulated that Opechancanough, with his people, had come from Spanish territory south of Virginia, but no anthropological evidence has been found to support the idea of such a migration. The Chickahominies' hostility to the Spaniards may have resulted from blaming them for the arrival of the belligerent Powhatan tribes.

[4] *painful*] distressed.

[5] *scandaled with*] slandered for having.

### 35. *Rolfe Marries Pocahontas to Convert Her—So He Claims*

[1] *pass*] care.

[2] *oblations*] prayers.

[3] *well-advised*] carefully considered.

[4] *motions*] arguments.

[5] *generation*] race.

[6] Actually, between the time of her capture in 1613 and her marriage to Rolfe in 1614, Pocahontas lived under the supervision of Sir Thomas Dale, where she received religious instruction and was baptized with the Christian name Rebecca.

[7] *talent*] abundance; see Matt. 25 : 14–30,

[8] *square*] measure.

### 36. *English Democratic Procedures in America*

[1] *manure*] occupy.

[2] The town was accordingly re-named Elizabeth City later in the same year. The modern name is Hampton.

[3] *howes*] i.e., hounds (?)

[4] A son of the antiquary, Sir Henry Spelman, he came to Virginia in 1609, 'being in displeasure of my friends and desirous to see other countries', as he put it in his own *Relation*. The *Relation*, containing some interesting details of Indian life from Spelman's observations while living with Powhatan and other chiefs for about a year, was not printed until 1872.

[5] *swinge*] control.

### 37. *Promise of Prosperity in Virginia*

[1] *calenture*] fever.

² *manure*] tillage.

³ *casual*] maintenance.

⁴ *absit invidia verbo*] may the utterance provoke no envy.

⁵ *si mens non laeva fuisset*] if my judgement had not been foolish.

⁶ Sir Dudley Carleton had been ambassador there since 1616.

⁷ *occurrents*] happenings.

39. *Fish, Furs, and Timber Better than Gold*

¹ In his *General History of Virginia* (1624) this reads 'five-and-forty', perhaps an example of Smith's tendency to make a good story better.

² *adventures*] investments.

³ *Easterlings*] inhabitants of the Baltic region.

⁴ *sword-pinks*] a variety of sea-going fishing-boat (Dutch *pincke*).

⁵ *todes*] another type of Dutch fishing vessel.

⁶ A peninsula on the north-west coast of Africa.

⁷ *puttargo*] a variant of 'botargo', a relish made from fish roe.

⁸ *fraught*] load.

⁹ *silly*] paltry.

¹⁰ *popular*] populous.

¹¹ *sallets*] greens.

¹² *untoward*] intractable.

¹³ Presumably Oporto.

¹⁴ *engines*] contrivances.

40. *The Pilgrims Seek a Refuge in America—and Find a Villain at Merrymount*

¹ See Num. 13 : 23–4.

² *cozen*] cheat.

³ *adventure*] investment.

⁴ *commons being but hard*] food being scanty.

⁵ Salem.

⁶ Chelsea.

⁷ Weymouth.

⁸ Hull.

⁹ *high*] arrogant.

¹⁰ *who had to do with him*] whose business was it.

42. *The Health-Preserving Climate of New England*

¹ *over*] beyond what.

² *cold and crude humours*] sluggish and improperly assimilated fluids.

³ *complexions*] physical constitutions.